Managing Nonprofit Organizations

Managing Nonprofit Organizations

edited by

Diane Borst
Patrick J. Montana

A Division of American Management Associations

Library of Congress Cataloging in Publication Data
Main entry under title:

Managing nonprofit organizations.

    1. Corporations, Nonprofit--Management--Addresses,
essays, lectures. I. Borst, Diane. II. Montana,
Patrick J.
HD38.M3188   658'.04'8   77-23169
ISBN 0-8144-5437-2

Fifth Printing

Preface

The concept for this book developed as a result of repeated requests from students in schools of public and business administration and from executives in nonprofit organizations for a comprehensive source of information on the management of these organizations. Coupled with these requirements were the authors' interests in the application of business management techniques to nonprofit organizations.

Most of the material available at the time consisted of articles in periodicals; these were widely scattered throughout the professional literature and served as points of reference in compiling this book.

The articles were selected from a variety of sources for their applicability and relevance to the management process, their ease of reading, and their understandability. All the articles are intended to reflect state-of-the-art information. With a few exceptions, they were published between 1973 and 1975.

We hope this book will be of benefit to the many thousands of people currently managing in nonprofit organizations. It is our intention that the book will prove helpful to students of management and to those who are considering a career in a nonprofit organization. We also recognize that there are gaps in available materials and would appreciate hearing from readers about new articles of interest on managing nonprofit organizations.

68503

Many people deserve credit for their contribution to this book. Those who wrote the original articles deserve special credit, for the book would be impossible without them. Special thanks are due to Steve Manning and Ray Cornbill for sharing their thoughts and ideas on the basic thrust and organization of the book and for countless discussions on management principles and their application in the nonprofit area. Our thanks go also to Barbara Kaplan, who oversaw all the details of obtaining permissions, typing, manuscript reading, and proofing.

DIANE BORST
PATRICK J. MONTANA

Contents

Introduction

The growth of nonprofit organizations and public service institutions in recent years has been astounding. In the year 1970, general government employed 14.3 million persons—or 17 percent of the total labor force. Health expenditures of $126 billion comprised 12 percent of the gross national product of the United States. Total educational services for the same year were $76 billion— or 5 percent of the total gross national product. Even allowing for overlaps and possible double counting, these three sectors alone accounted for nearly 25 percent of this country's total gross national product. This represents a phenomenal change from the manufacturing and production-oriented economy that characterizes the growth periods of the first half of the twentieth century. Continued growth is forecast for these sectors as well as for other nonprofit sectors, such as associations. Thus, the nonprofit sector is becoming a major portion of modern society and of the economy. These organizations must perform satisfactorily if society and the economy are to function efficiently and effectively.

Yet the evidence for satisfactory performance in the nonprofit fields is not impressive. Government, education, health care, associations, foundations, religious and charitable organizations, as well as quasi-governmental institutions are all huge beyond the imagination of an earlier generation. Many dispose of astronomical budgets. Almost everywhere they are "in crisis." Cities appear to

1

be leaning toward the brink of economic collapse; pressures for cost containment in the health care field can be read daily in newspapers and periodicals; education has come under heavy public criticism; tuition fees continually increase and the gap between income and expense continues to widen in many private educational institutions; some foundations have severely curtailed their grants; government seems ever-increasingly distrusted. These nonprofit organizations appear to be attacked on all sides for lack of performance. People are complaining louder and louder of "bureaucracy" and mismanagement in these institutions. "What are we getting for our dollars?" is a common question.

One of the clearest responses of the nonprofit sector to these criticisms has been to become more "management conscious." Nonprofit organizations increasingly turn to business to learn "management." In all nonprofit organizations, concepts and tools of business management are becoming more and more popular. These are wide in range and include management training and development, systems analysis, planning, management by objectives, project management, and participatory management techniques. This is a healthy sign, but it is no more than that. It does not mean that the nonprofit organizations understand the problems of management, nor does it mean that techniques that are well-proved in industry can be applied without modification. The increased interest in management does mean that executives of nonprofit organizations have begun to realize that at present, they may not be managing as well as they could be.

The purpose of this volume is to assemble selected articles, speeches, and periodicals on managing nonprofit organizations. The book is intended to provide the reader with information on various techniques and management tools now being applied in a variety of nonprofit organizations. The theme emerging from this selection of articles is that of the management process. Expressed in its most basic terms, the management process is generally described as planning, organizing, and controlling. This description is useful in considering management as an ongoing dynamic process.

Planning is an extremely important element of the management process and should occupy a significant percentage of any manager's time. Planning, simply defined, is the process of determining what an organization is, where it wants to go, and what alternatives exist toward that end. Planning exists on a variety of levels in each organization; strategic or long-range planning may look out over a five- to ten-year period; operational planning has a somewhat shorter time frame; and day-to-day planning is done within the organization's operational planning environment.

Organizing is the second major element in the management process. The organizing function implies the division of the work of the organization. Organizing, like planning, is process oriented; resources are allocated and reallocated; and authority and responsibility are integrated toward carrying out the organization's plans. The area of interpersonal relationships plays a large part in the organizing process, for this is how the manager actually combines the resources—the largest portion of which are people—to achieve the organization's plans.

Controlling is the third segment in the management process; it provides a link to the planning phase. Controlling, simply stated, answers the question "Did we achieve what we set out to?"—Were the objectives met? The function of the control process is to ensure effective and efficient use of resources. Controlling might include such activities as designing work plans and milestone charts, reviewing progress, scheduling, and performance appraisal. The results of each of these activities are then available for use as a link in terms of evaluation and feedback to the planning element of the management process. Thus, the last activity in the management process is to evaluate how well the organization has done in achieving its planning objectives, and then to prepare to repeat the entire process. The process and its links may be viewed this way:

These elements of the management process are widely accepted in the business world and, in fact, some very sophisticated techniques have been developed in each of the areas. These include such things as PERT (Program Evaluation and Review Technique) and CPM (Critical Path Method) in the controlling function, complex simulation models for planning, and operations research techniques, such as optimization formulas for use in the organizing function of management. This book is not addressed to these fairly advanced techniques, but rather to elements of the management process as they are currently being applied in the nonprofit sector.

The manager in a nonprofit organization may have an immediate and predictable reaction to applying generally accepted business management techniques in a nonprofit setting. This reaction may range from the opinion that "it's impossible" to the opinion that "nonprofits are different and cannot be managed like a business." Undoubtedly, there are significant differences between profit-making and non-profit-making businesses—just as there are significant differences among industries within the profit sector: management techniques and styles in the aircraft production sector are vastly different from those applied in production of garments. Yet they both use elements of the same management process. And, in the nonprofit organization, there *is* a uniqueness. The important notion is to recognize the uniqueness not as a stand-alone, single unit, but as a part of a larger process. Not *all* business management techniques will work in the nonprofit sector, but it is important to recognize that some business management techniques are, in fact, working very well in a variety of organizations within the nonprofit sector. The first section of this book addresses the question of whether or not nonprofits can, in fact, be managed.

Succeeding sections on Planning and Analysis, Management by Objectives, Project Management, and Participatory Management contain articles showing how these management concepts are now being applied in specific nonprofit sectors and organizations. Each section in itself can be viewed as a way to apply the management process in a nonprofit organization. While reading each of these sections, the reader is encouraged to bear in mind the basic elements of the management process—Planning, Organizing, and Controlling—so as to be able to apply these styles and approaches conceptually to his or her "own" nonprofit organization. The closing section of the book addresses itself to managing such unique organizations as the federal judicial system; the presidency; philanthropies; an art museum; and the Naval Shore Establishment.

The articles in each section were chosen from as many sectors as possible so as to be of interest to managers of a variety of nonprofit organizations. A wide scope of sources was used to provide the reader with a broad perspective on *Managing Nonprofit Organizations*.

Part 1

MANAGING
THE NONPROFIT ORGANIZATION

Can It Be Done?

BEFORE ADDRESSING THE "HOW TO" OF ANY PROBLEM, IT IS ALWAYS WISE TO step back and ask a question about whether the problem can be solved at all, with a given state of resource and technology. This notion is particularly important in addressing the question of managing the nonprofit organization. One of the most frequently heard comments has to do with the "uniqueness myth" propagated by many nonprofit organizations. It takes the form of "We're different from business—we don't make a profit," or "We don't have any objectives," or "We don't have any accountability," or "We don't have any shareholders or stockholders." Any or all of these may be true in varying degrees throughout the nonprofit sector, but, as shown in the articles in this section, these attributes of the "uniqueness myth" can be used in a positive sense in determining the kind of management techniques that are applicable and which can successfully be used.

The matrix below shows the titles and authors of the articles as well as the nonprofit sectors they address.

	Government	Education	Health	Religious and Charitable	Associations and Others
Can Nonprofit Organizations Be Well Managed? Robert N. Anthony	X	X	X	X	X
Managing the Public Service Institution Peter F. Drucker	X	X	X	X	X
Can a Scientific/Technical Executive from Industry Find Happiness in a Government Agency? Robert M. Schaffner	X				
The Academic Role of the Vice President for Health Sciences: Can a Walrus Become a Unicorn? Edmund D. Pellegrino, M.D.			X		
Managing for Results in the Federal Government Frederic V. Malek	X				

Can Nonprofit Organizations Be Well Managed?

Robert N. Anthony

There are at least two implications in the question: Can nonprofit organizations be well managed? First, the question implies that there is a basic difference between nonprofit organizations and profit-oriented organizations. I believe this to be the case. The fundamental distinction is one of purpose: A profit-oriented organization exists to earn a profit; its success is measured primarily by the amount of profit. A nonprofit organization exists to render a service; its success is measured primarily by how well it renders this service.

The second implication, of course, is that nonprofit organizations are not well managed. I can't prove by statistics that this is so, for there is no reliable way of measuring the excellence of management. I could point to stories with which most of you are familiar—the unnecessary red tape involved in getting an automobile registered; the public works irregularities in Somerville; the Middlesex County Courthouse; the welfare mess; the exorbitant increases in hospital costs; the condition of our city streets; and on and on. But anyone could counter these examples with equally depressing stories from the private sector: The Penn Central bankruptcy, the cost overruns at Lockheed, the

Reprinted with permission from *Vital Speeches of the Day,* February 18, 1971.

7

Brighton condominium that collapsed last month. So these stories by themselves don't prove anything.

Nevertheless, I think most informed persons would agree that the Penn Central, Lockheed, and Brighton situations are exceptions to the general rule, whereas the depressing stories about nonprofit organizations *are* the general rule.

I do not mean to imply there are no excellent managers in nonprofit organizations. I regard Robert McNamara as one of the great managers of this generation, and he does just as great a job in managing the World Bank or the Department of Defense, which are nonprofit organizations, as he did in managing the Ford Motor Company. John Knowles is a great manager of the Massachusetts General Hospital, and there are certainly others. But by and large, management of government organizations, educational organizations (present company excepted, of course), or health care organizations, and of the whole galaxy of organizations that make up the public sector is mediocre.

Is this situation inevitable? Or is there a likelihood that nonprofit organizations can become well managed? In exploring this question, I propose to list six reasons for the present deplorable state of affairs and to analyze what, if anything, can be done to rectify them. They are (1) the absence of a profit measure, (2) the absence of competition, (3) politics, (4) weak governing boards, (5) tradition, and (6) low management salaries.

The first reason is inherent in the very nature of a nonprofit organization, namely, that it does not exist for the purpose of earning a profit. Managers of profit-oriented companies often complain about the difficulty of measuring profits precisely, and all of you are aware of the frailties of even the best accounting systems. But despite these difficulties, the profit measure gives managers a control tool far superior to the tools that exist in a nonprofit organization. Industrial managers can make decisions in terms of their effect on profit, they can measure performance in terms of profit, and they have an automatic danger signal if profits decline.

In a nonprofit organization, the situation is quite different. Such organizations exist to render services. But "service" is a fuzzy concept. It is difficult for anyone to measure how much service was rendered, or to decide how much money needs to be spent to achieve a given level of service. As a case in point, can any of you judge whether spending 10 percent more at Boston University would give you a 10 percent better education, or whether spending 10 percent less would give you a correspondingly poorer education? Or can you decide what would be the best use of an incremental 10 percent if it became available: more teachers? higher faculty pay? more visual aids? more research? There is no analytical way of making such choices in a nonprofit organization. No one can establish a mathematical relationship between money spent and benefits received.

The difficulty of defining objectives, of deciding on the resources required to reach objectives, and of measuring the efficiency and effectiveness with which the organizations perform to meet objectives is, I believe, the most serious management problem in a nonprofit organization. It is an inherent problem; that is, there is no foreseeable way of developing a control structure in a nonprofit organization that is as good as a structure that can be built around the profit measure.

Although this problem will always be with us, I do believe that a great deal can be done to improve control systems in nonprofit organizations. Many of the techniques developed in the private sector are useful in nonprofit organizations, but they have been slow to adopt them. The unique problem in the public sector is to develop better measures of output—what the organization does, and how well it does it. A great deal of research into this problem is in progress, and some of this effort is already bearing fruit.

The driving force in our economy, the one thing that distinguishes it from pure socialist economies, is competition. In most nonprofit organizations, the force of competition is muted. Business companies compete for customers; they do everything they can to woo prospective customers. In many nonprofit organizations, the new client is not an opportunity; he is a problem. He is not a source of revenue; he is a source of headaches.

Internally, the spur of competition forces units within a business constantly to worry about giving better service and finding ways to cut costs. If they don't do this, a competitor will take the business away. Most nonprofit organizations have no such motivation because they have no competitors.

To some extent, this situation is inevitable. It is not likely that anyone would create a private army to compete with the U.S. Department of Defense. But if nonprofit managers appreciated what a powerful force competition is, they could do a great deal to harness it. They can do this on at least two levels.

First, a service might be transferred from the public to the private sector. We see stirrings in this direction in the field of elementary education, where, for example, contracts for the teaching of reading are let to private companies.

Second, much can be done to promote a spirit of competition *within* a nonprofit organization. In the Navy, for example, the several Navy shipyards now compete with one another for business. They bid for overhaul work with the ship commanders, and if their price is not low enough, or their service not good enough to obtain a satisfactory volume of overhaul work, this is a signal that something is wrong with the shipyard. A direct result of this competition was the shutting down of the Brooklyn Naval Shipyard.

Whenever units of an organization perform a similar service or whenever a unit performs a service that is also performed in the private sector, opportunities to promote competition exist.

Politics is an emotion-laden word, and this is unfortunate. The general public tends to think that politicians are not quite as good as other people. They tend to forget that we live in a democracy and that the democratic process can't operate without politicians.

It is a simple fact that a politician can't do his job if he is not reelected. He therefore must please his constituency. He must do favors for them, and he must sometimes vote for measures that support his own district, even though he is not convinced that they are in the best interest of the whole country. Furthermore, a good politician sometimes supports bills that he personally is not enthusiastic about as a trade for support from his colleagues for his own pet bills. This is the way the system works, and it cannot work any other way.

Not all public-sector organizations are political, but in those that are, political considerations impede good management. The Portsmouth Navy Yard is kept open, even though Defense managers do not see a compelling economic reason for doing so. Favors are repaid by putting people on the public payroll. Managers must endure unfair attacks just so that a politician can get his name in the headlines.

These are serious problems, but I do not think they need be as serious as some people make them out to be. The Military Services kowtowed to Chairman Rivers of the House Armed Services Committee. They spent many millions of dollars of the taxpayers' money in Charleston, South Carolina, and on junkets of various kinds, justifying all this in the name of politics. But at the same time, scarcely any favors were given to Chairman Mahon, of the House Appropriations Committee, a much more powerful man, actually, than Chairman Rivers. The reason was simply that Chairman Mahon is not the type of man who asks for favors. I rather suspect that if the military had shown more backbone in standing up to Chairman Rivers, no dire consequences would have resulted, and much of the taxpayers' money would have been saved.

Although politics is inevitable in a democracy, I don't want anyone to make the inference that the way to cure this problem is to eliminate the democratic process. As Winston Churchill said: "Democracy is the worst form of government there is, except for all the others."

About 30 years ago, there was some support for a movement called technocracy, whose advocates painted a glowing picture of a society run by engineers, the same way a factory is run. Most people realize that such a society would not be a very nice place to live in. Some people also laud the efficiency of the socialist system as practiced in the Soviet Union. Such a system seems to work well when a nation is in the "take-off" stage, that is, when it is making the transition from a primitive to an industrial state; but it doesn't work well at all in a highly developed society such as we have, and such as exists in the countries of Western Europe. Indeed, the evidence is pretty conclusive that it has not worked very well in the Soviet Union, and that the Soviets are shifting their system to one that resembles ours.

Politics is inevitable and necessary, but there are opportunities to lessen the political influence on nonprofit organizations. The recent creation of the U. S. Postal Service, with the likelihood that postmaster selection will become nonpolitical—and, more importantly, the likelihood that postal wage rates will be set through normal bargaining rather than through pressure on Congressional Committees—is one desirable step. The creation of authorities, such as the Massachusetts Bay Transportation Authority, is another, although the history of MBTA demonstrates that this device does not by itself guarantee good management.

Another desirable movement is the tendency to reduce the number of officials elected and to increase the number who are appointed. The qualifications required to get elected and the qualifications required to manage an organization are quite different. If a sheriff, or a school superintendent, or a state treasurer is chosen by the electorate, he is less likely to be a good manager than if he is selected by the county commissioners, the school board, or the governor.

In all organizations, the top management is responsible to some policy-making and review body. In a profit-oriented company, this is the board of directors. In federal, state, and local governments, it is the legislative body, or in the case of municipalities, the voters directly, and I have already referred to their influence earlier.

In other types of nonprofit organizations—hospitals, churches, universities, charitable organizations of various kinds, and art museums—there is a board of governors, board of trustees, or body with a similar title. Its function is to set policy and to check up on how well this policy is carried out. By and large, these boards do not do a very good job.

The trustees of a nonprofit organization should have a more important role than the board of directors of a corporation. In a nonprofit organization, the objectives are difficult to define, and there is no automatic danger signal comparable to the profit measure, so an appraisal of policies and of management performance depends on the soundness of the judgment of the board of trustees.

Despite the innate importance of their role, board members typically are not selected for their sound judgment. In some cases election is regarded as an honor in recognition of outstanding community service. In other cases, board members are selected primarily because they are good fund raisers. Such board members are competent individuals in their own field, but only by chance do they possess the skills that are necessary to do the job that the board should do.

Furthermore, since board membership is supposed to be regarded as an honor, members are rarely paid for their services. This means that only the wealthy can afford to give much time to board activities; the others have only a limited amount of time that they can afford to divert from their main endeavors.

Boards therefore tend to rubber-stamp the policies of the institution's top management. The have neither the time nor the special competence to do otherwise. Indeed, university trustees are sometimes told, "You have two functions: (1) to select a good president, and (2) to support him. Period."

This situation badly needs correcting, and there are a number of forces at work that well may lead to correction. The disturbances on university campuses in the spring of 1970 awakened the eyes of many boards to the fact that they needed to know more about what was going on and that they had a more important responsibility than they realized.

I hope these trends continue. The governing boards of nonprofit organizations need beefing up. Either the full board, or an executive meeting thereof, should meet at least monthly, and the meetings should be long enough so that there can be a thorough discussion of policies and a probing of actual management performance.

Some university presidents and other nonprofit managers regard such activities as infringement on their prerogatives, and they are upset about the possibility. The changes that are occurring *do* require a different relationship between the president and the board, and problems are likely to arise in adjusting to the new relationships, but there is no inherent reason why a board functioning as it should, should not actually be an aid to the president.

I have two suggestions that might speed up the process of improving the performance of boards of trustees. The first is that boards might seek out recently retired executives for membership. Many executives are by company policy required to retire at a set age, even though they may still be vigorous. They have the qualifications to be good board members, and they have the time. The second suggestion is that boards consider adding professional board members, persons whose principal occupation is serving on boards. They would, of course, be paid. Many companies find it useful to have a few professional directors on their board, men who have the knowledge and the personal qualifications that make them especially effective in such a role.

Mrs. Esther Weltman, one of the members of the Boston University Board, is an example of a real professional, except that she is not paid. She is a member of several college and university boards, she gives most of her time to this work, and the insights that she brings to the board meeting are extraordinarily valuable contributions.

Traditions have accumulated in nonprofit organizations that inhibit good management.

Many people in nonprofit organizations don't even know what the word "manager" is supposed to mean. As we use the term in business, the manager is the boss; he is number 1. His job is not to do the work, but to see to it that the work gets done. The Boston University football team has a person called the "manager," but he is not really the manager in the usual sense. The quarterback or the coach are the closest equivalents.

This misunderstanding of the nature of management results in the wrong people being appointed managers. In a hospital, the number 1 man should not be chosen because he is the best surgeon; he should be chosen because he is the best manager. In a school system, the superintendent need not be an expert on curriculum design, and the fact that he has successfully completed x number of courses in a school of education is largely irrelevant, unless these courses relate specifically to educational management. The primary qualification of a good superintendent is that he be a good manager.

But some very prominent people do not understand this distinction. My colleague John Kenneth Galbraith is quoted as saying, "The Harvard Business School is a good school. We should be grateful to it for training people who will shoulder the dull, tedious administrative jobs in organizations." It saddens me to read such a complete misconception. The manager is not the person who does "dull, tedious jobs"; he is the boss.

The tradition that the head of an organization should be a technical specialist disappeared from business companies early in the twentieth century. It persists in nonprofit organizations, and results in the selection of top men who simply are not qualified to manage. Indeed, many of these technical experts don't even enjoy management. They would be happier working at their specialty.

A second influence of tradition is that nonprofit organizations have been slow to adopt modern management techniques. Nonprofit organizations do differ from profit-oriented companies, but they also have much in common. They both have objectives, they both make decisions about the use of resources to accomplish these objectives, and in both cases an important management function is to see to it that the organization uses these resources efficiently and effectively. Business companies have developed a number of valuable tools for aiding management in this process: budgets, responsibility centers, cost analyses, standard costs, analyses of variances, management by objectives, linear programming, probability analysis—I could extend this list indefinitely. Most of these can be used, or adapted for use, in nonprofit organizations, but nonprofit organizations are slow to do so.

To take just one example: Nonprofit organizations are now hearing a lot about a control system called PPBS or Program Budgeting. A research report in a recent issue of *Science*[1] lists the development of PPBS as one of the 62 leading achievements in the social sciences. Anyone familiar with business practice knows that there is nothing fundamentally new about PPBS; it is an adaptation to nonprofit organizations of techniques that many profit-oriented companies have been using for at least 20 years.

The mere statement of this problem suggests the solution: Get rid of the

1. Karl W. Deutsch, John Platt, and Dieter Senghaas, "Conditions Favoring Major Advances in Social Sciences," *Science,* Feb. 5, 1971.

traditional ways of thinking about management; recognize the management function for what it is, and use the modern management techniques that are available. This is, of course, much easier said than done. It requires education. It requires pressure, and this is where the revitalized Board of Trustees can play a key role. And above all, it requires a new breed of managers.

This brings me to my final point: pay. We need better managers in nonprofit organizations. In order to get them, we need to make the profession of management in nonprofit organizations more attractive to young people who are choosing a career. The principal way of doing this is to increase management salaries. Not the starting pay, for starting pay, and indeed pay at most levels except the top, are quite competitive with those in business companies. Rather, the crucial amount is the salary that the top management earns, for this is the goal which the young person thinks about in career selection. Pay is partly attractive for its own sake, of course, but perhaps more importantly, pay is a signal of the importance that society attaches to a job.

The president of a fairly large business company can expect to earn $100,000, $200,000, or more a year. The stockholders are glad to authorize such payments because they know that management talent is scarce, and that they benefit when they attract and hold an outstanding manager. In the public sector, there is a feeling that $30,000 is a generous salary for the top manager of an organization of comparable size and responsibility. A salary of $60,000 is regarded as unusually lucrative, and $85,000 is, so far as I know, the top.

The average citizen doesn't appreciate the scarcity of management talent. He tends to think that any salary much higher than his own is a "political plum." He thinks that a school superintendent, a university president, a hospital administrator, or the administrator of a government organization should do his job as a public service; he should value the honor of the position, and not be so crass as to think about money. This is a long-standing tradition, and it is most unfortunate. Happily, this attitude is changing, and it is changing rapidly. As a class, school superintendents are perhaps the category in which the change is most visible. Some of them now earn $50,000, a few make more. Until recently, the head of the state prison system in New Hampshire was paid less than $15,000; his pay is now $19,000. The pay for managers of state government agencies has reached the $50,000 level. I hope and believe this trend will continue. Twenty years ago, I said that the salaries of top managers in government should be quadrupled. As a measure of the improvement, my present feeling is that the salaries should be about doubled.

The effects of adequate salary policy are not felt for a whole generation, unfortunately. Although its real purpose is to attract outstanding people to the profession—an infusion of new blood—the immediate effect of a salary increase, of course, is simply to pay more money to the people who are already there. Thus, we must be patient and not expect results too rapidly.

That completes my list, but I want to point out an intentional omission from it. To some people, "bureaucracy" is a very bad word, and they attribute the poor performance of nonprofit organizations to the "bureaucrat" and to the "civil service regulations" that allegedly guarantee lifetime jobs to incompetent people. Now, any large organization is technically called a bureaucracy, and the people who work in it are bureaucrats. Except for the top managers, I do not observe a significant difference between the average ability of people in a nonprofit organization and people in a business company. Nor do I see any great difference between the impact of federal civil service regulations and the impact of the personnel regulations in a large private company.

In general, the top managers of nonprofit organizations are not as able as their business counterparts, nor is it likely that management talent will be identified and rewarded as quickly. Influential people are beginning to recognize that if this situation is corrected, the new managers will correct the other problems.

My answer to the question "Can nonprofit organizations be well managed?" is thus a qualified "yes." It is qualified because the problems of measuring performance and the inevitable political considerations make the management job inherently more difficult. But the quality of management can be a lot better than it now is. I have suggested some ways in which I think improvement might be brought about—the adoption of modern management methods, increased competition, a new role for the board of trustees, and greater public recognition of the management skill.

Above all, I mean to suggest to you that nonprofit organizations are becoming a more attractive and more challenging place in which to work and that they are offering correspondingly better rewards for those who decide to make a career there. I hope that some of you will look into the possibilities.

Managing the Public Service Institution

Peter F. Drucker

Service institutions are an increasingly important part of our society. Schools and universities; research laboratories; public utilities; hospitals and other health-care institutions; professional, industry, and trade associations; and many others—all these are as much "institutions" as is the business firm, and are therefore equally in need of management.* They all have people who are designated to exercise the management function and who are paid for doing the management job—even though they may not be called "managers," but "administrators," "directors," "executives," or some other such title.

These "public service" institutions—to give them a generic name—constitute the real growth sector of a modern society. Indeed, what we have now is a "multi-institutional" society rather than a "business" society. The traditional

* Government agencies and bureaus are also "service institutions," of course, and have management problems which are comparable to those of the institutions I have mentioned. But because they also partake of a general "governmental" purpose, not usefully defined in management terms, I shall not be dealing with them in this article. I shall feel free, however, to include such quasi-governmental organizations as the TVA or the post office in my discussion.

Reprinted with permission of the author and publisher from *The Public Interest*, No. 33, Fall 1973.

title of the American college course still tends to read Business and Government. But this is an anachronism. It should read Business, Government, and Many Others.

All public service institutions are being paid for out of the economic surplus produced by economic activity. The growth of the service institutions in this century is thus the best testimonial to the success of business in discharging its economic task. Yet unlike, say, the early nineteenth-century university, the service institutions are not mere "luxury" or "ornament." They are, so to speak, main pillars of a modern society, load-bearing members of the main structure. They *have* to perform if society and economy are to function. It is not only that these service institutions are a major expense of a modern society; half of the personal income of the United States (and of most of the other developed countries) is spent on public service institutions (including those operated by the government). Compared to these "public service" institutions, both the "private sector" (i.e., the economy of goods) and the traditional government functions of law, defense, and public order, account for a smaller share of the total income flow of today's developed societies than they did around 1900—despite the cancerous growth of military spending.

Every citizen in the developed, industrialized, urbanized societies depends for his very survival on the performance of the public service institutions. These institutions also embody the values of developed societies. For it is in the form of education and health care, knowledge and mobility—rather than primarily in the form of more "food, clothing, and shelter"—that our society obtains the fruits of its increased economic capacities and productivity.

Yet the evidence for performance in the service institutions is not impressive, let alone overwhelming. Schools, hospitals, and universities are all big beyond the imagination of an earlier generation. They all dispose of astronomical budgets. Yet everywhere they are "in crisis." A generation or two ago, their performance was taken for granted. Today, they are being attacked on all sides for lack of performance. Services which the nineteenth century managed with aplomb and apparently with little effort—the postal service, for instance—are deeply in the red, require enormous and ever-growing subsidies, yet give poorer service everywhere. In every country the citizen complains ever more loudly of "bureaucracy" and mismanagement in the institutions that are supposed to serve him.

ARE SERVICE INSTITUTIONS MANAGEABLE?

The response of the service institutions to this criticism has been to become "management conscious." They turn increasingly to business to learn "management.'' In all service institutions, ''manager development,'' ''management by objectives,'' and many other concepts and tools of business management are becoming increasingly popular. This is a healthy sign—but no more than that. It does not mean that the service institutions understand the problems of managing themselves. It only means that they have begun to realize that, at present, they are not being managed.

Yet, though ''performance'' in the public service institutions is the exception rather than the rule, the exceptions do prove that service institutions can perform. Among American public service agencies of the last 40 years, for instance, there is the Tennessee Valley Authority (TVA), the big regional electric-power and irrigation project in the Southeastern United States. (TVA's performance was especially notable during its early years, in the 1930s and 1940s, when it was headed by David Lilienthal.) Whereas a great many—perhaps most—schools in the inner-city, black ghettos of America deserve all the strictures of the ''deschooling'' movement, a few schools in the very worst ghettos (e.g., in New York's South Bronx) have shown high capacity to help the most ''disadvantaged'' children to acquire the basic skills of literacy.

What is it that the few successful service institutions do (or eschew) that makes them capable of performance? This is the question to ask. And it is a *management* question—of a special kind. In most respects, the service institution is not very different from a business enterprise. It faces similar—if not precisely the same—challenges in seeking to make work productive. It does not differ significantly from a business in its ''social responsibility.'' Nor does the service institution differ very much from business enterprise with respect to the manager's work and job, to organizational design and structure, or to the job and structure of top management. *Internally,* the differences tend to reside in terminology rather than in substance.

But the service institution is in a fundamentally different ''business'' from business. It is different in its purpose. It has different values. It needs different objectives. And it makes a different contribution to society. ''Performance and results'' are quite different in a service institution from what they are in a business. ''Managing for performance'' is the one area in which the service institution differs significantly from a business.

WHY SERVICE INSTITUTIONS DO NOT PERFORM

There are three popular explanations for the common failure of service institutions to perform:

>   Their managers aren't ''businesslike.''
>   They need ''better men.''
>   Their objectives and results are ''intangible.''

All three are alibis rather than explanations.

The service institution will perform, it is said again and again, if only it is managed in a "businesslike" manner. Colbert, the great minister of Louis XIV, was the first to blame the performance difficulties of the nonbusiness—the service—institution on this lack of "businesslike" management. Creator of the first "modern" public service in the West, Colbert never ceased to exhort his officials to be "businesslike." The cry is still being repeated every day—by chambers of commerce, by presidential and royal commissions, by ministers in the Communist countries, and so on. If only, they all say, their administrators were to behave in a "businesslike" way, service institutions would perform. And of course, this belief also underlies, in large measure, today's "management boom" in the service institutions.

But it is the wrong diagnosis, and being "businesslike" is the wrong prescription for the ills of the service institution. The service institution has performance trouble precisely because it is *not* a business. What being "businesslike" usually means in a service institution is little more than control of cost. What characterizes a business, however, is focus on results—return on capital, share of market, and so on.

To be sure, there is a need for efficiency in all institutions. Because there is usually no competition in the service field, there is no outward and imposed cost control on service institutions as there is on business in a competitive (and even an oligopolistic) market. But the basic problem of service institutions is not high cost but lack of effectiveness. They may be very efficient—some are. But they then tend not to do the right things.

The belief that the public service institution will perform if only it is put on a "businesslike" basis underlies the numerous attempts to set up many government services as separate "public corporations"—again an attempt that dates back to Colbert and his establishment of "Crown monopolies." There may be beneficial side effects, such as freedom from petty civil service regulation. However, the intended main effect, performance, is seldom achieved. Costs may go down (though not always; setting up London Transport and the British Post Office as separate "businesslike" corporations, and thereby making them defenseless against labor union pressures, has led to skyrocketing costs). But services essential to the fulfillment of the institution's purpose may be slighted or lopped off in the name of "efficiency."

The best and worst example of the "businesslike" approach in the public service institution may well be the Port of New York Authority, set up in the 1920s to manage automobile and truck traffic throughout the two-state area (New York and New Jersey) of the Port of New York. The Port Authority has, from the beginning, been "businesslike" with a vengeance. The engineering of its bridges, tunnels, docks, silos, and airports has been outstanding. Its construction costs have been low and under control. Its financial standing has been extremely high, so that it could always borrow at most advantageous rates of interest. It made being "businesslike"—as measured, above all, by its standing with the banks—its goal and purpose. As a result, it did not concern itself with transportation policy in the New York metropolitan area, even though its bridges, tunnels, and airports generate much of the traffic in New York's streets. It did not ask, "Who are our constituents?" Instead it resisted any such question as "political" and "unbusinesslike." Consequently, it has come to be seen as the villain of the New York traffic and transportation problem. And when it needed support (e.g., in finding a site for New York's badly needed fourth airport), it found itself without a single backer, except the bankers. As a result the Port Authority may well become "politicized," that is, denuded of its efficiency without gaining anything in effectiveness.

"Better People"

The cry for "better people" is even older than Colbert. In fact, it can be found in the earliest Chinese texts on government. In particular, it has been the constant demand of all American "reformers," from Henry Adams shortly after the Civil War, to Ralph Nader today, all of whom have believed that the one thing lacking in the government agency is "better people."

But service institutions cannot, any more than businesses, depend on "supermen" to staff their managerial and executive positions. There are far too many institutions to be staffed. If service institutions cannot be run and managed by men of normal—or even fairly low—endowment, if, in other words, we cannot organize the task so that it will be done on a satisfactory level by men who only try hard, it cannot be done at all. Moreover, there is no reason to believe that the people who staff the managerial and professional positions in our "service" institutions are any less qualified, any less competent or honest, or any less hard-working than the men who manage businesses. By the same token, there is no reason to believe that business managers, put in control of service institutions, would do better than the "bureaucrats." Indeed, we know that they immediately become "bureaucrats" themselves.

One example of this was the American experience during World War II, when large numbers of business executives who had performed very well in their own companies moved into government positions. Many rapidly became "bureaucrats." The men did not change. But whereas in business they had been capable of obtaining performance and results, in government they found themselves producing primarily procedures and red tape—and deeply frustrated by the experience.

Similarly, effective businessmen who are promoted to head a "service staff" within a business (e.g., the hard-hitting sales manager who gets to be "Vice President—marketing services") tend to become "bureaucrats" almost overnight. Indeed, the "service institutions" within business—R&D departments, personnel staffs, marketing or manufacturing service staffs, and the like—apparently find it just as hard to perform as the public service institutions of society at large, which businessmen often criticize as being "unbusinesslike" and run by "bureaucrats."

"Intangible" Objectives

The most sophisticated and, at first glance, the most plausible explanation for the nonperformance of service institutions is the last one: The objectives of service institutions are "intangible," and so are their results. This is at best a half-truth.

The definition of what "our business is" is always "intangible," in a business as well as in a service institution. Surely, to say, as Sears Roebuck does, "Our business is to be the informed buyer for the American family," is "intangible." And to say, as Bell Telephone does, "Our business is service to the customers," may sound like a pious and empty platitude. At first glance, these statements would seem to defy any attempt at translation into operational, let alone quantitative, terms. To say, "Our business is electronic entertainment," as Sony of Japan does, is equally "intangible," as is IBM's definition of its business as "data processing." Yet, as these businesses have clearly demonstrated, it is not exceedingly difficult to derive concrete and measurable goals and targets from "intangible" definitions such as those cited previously.

"Saving souls" as the definition of the objectives of a church is, indeed, "intangible." At least the bookkeeping is not of this world. But church attendance is measurable. And so is "getting the young people back into the church."

"The development of the whole personality" as the objective of the school is, indeed, "intangible." But "teaching a child to read by the time he has finished third grade" is by no means intangible; it can be measured easily and with considerable precision.

"Abolishing racial discrimination" is equally unamenable to clear operational definition, let alone measurement. But to increase the number of black apprentices in the building trades is a quantifiable goal, the attainment of which can be measured.

Achievement is never possible except against specific, limited, clearly defined targets, in business as well as in a service institution. Only if targets are defined can resources be allocated to their attainment, priorities and deadlines be set, and somebody be held accountable for results. But the starting point for effective work is a definition of the purpose and mission of the institution—which is almost always "intangible," but nevertheless need not be vacuous.

It is often said that service institutions differ from businesses in that they have a plurality of constituencies. And it is indeed the case that service institutions have a great many "constituents." The school is of vital concern not only to children and their parents, but also to teachers, to taxpayers, and to the community at large. Similarly, the hospital has to satisfy the patient, but also the doctors, the nurses, the technicians, the patient's family—as well as taxpayers or, as in the United States, employers and labor unions who through their insurance contributions provide the bulk of the support of most hospitals. But business also has a plurality of constituencies. Every business has at least two different customers, and often a good many more. And employees, investors, and the community at large—even management itself—are also "constituencies."

MISDIRECTION BY BUDGET

The one basic difference between a service institution and a business is the way the service institution is paid. Businesses (other than monopolies) are paid for satisfying the customer. They are only paid when they produce what the customer wants and what he is willing to exchange his purchasing power for. Satisfaction of the customer is, therefore, the basis for performance and results in a business.

Service institutions, by contrast, are typically paid out of a budget allocation. Their revenues are allocated from a general revenue stream that is not tied to what they are doing, but is obtained by tax, levy, or tribute. Furthermore, the typical service institution is endowed with monopoly powers; the intended beneficiary usually has no choice.

Being paid out of a budget allocation changes what is meant by "performance" or "results." *"Results" in the budget-based institution means a larger budget. "Performance" is the ability to maintain or to increase one's budget.* The first test of a budget-based institution and the first requirement for its survival is to obtain the budget. And the budget is, by definition, related not to the achievement of any goals, but to the *intention* of achieving those goals.

This means, first, that efficiency and cost control, however much they are being preached, are not really considered virtues in the budget-based institution. The importance of a budget-based institution is measured essentially by the size of its budget and the size of its staff. To achieve results with a smaller budget or a smaller staff is, therefore, not "performance." It might actually endanger the institution. Not to spend the budget to the hilt will only convince the budget-maker—whether a legislature or a budget committee—that the budget for the next fiscal period can safely be cut.

Thirty or forty years ago, it was considered characteristic of Russian planning, and one of its major weaknesses, that Soviet managers, toward the end of the plan period, engaged in a frantic effort to spend all the money allocated to them, which usually resulted in total waste. Today, the disease has become universal, as budget-based institutions have become dominant everywhere. And "buying-in"—that is, getting approval for a new program or project by grossly underestimating its total cost—is also built into the budget-based institution.

"Parkinson's law" lampooned the British Admiralty and the British Colonial Office for increasing their staffs and their budgets as fast as the British Navy and the British Empire went down. "Parkinson's law" attributed this to inborn human perversity. But it is perfectly rational behavior for someone on a budget, for it is the budget, after all, that measures "performance" and "importance."

It is obviously not compatible with *efficiency* that the acid test of performance should be to obtain the budget. But *effectiveness* is even more endangered by reliance on the budget allocation. It makes it risky to raise the question of what the "business" of the institution should be. That question is always "controversial"; such controversy is likely to alienate support and will therefore be shunned by the budget-based institution. As a result, it is likely to wind up deceiving both the public and itself.

Take an instance from government: The U.S. Department of Agriculture has never been willing to ask whether its goal should be "farm productivity" or "support of the small family farm." It has known for decades that these two objectives are not identical as had originally been assumed, and that they are, indeed, becoming increasingly incompatible. To admit this, however, would have created controversy that might have endangered the Department's budget. As a result, American farm policy has frittered away an enormous amount of money and human resources on what can only (and charitably) be called a public relations campaign, that is, on a show of support for the small family farmer. The effective activities, however—and they have been very effective indeed—have been directed toward eliminating the small family farmer and replacing him by the far more productive "agribusinesses," that is, highly capitalized and highly mechanized farms, run as a business and not as a "way of life." This may well have been the right thing to do. But it certainly was not what the Department was founded to do, nor what the Congress, in approving the Department's budget, expected it to do.

Take a nongovernmental example—the American community hospital— which is "private" though "nonprofit." Everywhere it suffers from a growing confusion of missions and objectives, and the resulting impairment of its effectiveness and performance. Should a hospital be, in effect, a "physician's facility"—as most older American physicians still maintain? Should it focus on the major health needs of a community? Or should it try to do everything and be "abreast of every medical advance," no matter what the cost and no matter how rarely certain facilities will be used? Should it devote resources to preventive medicine and health education? Or should it, like the hospital under the British health service, confine itself strictly to repair of major health damage after it has occurred?

Every one of these definitions of the "business" of the hospital can be defended. Every one deserves a hearing. The effective American hospital will be a multipurpose institution and strike a balance between various objectives. What most hospitals do, however, is pretend that there are no basic questions to be decided. The result, predictably, is confusion and impairment of the hospital's capacity to serve any function and to carry out any mission.

PLEASING EVERYONE AND ACHIEVING NOTHING

Dependence on a budget allocation militates against setting priorities and concentrating efforts. Yet nothing is ever accomplished unless scarce resources are concentrated on a small number of priorities. A shoe manufacturer who has 22 percent of the market for work shoes may have a profitable business. If he succeeds in raising his market share to 30 percent, especially if the market for his kind of footwear is expanding, he is doing very well indeed. He need not concern himself too much with the 78 percent of the users of work shoes who buy from somebody else. And the customers for ladies' fashion shoes are of no concern to him at all.

Contrast this with the situation of an institution on a budget. To obtain its budget, it needs the approval, or at least the acquiescence, of practically everybody who could remotely be considered a "constituent." Whereas a market share of 22 percent might be perfectly satisfactory to a business, a "rejection" by 78 percent of its "constituents"—or even by a much smaller proportion—would be fatal to a budget-based institution. And this means that the service institution finds it difficult to set priorities; it must instead try to placate everyone by doing a little bit of everything—which, in effect, means achieving nothing.

Finally, being budget-based makes it even more difficult to abandon the wrong things, the old, the obsolete. As a result, service institutions are even more encrusted than are businesses with the barnacles of inherently unproductive efforts.

No institution likes to abandon anything it does. Business is no exception. But in an institution that is being paid for its performance and results, the unproductive, the obsolete, will sooner or later be killed off by the customers. In a budget-based institution no such discipline is being enforced. The temptation is great, therefore, to respond to lack of results by redoubling efforts. The temptation is great to double the budget, precisely *because* there is no performance.

Human beings will behave as they are rewarded for behaving—whether the reward be money and promotion, a medal, an autographed picture of the boss, or a pat on the back. This is one lesson the behavioral psychologist has taught us during the last 50 years (not that it was unknown before). A business, or any institution that is paid for its results and performance in such a way that the dissatisfied or uninterested customer need not pay, has to "earn" its income. An institution that is financed by a budget—or that enjoys a monopoly which the customer cannot escape—is rewarded for what it "deserves" rather than for what it "earns." It is paid for good intentions and for "programs." It is paid for not alienating important constituents rather than for satisfying any one group. It is misdirected, by the way it is paid, into defining "performance" and "results" as what will maintain or increase its budget.

WHAT WORKS

The exception, the comparatively rare service institution that achieves effectiveness, is more instructive than the great majority that achieve only "programs." It shows that effectiveness in the service institution is achievable—though by no means easy. It shows what different kinds of service institutions can do and need to do. It shows limitations and pitfalls. But it also shows that the service institution manager can do unpopular and highly "controversial" things if only he makes the risk-taking decision to set priorities and allocate resources.

The first and perhaps simplest example is that of the Bell Telephone System. A telephone system is a "natural" monopoly. Within a given area, one supplier of telephone service must have exclusive rights. The one thing any subscriber to a public telephone service requires is access to all other subscribers, which means territorial exclusivity for one monopolistic service. And as a whole country or continent becomes, in effect, one telephone system, this monopoly has to be extended over larger and larger areas.

An individual may be able to do without a telephone—although in today's society only at prohibitive inconvenience. But a professional man, a tradesman, an office, or a business *must* have a telephone. Residential phone service may still be an "option." Business phone service is compulsory. Theodore Vail, the first head of the organization, saw this in the early years of this century. He also saw clearly that the American telephone system, like the telephone systems in all other industrially developed nations, could easily be taken over by government. To prevent this, Vail thought through what the telephone company's business was and should be, and came up with his famous definition: "Our business is service." * This totally "intangible" statement of the telephone company's "business" then enabled Vail to set specific goals and objectives and to develop measurements of performance and results. His "customer satisfaction" standards and "service satisfaction" standards created nationwide competition between telephone managers in various areas, and became the criteria by which the managers were judged and rewarded. These standards measured performance as defined by the customer, for example, waiting time before an operator came on the line, or time between application for telephone service and its installation. They were meant to direct managers' attention to results.

Vail also thought through who his "constituents" were. This led to his conclusion—even more shocking to the conventional wisdom of 1900 than his "service" objectives—that it was the telephone company's task to make the public utility commissions of the individual states capable of effective rate regulation. Vail argued that a national monopoly in a crucial area could expect to escape nationalization only by being regulated. Helping to convert the wretchedly ineffectual, corrupt, and bumbling public utility commissions of late nineteenth-century populism into effective, respected, and informed adversaries was in the telephone company's own survival interest.

Finally, Vail realized that a telephone system depends on its ability to obtain capital. Each dollar of telephone revenue requires a prior investment of three to four dollars. Therefore, the investor too had to be considered a "constituent," and the telephone company had to design financial instruments and a financial policy that focused on the needs and expectations of the investor, and that made telephone company securities, whether bonds or shares, a distinct and preferred financial "product."

THE AMERICAN UNIVERSITY

The building of the American university from 1860 to World War I also illustrates how service institutions can be made to perform. The American university as it emerged during that era was primarily the work of a small number of men: Andrew D. White (President of Cornell, 1868–1885); Charles W. Eliot (President of Harvard, 1869–1909); Daniel Coit Gilman (President of Johns Hopkins, 1876–1901); David Starr Jordan (President of Stanford, 1891–1913);

---

* This was so heretical that the directors of the telephone company fired Vail when he first propounded his thesis in 1897—only to rehire him 10 years later when the absence of clear performance objectives had created widespread public demand for telephone nationalization even among such nonradicals as the Progressive wing of the Republican Party.

William Rainey Harper (President of Chicago, 1892–1904); and Nicholas Murray Butler (President of Columbia, 1902–1945).

These men all had in common one basic insight: The traditional "college"—essentially an eighteenth-century seminary to train preachers—had become totally obsolete, sterile, and unproductive. Indeed, it was dying fast; America in 1860 had far fewer college students than it had had 40 years earlier with a much smaller population. The men who built the new universities shared a common objective: to create a new institution, a true "university." And they all realized that while European examples, especially Oxford and Cambridge and the German university, had much to offer, these new universities had to be distinctively American institutions.

Beyond these shared beliefs, however, they differed sharply on what a university should be and what its purpose and mission were. Eliot, at Harvard, saw the purpose of the university as that of educating a leadership group with a distinct "style." His Harvard was to be a "national" institution rather than the parochial preserve of the "proper Bostonian" that Harvard College had been. But it also was to restore to Boston—and to New England generally—the dominant position of a moral elite, such as in earlier times had been held by the "Elect," the Puritan divines, and their successors, the Federalist leaders in the early days of the Republic. Butler, at Columbia—and, to a lesser degree, Harper at Chicago—saw the function of the university as the systematic application of rational thought and analysis to the basic problems of a modern society, from education to economics, and from domestic government to foreign affairs. Gilman, at Johns Hopkins, saw the university as the producer of, advanced knowledge; indeed, originally Johns Hopkins was to confine itself to advanced research and was to give no undergraduate instruction. White, at Cornell, aimed at producing an "educated public."

Each of these men knew that he had to make compromises. Each knew that he had to satisfy a number of "constituencies" and "publics," each of whom looked at the university quite differently. Both Eliot and Butler, for instance, had to build their new university on an old foundation (the others could build from the ground up) and had to satisfy—or at least to placate—existing alumni and faculty. They all had to be exceedingly conscious of the need to attract and hold financial support. It was Eliot, for instance, with all his insistence on "moral leadership," who invented the first "placement office" and set out to find well-paying jobs for Harvard graduates, especially in business. It was Butler, conscious that Columbia was a late-comer and that the millionaire philanthropists of his day had already been snared by his competitors (e.g., Rockefeller by Chicago), who invented the first "public relations" office in a university, designed—and most successfully—to reach the merely well-to-do and get their money.

These founders' definitions did not outlive them. Even during the lifetime of Eliot and Butler, for instance, their institutions escaped their control and began to diffuse objectives and to confuse priorities. In the course of this century, all these universities—and many others, like the University of California and other major state universities—have converged toward a common type. Today, it is hard to tell one "multiversity" from another. Yet the imprint of the founders has still not been totally erased. It is hardly an accident that the New Deal picked faculty members primarily from Columbia and Chicago to be high-level advisors and policy makers; for the New Deal was, of course, committed to the application of rational thought and analysis to public policies and problems. And 30 years later, when the Kennedy Administration came in with an underlying belief in the "style" of an "elite," it naturally turned to Harvard. For while each of the founding fathers of the modern American university made compromises and adapted to a multitude of constituencies, each had an objective and a definition of the university to which he gave priority and against which he measured performance. Clearly, the job the founders did almost a century ago will have to be done again for today's "multiversity," if it is not to choke on its own services.

SCHOOLS, HOSPITALS, AND THE TVA

The English "open classroom" is another example of a successful service institution. It is being promoted in this country as the "child-centered" approach to schooling, but its origin was in the concern with performance, and that is also the secret of its success. The English "open classroom" demands that each child—or at least each normal child—acquire the same measurable proficiency in the basic skills of literacy at roughly the same time. It is then the teacher's task to think through the learning path best suited to lead each child to a common and preset goal. The objectives are perfectly clear: the learning of specific skills, especially reading, writing, and figuring. They are identical for all children, measurable, and measured. Everything else is, in effect, considered irrelevant. Such elementary schools as have performed in the urban slums of this country—and there are more of them than the current "crisis in the classroom" syndrome acknowledges—have done exactly the same thing. The performing schools in black or Puerto Rican neighborhoods in New York, for instance, are those that have defined one clear objective—usually to teach reading—have eliminated or subordinated everything else, and then have measured themselves against a standard of clearly set performance goals.

The solution to the problem of the hospital, as is becoming increasingly clear, will similarly lie in thinking through objectives and priorities. The most promising approach may well be one worked out by the Hospital Consulting Group at Westinghouse Electric Corporation, which recognizes that the American hospital has a multiplicity of functions, but organizes each as an autonomous "decentralized" division with its own facilities, its own staff, and its own objectives. There would thus be a traditional-care hospital for the fairly small number of truly sick people who require what today's "full-time" hospital offers; an "ambulatory" medical hospital for diagnosis and outpatient work; an "ambulatory" surgical hospital for the large number of surgical patients— actually the majority—who, like patients after cataract surgery, a tonsilectomy, or most orthopedic surgery, are not "sick" and need no medical and little nursing care, but need a bed (and a bedpan) till the stitches are firm or the cast dries; a psychiatric unit—mostly for outpatient or overnight care; and a convalescent unit that would hardly differ from a good motel (e.g., for the healthy mother of a healthy baby). All these would have common services. But each would be a separate health care facility with different objectives, different priorities, and different standards of performance.

But the most instructive example of an effective service institution may be that of the early Tennessee Valley Authority. Built mainly during the New Deal, the TVA today is no longer "controversial." It is just another large power company, except for being owned by the government rather than by private investors. But in its early days, 40 years ago, the TVA was a slogan, a battle cry, a symbol. Some—friends and enemies alike—saw in it the opening wedge of the nationalization of electric energy in the United States. Others saw in it the vehicle for a return to Jeffersonian agrarianism, based on cheap power, government paternalism, and free fertilizer. Still others were primarily interested in flood control and navigation. Indeed, there was such a wealth of conflicting expectations that TVA's first head, Arthur Morgan, a distinguished engineer and economist, completely floundered. Unable to think through what the business of the TVA should be and how varying objectives might be balanced, Morgan accomplished nothing. Finally, President Roosevelt replaced him with an almost totally unknown young lawyer, David Lilienthal, who had little previous experience as an administrator.

Lilienthal faced up to the need to define the TVA's business. He concluded that the first objective was to build truly efficient electric plants and to supply an energy-starved region with plentiful and cheap power. All the rest, he decided, hinged on the attainment of this first need, which then became his operational priority. The TVA of today has accomplished a good many other objectives as well, from flood control and navigation to fertilizer production and, indeed, even balanced community development. But it was Lilienthal's insistence on a clear definition of the TVA's business and on setting priorities that explains why today's TVA is taken for granted, even by the very same people who, 40 years ago, were among its implacable enemies.

THE REQUIREMENTS FOR SUCCESS

Service institutions are a most diverse lot. The one and only thing they all have in common is that, for one reason or another, they cannot be organized under a competitive market test.* But however diverse the various kinds of "service institutions" may be, all of them need first to impose on themselves the discipline practiced by the managers and leaders of the institutions in the examples presented above.

1. They need to answer the question, *"What is our business and what should it be?"* They need to bring out into the open alternative definitions and to think them through carefully, perhaps even to work out (as did the presidents of the emerging American universities) the balance of different and sometimes conflicting definitions. What service institutions need is not to be more "businesslike." They need to be more "hospital-like," "university-like," "government-like," and so on. They need to be subjected to a performance test—if only to that of "socialist competition"—as much as possible. In other words, they need to think through their own specific function, purpose, and mission.

2. Service institutions need to derive *clear objectives and goals* from their definition of function and mission. What they need is not "better people," but people who do the management job systematically and who focus themselves and their institutions purposefully on performance and results. They do need efficiency—that is, control of costs. But, above all, they need effectiveness—that is, emphasis on the right results.

3. They then have to think through *priorities* of concentration which enable them to select targets; to set standards of accomplishment and performance (that is, to define the minimum acceptable results); to set deadlines; to go to work on results; and to make someone accountable for results.

4. They need to define *measurements of performance*—the "customer satisfaction" measurements of the telephone company, or the figures on reading performance by which the English "open classroom" measures its accomplishments.

5. They need to use these measurements to *"feed back"* on their efforts—that is, *they must build self-control from results into their system.*

6. Finally, they need an organized audit of *objectives and results,* so as to identify those objectives that no longer serve a useful purpose or have proven unattainable. They need to identify unsatisfactory performance, and activities which are obsolete, unproductive, or both. And they need a mechanism for

* This may no longer be necessarily true for the postal service. At last an independent postal company in the United States is trying to organize a business in competition to the government's postal monopoly. Should this work out, it might do more to restore performance to the mails than the recent setting up of a postal monopoly as a separate "public corporation" which is on a "businesslike" basis.

sloughing off such activities rather than wasting their money and their energies where the results are not.

This last requirement may be the most important one. The absence of a market test removes from the service institution the discipline that forces a business eventually to abandon yesterday's products—or else go bankrupt. Yet this requirement is the least understood.

No success lasts "forever." Yet it is even more difficult to abandon yesterday's success than it is to reappraise failure. Success breeds its own hubris. It creates emotional attachments, habits of thought and action, and, above all, false self-confidence. A success that has outlived its usefulness may, in the end, be more damaging than failure. Especially in a service institution, yesterday's success becomes "policy," "virtue," "conviction," if not indeed "Holy Writ," unless the institution imposes on itself the discipline of thinking through its mission, its objectives, and its priorities, and of building in feedback control from results over policies, priorities, and action. We are in such a "welfare mess" today in the United States largely because the welfare program of the New Deal had been such a success in the 1930s that we could not abandon it, and instead misapplied it to the radically different problem of the black migrants to the cities in the 1950s and 1960s.

To make service institutions perform, it should by now be clear, does not require "great men." It requires instead a system. The essentials of this system may not be too different from the essentials of performance in a business enterprise, as the present "management boom" in the service institutions assumes. But the application will be quite different. For the service institutions are not businesses; "performance" means something quite different for them.

Few service institutions today suffer from having too few administrators; most of them are overadministered and suffer from a surplus of procedures, organization charts, and "management techniques." What now has to be learned—it is still largely lacking—is to manage service institutions for performance. This may well be the biggest and most important management task for the remainder of this century.

Can a Scientific/Technical Executive from Industry Find Happiness in a Government Agency?

Robert M. Schaffner

Since the 1930s, both Republican and Democratic administrations have been bringing career business managers into the federal government in the hope that the management techniques that produce profits in the private sector can be adapted to the public sector. Lately, as the cry for higher productivity has intensified, the drive for experienced executive talent has intensified also. This trend, coupled with the increasing mobility of managers, has heralded an era in which more and more business-experienced people are leaving industry to start a "second career" in public service.

The professional civil servant who has been drawn from business management has found that management in government is indeed different from management in industry, and that it is well to be prepared for the differences. High and frequent turnover in top levels of government and in Congress, political considerations, complicated bureaucratic procedures, and media limelight all contribute to the rarefied climate in the public sector. For an executive who comes from a scientific/technical organization to take a comparable position in

Reprinted by permission of the publisher from *Management Review*, March 1975, © 1975 by AMACOM, a division of American Management Associations.

the federal government, there are some very specific differences. As one who has experienced this kind of transition, let me describe the conditions a scientific/technical manager will face when he or she heeds the call to public service.

THE HORIZONTAL AND THE VERTICAL

Perhaps the most obvious differences are in the organizational structure and work environment. Both private and public institutions have hierarchical structures, and both groups work with others in so-called horizontal relationships. But the balances between the two kinds of structure are different. In industry, an executive in the research and development division of a company may perform some task force work with marketing, or discuss start-up problems with production when a new product is being developed; however, his horizontal relationships are not ordinarily a sustained major element of his job. Public administration bureaucracy has a hierarchical structure for the clearance of reports, regulations, and similar matters, but there is also a much larger horizontal structure.

An agency research and development executive works with other scientific disciplines in the agency and has many contacts with the agency's field organization (which frequently has regulatory responsibilities). Outside the immediate agency or department, he must be involved with other governmental agencies that have overlapping concerns, often authorized by Congress. It is frequently necessary for several agencies to work together in formal task forces to determine who is going to carry out a given area of research and who will be involved in regulation and enforcement. Ultimately, these task forces must work out "memos of agreement and understanding" between two government departments to specify these responsibilities and actions." For example, my own agency, the Food and Drug Administration of the Department of Health, Education and Welfare, has working agreements with the Departments of Agriculture, Commerce, and the Treasury and also with the Environmental Protection Agency, the Consumer Product Safety Commission, and the Federal Trade Commission. Numerous discussions must be held and compromises made, and in some situations the two cabinet offices involved ultimately sign a written agreement.

In addition to sister agencies or departments, the public executive must work with Congress, or at least committees and members of Congress who are interested in his operations. Congresspeople may also have a direct interest in arranging discussions and meetings with their constituents to express opinions about regulations, to solve problems, or to ask for some form of scientific help.

Another large part of this horizontal structure is the industry regulated by the agency. The government administrator must work not with a homogeneous group, but with a collection of company representatives with widely diverse opinions. Again, considerable discussion is usually necessary in order to reach workable compromises.

CONSUMER GROUPS AND NEWS MEDIA

Add to this horizontal structure the increasing role of consumer advocates. They may often be useful in helping to set public policy and regulation, and they certainly help to balance the pressures from industry. But many of the consumer-advocate groups are not technically trained, so the public administrator is faced with the task of explaining the scientific reasons for certain regulations. Here, a problem often arises: Not only may there be differences among the scientific findings of the agency, the industry, and the academic world, but these various findings may also be at odds with the convictions of the consumer-advocate groups.

Occasionally resolution is reached in face-to-face discussions with consumer advocates. The FDA has organized an ad hoc Consumer Representatives Group composed of consumer-advocate organizations. Members of this group meet once a month with key members of the FDA to discuss problems in foods, drugs, and cosmetics. Frequently, the agency's priorities from a scientific standpoint are quite different from those of the consumer advocate, and long discussions are required to reach an understanding.

Beyond these considerations, the government executive's relationship with the news media is different from that of his industry days. Nearly all government activities are funded, of course, by taxpayers; consequently, the public administrator must work in a much more open environment than is true of private industry. The average research executive in the scientific field in industry has few contacts with the press—the contacts usually occur either when a new product is introduced or when a company has some form of emergency resulting from a product defect. The public administrator, however, has to work with the press on a day-to-day basis, particularly on items of current interest to the public.

Since the press and the public are entitled to information, the agency must be guided by the Freedom of Information Act and the particular agency regulation implementing this Act. In private industry, if a company is not prepared to talk about some new research development or to give details about a manufacturing process, it can decline to do so on the basis of "trade secrets." However, except for national security matters, the government does not have trade secrets, and it must release information, as soon as it is complete, in the form of research reports, investigations, regulations, or statements of enforcement actions. Good relationships with the press are vital for any agency's reputation with the general public and with its representatives, the members of Congress.

SETTING AND MEETING OBJECTIVES

Another difference in administration is the matter of setting objectives and goals. In private industry, the goal can usually be expressed in some rather definite language—for example, the development of new products to generate certain sales volume and profits or the expansion of the business to capture a specified percentage of the market. In public administration prior to the 1960s, objectives were essentially only those general legislative purposes spelled out by Congress. In recent years, more up-to-date management techniques have been applied to government agencies, and today some form of "management by objectives" procedure is being used throughout the federal government. However, some government managers and employees still find it difficult to employ MBO effectively.

The first problem for the manager is to relate his project to the agency's specific objective. For example, he may have to "sell" chemists the idea that the objective is not just the performance of a given number of analyses of food samples, but rather the completion of an investigation to determine whether a health hazard exists. When this idea has been sold, the manager must then work with his staff in setting "milestone dates" when certain parts of the project will be completed so they will fit into the overall schedule. Although the setting of fixed dates is often resented by bench scientists who feel that their boss is using this method to make them "punch a factory time clock," if the manager can get them to understand how their segment of the larger program results in an overall benefit to the welfare of the public, they can usually be persuaded of the necessity for deadlines.

Because the government organization receives its budget on an annual basis, many objectives have to be short-range so that accomplishment can be reported to Congress. The problem here is that the effectiveness of regulations, research findings, and the like is frequently difficult to measure, especially within a short period of time. For instance, to determine the effectiveness of a new regulation to improve the conditions in an industry, it is necessary first to measure the industry before the regulations are put into effect, allow a suitable period for industry response to the regulation, and then measure the industry again. This "measure–act–measure" procedure will cover a period of at least three years, and it is frequently difficult to measure the concurrent influences of factors other than the regulation.

To take another example from my own agency, the FDA is interested in seeing that various segments of the food manufacturing industry improve their operations so that filth and health hazards are eliminated. In 1971 there were two incidents of botulism from canned foods, and investigations showed that some canners were not following some of the basic principles of satisfactory thermal processing. The FDA issued a detailed Good Manufacturing Practice Regulation for the canning industry. Hundreds of canning plants are now being inspected to see if they are in compliance with the new regulations. The entire "measure–act–measure" procedure will take four or five years.

MOTIVATION AND INTERACTION

Thus far, we have talked only about the differences in organization, environment, and procedures involved in public administration as compared to the private sector. But any discussion on executive roles is incomplete, of course, without consideration of the most vital element—how one works with the people in these organizations.

Many behavioral scientists believe that motivation depends on how well an organization meets the employees' needs. There is some difference, I have found, between the ways in which public and private organizations meet such needs, and these differences can affect managerial behavior.

The most basic set of needs, the physiological, are certainly met by today's civil service pay scales; salaries are about equal to those in industry for all but the top levels of administration. The second need level, security, is amply met in the federal government by the tenure received after three years and also by an excellent retirement system. (Some people believe, in fact, that the public sector has overdone the security provision and provided a haven for mediocrity. In my experience, this criticism, although to some extent just, has been given undue emphasis.)

The physiological and security needs of the scientific public worker are met so well by the civil service and agency rules and regulations that it behooves managers to motivate their subordinates by emphasizing recognition and fulfillment needs. In some ways, the public sector executive has an advantage here over his counterpart in the private sector. In industry, technical goals are usually limited by the practical necessity of profit potential, but in government the goal is public benefit, and that presents a broader opportunity to apply scientific expertise and effort. For example, analytical chemists in industry may be called on to develop techniques to detect impurities only in the products that the company buys or sells. But government chemists have to devise methods for detecting contaminants that may be present in a wide variety of products.

A great deal of creativity is called for, and the chemists know they are responsible for protecting the public's health.

Also, government agencies afford a greater opportunity than industry for satisfying the recognition need by encouraging people to give speeches and publish papers. Government agencies can and do encourage such presentations, whereas many industrial firms restrict them as a matter of policy, for competitive reasons.

Finally, however, I must point out one significant advantage enjoyed by the industrial technical administrator over his government counterpart—He has much greater freedom of action in such matters as personnel selection and hiring, compensation adjustments, organizational revision, and program adjustment. The checks and balances built into government service are wisely conceived, but they often inhibit corrective action.

The Academic Role of the Vice President for Health Sciences

Can a Walrus Become a Unicorn?

Edmund D. Pellegrino, M.D.

While it is a very recent newcomer to the realm of academic administration, the job of vice president for health sciences* is perhaps the most exciting and interesting administrative post in the modern university. Yet, it was conceived as a child of frustration and necessity, and in the manner of such children vice presidents are deeply immersed in the familiar questions of their identity and purpose within the university family. These uncertainties, together with the conflict of authority and responsibility inherent in the vice president's functions, are in large measure at the base of a rapid turnover rate in these posts, a rate approaching that of medical school deans.

The purpose of this essay is to review the genesis of the job, the factors in its transformation to its present state, and the tensions this newest member of

* The term "vice president for health sciences" is used throughout as a convenient shorthand for the chief administrative officer of the multischool health sciences component of a university, not excluding those few unassociated with a university. Titles include president, chancellor, vice president, vice chancellor, and provost, all of which are subsumed here under the rubric of "vice president."

Reprinted with permission of the author and publisher from *Journal of Medical Education*, March 1975.

the academic community inevitably generates as it gains strength, maturity, and a larger measure of visibility as well as identity.

There are several ways to view the position of the vice president for health sciences, not all of them benign or congenial. To medical deans and faculties, vice presidents may seem a herd of tuskless walruses, occupying a large volume of space, surrounded by a flock of adulatory assistants, uttering accommodating noises, and accomplishing little of visible benefit. No longer fit for the hunt, they engage in mystical pursuit of "coordination" and "management." To the university president, these vice presidents are like the sheiks of fabulous empires, controlling vast storehouses of federal and clinical dollars but only feebly restraining the pragmatic and sometimes rowdy band of clinicians they supposedly command. To the deans of the schools other than medicine, the vice president may be seen either as a super-dean of medicine thinly veiling his preferences for extending the barony of the medical school or, in rarer instances, as a new St. George who will keep the dragon of the medical school at bay and encourage the rightful growth of all the other health professions. For the general university faculty, this new vice president is simply another administrative encumbrance, further cluttering the academic scene and weakening the academic supremacy of the academic vice president or provost and thereby the supremacy of the academic "heart" of the university.

In each of these contrary views, there is some measure of truth and reality which is derived from the telescoped history and rapid transformations of the position of vice president for health sciences. There is little wonder that the incumbents should themselves be a bit confused, as they attempt to conform to, or resist, the multiple images thrust upon them. What about the vice president's view of himself?

Here too, there is no clear picture. Some vice presidents, coming straight from the deanship of medicine, see themselves as the protectors of the rightful dominance of the medical school, benignly and paternalistically "coordinating" the other health professions. Others assume a variety of postures as the university president's adviser on health affairs or the extramural and community representative of the medical center or the semiautonomous executive of a large multi-institutional enterprise, deploying large budgets, personnel, and facilities and thereby influencing the whole spectrum of health care and its provision to the community.

There is partial truth and reality in these views, too; no single vision of the vice presidency is the "right one." Nonetheless, there is growing necessity to define and delimit more clearly the academic role of the vice president for health sciences. This definition must concentrate on those things unique and essential to the emergent conception of a true academic health sciences center.[1,2]

The lineaments of this new image are as yet quite unclear, but they promise to become less vague in the decade ahead. The unicorn might provide a good counterimage to that of the tuskless walrus fashioned by medical deans and faculties. The unicorn is a bit mythical; no one has actually seen one, and it takes particular care to find one since from behind it looks like any other equine and it is only unique when seen in profile. Is the walrus on the way to becoming a unicorn, improbable as that metamorphosis may appear?

Let us examine features of this strange creature by looking at the forces which are shaping it even now—its genesis in the university and the tensions created as vice presidents begin to perceive the nature of an academic health center and move more strenuously toward its realization.

GENESIS

Several decades ago most medical schools in this country moved to a closer relationship with their parent universities. Whereas the degree of this integration has been variable, some common problems were created for the university administration. University presidents were faced more squarely with the resolution of a viper's tangle of unfamiliar problems—affiliation agreements, community demands for medical care, private practice plans, reimbursement formulas, hospitals with deficits, demands of the practicing commumity—the whole mixture of exciting and often frustrating exercises that constitute normal daily fare for vice presidents in the health sciences. The whole mix was made a little more vexing by emanating from a professional faculty not yet entirely respectable to its university colleagues.

Predictably, and somewhat in self-defense, the university president conceived the need for a member of his staff—the academic vice president, the provost, a special assistant, or the dean of medicine—to coordinate, consolidate, and screen these new problems for him. Whatever his own discipline, the president did not have the requisite knowledge or time to devote to such a rapidly growing and unpredictable element in his organization as the medical schools and university hospitals were becoming.

Matters were further complicated as other schools were added—nursing, pharmacy, dentistry. These schools began to relate to each other and to the medical school in a new but vague entity called the "medical" or "health sciences center." The energies created by the vigorous expansion of the health professions soon overwhelmed the buffering capacity of the president's staff man. More and more of the decisions arising in the new "centers" had to be referred to his desk since they impinged increasingly upon the operation of the entire university. Clearly, more line of authority was needed and more authority had to be delegated.

Presidents now selected a medical person, still largely as a staff administrator, who usually was from the ranks of distinguished or fatigued deans of medicine or was a retired military or hospital administrator. To avoid the inevitable proliferation of vice presidents to which organizations are so susceptible, this new person was made a director of the medical center and had certain limited decision-making powers.

But health sciences centers continued to grow exponentially in the sixties, to become more deeply involved in community service and in large building programs, and to receive larger amounts of external financial support. The range of problems widened proportionately; an array of new academic problems arose in the interrelationships of the several schools of the health sciences centers and the university departments. Today the academic health center is a giant, still unsure of its mission and still evolving in complexity if not in size.

Chief administrative officers of health sciences centers had to assume more line authority, make more decisions on their own, and manage enterprises often equal in complexity to those of the rest of the university. Today, almost all centers have chief executive officers with decentralized authority of significant proportions. The president of the university faces new problems with his schools in the health professions—a new kind of isolation from the university based on size and complexity of mission but nonetheless potentially divisive and threatening in several vital respects. The full potentialities of the health sciences centers are still evolving. The administrative authority, responsibility, and functions of the vice presidents for health sciences have moved decidedly from staff to line function and then to those of executive officer of a mini-university within the larger total university. A closer look at the forces effecting this transformation will help to define the vectors which will, in turn, determine the future evolution of the position.

TRANSFORMING FACTORS

While the responses of individual academic health centers and individual vice presidents to them are as yet variable, a clear set of forces is operating to transform the academic health center. In so doing, those forces will transform the functions of its chief administrative officer. An enumeration of these factors will suffice to make the point.

The first is the sheer growth in size. Most centers started with a medical school and hospital. Now they may include as many as eight different professional schools, affiliations with half a dozen or more hospitals, academic relationships with community colleges, and regional responsibilities for health maintenance organizations, area health education centers, regional medical programs, comprehensive health planning, and other community organizations.

Budgets and physical facilities have paralleled the growth in size and complexity of programs. These may in many instances equal those of the entire university or even surpass them. These budgets consist of funds from sources external to the university, and in large part their use is dictated by demands often only indirectly related to the needs of the rest of the university. The management of these funds requires a familiarity with intricacies of third party payers, clinical practice funds, and billing and collection from a wide range of consumers—all problems of a different genre than those familiar to university business officers.

The second factor is the increasing assumption of responsibility for service to the communities in which academic health centers reside. They are expected to provide health care services, modify patterns of care, effect a better distribution of manpower, and generally engage in a host of activities directly or indirectly related to the health of the community. The vice president must in consequence deal with a large number of organizations, legislative officers, boards, and executive officers, whose variety and number equal or exceed those with which the president of the university may deal.

A third factor is the mounting pressure to effect some equality between the needs of society for certain kinds of manpower and the rate at which that manpower is produced. The endless proliferation of categories of health workers and the overlap and duplication of functions and increased costs which follow upon uncontrolled growth must be countered. This requires a coordination of the efforts of the several professional schools, development of new educational continua, consortium arrangements with other institutions preparing health workers, realignment of roles of existing professions, and operation of new models of patient care. Since these are matters which transcend the interests of individual schools, they fall to the office of the vice president, the only place where professional leadership can be exerted in such matters as interdisciplinary education, common courses for several professions, and long-range manpower-planning.

A fourth factor is the appearance of the concept of professional accountability, which is rapidly being translated into institutional accountability as well. Heretofore, professionals and institutions might vest themselves with responsibilities and be their own judges of the degree to which those responsibilities were fulfilled. Community and consumer participation, federal legislation, and such things as the patient's "bill of rights" underscore the new public interest in continuing assessment and external review of the adequacy of the performance of professionals and institutions. The vice president for health sciences is now the focal point of institutional accountability for quality of patient care, competence of professionals, and continuing education as well as efficiency of management, cost confinement, hospital and laboratory utilization, and a host of other matters of acute public concern.

In clinical matters, the call for accountability and the concomitant fixing of liability are squarely with the ranking clinical administrator and can be shifted to the president and the board of trustees only with difficulty. If the vice president for health sciences is a clinician, the president must of necessity delegate authority for decisions to him or carry the onus of errors in clinical decision making himself.

These are just some examples of the powerful forces which are now transforming the role of the vice president for health sciences into one of the most important and vital in the university and in the community as well. In certain matters, especially those with clinical dimensions, his authority is at least equal to and may exceed that of the university president; at least it will seem so to those who demand accountability.

No longer is a staff position equal to the span of these demands. Nor can the office be a passive conduit for papers from deans to the president of the university, though some presidents and vice presidents might wish it that way. The vice president for health sciences is clearly not "another" vice president in the university. He must be a peculiar type of vice president who somehow has to meet all the external and internal demands imposed on the chief executive officer of a large and complex clinical and educational undertaking and still do so as a university officer.

When the enlarging dimensions of the functions of the vice president for health sciences are taken seriously, there are bound to be tensions with the regular academic structures of the university, which is attuned to adherent sets of values. These tensions in their turn are now shaping the image of the vice presidency, and a brief look at them is worthwhile.

NEED FOR DEFINING ROLE

A conscious decision must be made in each university about the nature of the position of vice president for health sciences rather than waiting for resolution of ambiguities during some crisis. The expectations of the university president and his other vice presidents may be inconsistent with some of the newer and expanded responsibilities of the position. Does the university want a staff or line position, a matter too often left ambiguous, creating conflict with other vice presidents? Are the other vice presidents in line with authority over the vice president for health sciences, actually or by default of definition? Can he expect them to serve him as they do the president for those functions he needs and in terms dictated by the special climate of a clinical setting? Lack of clarity on this point creates ill will and animosities in a position too large in scope for a vague assignment.

Opinions will differ among those who hold this post and among university presidents, but the author believes that if the job is to be done properly, the position must have clear line authority for each of the schools which make up the health sciences center. The vice president for the health sciences is unique in this respect among the other vice presidents in a university, who usually function as the president's staff officers. In fact, if he is to be accountable as the public requires and if he is to create a team out of the diverse schools over which he presides, the vice president for health sciences is really the chief executive and academic officer of a compact but complex mission-oriented mini-university within a larger university.

This fact is not discussed openly enough. It implies considerable overlap with the functions of other vice presidents—for academic affairs, for business and finance, and for graduate studies. The latter positions carry responsibility for the "whole" university. But to what extent should these responsibilities be decentralized to meet the urgent needs of the health sciences centers, especially where there is a hospital along with other programs providing health care to the community? How much duplication is sensible, and how much is divisive? To what extent should policies apply uniformly to all segments of the university, and to what extent do the special needs of the health sciences justify exceptions?

These questions are pertinent to every facet of the operation of a modern-day health sciences center. While there is no one "right" pattern, these questions cannot be answered by default.

SOME ACADEMIC CHALLENGES

Vice presidents for the health sciences have several unique and exciting academic challenges. One is to use their unique position to define a common mission and purpose toward which all the schools in a center may direct their efforts. A multischool center needs a definition of its commitments, that is, of the choices it has made among the things it wishes to achieve as an institution. These are essential benchmarks in planning, allocating resources, and coordinating the efforts of disparate schools and programs. Each school cannot be completely free to devise its own answers to social needs. The result of this libertarian view is an inevitable multiplication of categories of health professionals, endless territorial fracases, and confusion in the public mind about the vice president's purposes.

The vice president is the person best situated to take leadership in defining the mission and common goals of his center. His most important academic task is to articulate this mission, symbolize it, and by persuasion unite all schools in its pursuit. He is expected to adjudicate and balance interschool and supra-school aspirations. In that endeavor he really adumbrates the specific image and physiognomy of the entire center, as the deans and faculty are expected to do within their own schools. Each school is a part of the mosaic. But if the pieces are to fit into a comprehensible whole, the total pattern has to be known to all and accepted by them.

RELATIONSHIP WITH UNIVERSITY

In tackling this difficult and sometimes elusive task, the vice president must somehow remain faithful to the larger mission of the university as a whole. This mission is only too rarely articulated, except in the most general terms. The vice president for health sciences faces a paradox. If he really creates a unity within the health sciences, he will induce friction with respect to the unity of the health sciences and that of the university as a whole. In fact, where no friction exists, the job is probably not being done. The trick is to make the resultant tension a positive stimulus for both the university and the health sciences.

University presidents and their faculties find this last fact difficult to accept. They see the health sciences as only one of a wide spectrum of programs in which the university is engaged. They fail to understand why academic programs in the health sciences should not be handled precisely as they are in English, physics, or classics. Pleas for "uniqueness" often seem like self-serving bids for preferred status, equally arguable, it is thought, by all other disciplines.

The matter is most vexing when it comes to appointments, promotion, and tenure, that triad of staunchly defended prerogatives over which faculties bleed and die. Health sciences centers, and especially schools other than medicine, seem to use criteria which would lower the standards of appointment. Research productivity or scholarly publication are not as indispensable as they have become on the general campus.

This is true, and necessarily so. If health sciences faculties are to take new directions in clinical education, experiment with new models of care, or teach clinical craftmanship, their faculty members must have requisite experience and skills. The measures of excellence for these people are not the same ones applied to the usual university professor. The needed people are less apt to be involved in standard types of research. When they are so involved, their papers strike the university faculty members as nonacademic or naive and unsophisticated.

A special example appears when a medical school establishes a department of family medicine. The number of skilled family practitioners with academic credentials is very small. Yet, this field must be taught by competent clinicians. Their presence on medical faculties is essential if models of family care are to be developed and students are to see this field adequately represented on the academic scene. The same problems are encountered when clinicians in nursing, allied health, dentistry, and pharmacy are appointed to the faculties.

Another point of tension is in faculty governance. To develop a health sciences center as a unified entity directed toward achieving certain common goals, there is need for some sort of unified governance within the center's faculty. A common complaint is that there is not enough communication among the faculties in the health sciences center. A health sciences center governance structure dealing with problems common to all the health professional schools is essential. This then raises the question of the relationship of that senate and that governance procedure to the university senate and its governance procedures.

INTRARELATIONSHIPS

There are tensions within the center as well which flow from some of the special and unique responsibilities of the vice president. One of the major examples is the relationship of the vice president for health sciences to the dean of medicine. If the kind of coordination that has been suggested is to be achieved, the vice president for the health sciences ought to be symbolically and actually the academic leader of a group of health professions. He cannot identify with any one profession, or he loses his effectiveness as the leader of all.

One of the recurrent errors is to fail to make the separation between the role of the vice president and that of the dean of medicine. Medicine needs to play a central role in the health sciences center. The other schools readily realize that without medicine there can be no genuine health sciences center. What the other health professions urgently need, however, is the support of the vice president for health sciences to make them more equal partners in the development of the center. A truly cooperative effort among all health professionals is indispensable to optimal utilization of health manpower and a coordinated set of academic programs.

The vice president for the health sciences cannot perform this vital function if he is identified too personally with the medical school. He must not "run" the medical school. Even indirectly, he must not favor its purposes apart from those of other schools. This requirement is especially difficult for those with the medical degree. Yet, this distinction in function between vice president and dean of medicine is the most crucial determinant of whether the health sciences center really functions as an entity or not. The higher responsibility of the vice president is to represent all the health professions. That is his unique academic contribution, a contribution no other administrative officer in the university can make. If he does not meet this requirement, there is a valid question about the viability of the post, except to perform a mediator's function for the president; for the vice president to do so would mean a return to the situation that prevailed in the beginning days of the job, and it would abnegate all the changes in its potentialities since then.

The vice president for the health sciences must concern himself with all those matters which transcend the concerns of individual schools and professions. His success will increasingly be measured by the extent to which he can make the interactions between the component schools of the health sciences center act synergistically and not antagonistically.

CONCLUSION

This essential internal function and his function at the intersections with the university, the community, and government clearly define a set of tasks beyond the capabilities of ponderous old walruses. As the advertisements say, the vice presidents have "come a long way" from the staff position or special assistant category of a little while back. Whether or not something as unique and dramatic as a unicorn will emerge is an open question. But at least we can be sure that a significant transformation has occurred and is still occurring.

The final outlines of the job of vice president are still not clearly visible. Those who occupy these posts have the responsibility to create that new outline simultaneously with solving their many complex operational problems. The forces shaping the position seem clear enough. Harnessing them in a new way is surely one of the most interesting and exciting assignments in academia.

REFERENCES

1. L. T. Coggeshall, *Planning for Medical Progress Through Education* (Evanston, Ill.: Association of American Medical Colleges, 1965).
2. E. D. Pellegrino, "The Regionalization of Academic Medicine: The Metamorphosis of a Concept." *Journal of Medical Education,* 48:119–133, 1973.

Managing for Results
in the Federal Government

Frederic V. Malek

> A government without good management is a house built on sand.
> —*Franklin D. Roosevelt, 1937*

> Effective action must be taken to improve efficiency.
> —*Dwight D. Eisenhower, 1957*

> I mean to ensure that in each of the various Federal programs, objectives are achieved.
> —*John F. Kennedy, 1963*

> There is no subject of greater importance to the people of this country and to me than the efficient operation of our programs.
> —*Lyndon B. Johnson, 1966*

> I am now asking each department and agency head to seek a sharper focus on *results*.
> —*Richard M. Nixon, 1973*

Reprinted with permission from *Business Horizons,* April 1974.

The period from 1789 to 1849 was a most active time in the development of this country: a new government was formed under George Washington, and a great city bearing his name was constructed on the swamplands of the Potomac River; Thomas Jefferson almost doubled the size of the nation with the purchase of the 800,000-square-mile Louisiana Territory from France in 1803; and we fought an important war with Britain in 1812 and another with Mexico in 1846. A good deal of money was needed to finance these activities; the total cumulative expenditures by the federal government came to a little more than $1 billion over the sixty-year period. However, even this impressive sum becomes relatively insignificant by today's standards. In 1973 our expenditures averaged over $1 billion *each working day*.

Certainly the people deserve and have a right to expect the highest quality service possible, whether we are spending $1 billion a day or $1 million a day. However, there is no question that this enormous expansion in the cost of running the federal bureaucracy is at least partly responsible for the elevation of better management to its current position as a major presidential level priority. The creation of the Brownlow Committee by Franklin Roosevelt in the mid-1930s is generally conceded to be the first major expression of concern by a Chief Executive in the management field.

During his first Administration, President Nixon formed the Ash Council to take a fresh look at the problem of management effectiveness within the federal government. Based upon its recommendations, he introduced sweeping legislation to realign and revitalize the Executive Branch. He also created a central point of reference for all management policy by establishing the Office of Management and Budget (OMB) within the Executive Office of the President.

At the start of his second Administration, the President was determined to further build on the organizational framework he had established in 1970. When Roy Ash and I were appointed as director and deputy director of OMB in February 1973, we were given a mandate by the President to develop a program whereby the American public could be certain that the best possible benefits were resulting from the expenditure of their tax dollars.

THE BUREAUCRATIC ENVIRONMENT

In order to understand the nature of the program that was undertaken in response to the President's directive, it is important to note the unique environment that exists within the federal government. It is significantly different from the private sector, and these differences tend to create three problems that are especially critical:

◇ The highest priority items are often subsumed by the welter of routine tasks.
◇ Managers are frequently not held accountable for producing a specific result.
◇ There is poor follow-through on major programs.

Establishing Priorities

Columnist Joseph Alsop has described the Executive Branch as "the essential great engine of the U.S. government." Few people realize just how complex and cumbersome this machine really is. In terms of sheer size alone, it involves a civilian workforce of approximately 2 million people.

Like any large organization, there is a tendency for management to become totally immersed in the maze of everyday business. All too often, the important breakthrough opportunity is lost in the ongoing routine. Therefore, we felt an urgent need to counteract this tendency by selectively spotlighting high priority initiatives in each agency so that they can be given special attention by managers at all levels, right up to and including the President.

Accountability for Results

The practice of setting specific objectives, measuring the results attained, and then rewarding outstanding performance is perhaps the most significant difference between private and public sector operations. Generally, the problem of developing a specific, results-oriented objective is considerably more difficult in a public institution because it deals to a great extent with intangibles. The chief executive officer in a private company has a wide variety of quantitative yardsticks to measure performance (for example, profit and market share) that are not available in the public sector.

Consequently, objectives are rarely set and progress is measured in terms of activities rather than accomplishments. You can always find a manager who is responsible for performing a certain function, but you can almost never find one who is accountable for producing the end result.

There had to be, in our view, a renewed emphasis on setting objectives and then holding the responsible managers accountable for their attainment. Granted, there is a measurability problem, but a lot can be done with nonquantifiable or subjective evaluation techniques if the problem is approached sensibly.

Effective Follow-through

Effective management follow-through is an especially difficult task in the public sector. First, there is always a crisis to deal with. The outbreak of hostilities in the Middle East, the demands of the energy crisis, the truckers' strike, an unusually large monthly growth in unemployment, and so on are all recent examples that required federal managers to turn their attention away from important long-term goals to deal with short-term contingencies. The practice of jumping from one hot, highly visible issue to another without returning to the high priority objective is a luxury that the government executive can afford without penalty.

Second, statistics show that the average time in office for the appointee who takes an executive position in Washington will be on the order of twenty-two months. This fact of life also tends to destroy continuity and executive follow-through. We felt better ways had to be devised to get an executive up to speed quickly, enable him to effectively delegate and decentralize his operations without abrogating his management responsibility in the agency, and help him to constantly focus on the progress being made toward the achievement of his objectives.

A PRESIDENTIAL INITIATIVE

These are the problems that motivated the President when he directed Roy Ash and me to launch a major new management initiative in the spring of 1973. The approach we worked out with him was a selective adaptation of the management-by-objectives concept that has been successfully introduced into a wide variety of private and public institutions. MBO offers many answers to the problems noted above.

First of all, it is a selective process that requires the segregation of important items from those that are more routine. Second, it is based on the development of objectives by the same manager who will ultimately be held responsible for their achievement. Since it requires action plans for achieving objectives, it does provide the executive with a simple method for keeping his eye on the ball despite the distractions that may arise during the year. Finally, it enables the President to delegate more to his agency heads with confidence since he has agreed in advance as to what they will achieve and has the means to follow their progress toward achievement.

As in any mammoth organization, major changes cannot be installed overnight, particularly when they affect something as fundamental as the way the organization is conducting its business. But we have made substantial progress toward creating a new style of public management as illustrated by the following discussion.

The Planning Phase

Twenty-one of the major departments and agencies were selected to participate in the new management initiative. Together, these agencies account for more than 95 percent of all federal government expenditures.

Request for results-oriented objectives. The President personally launched the initative with a memorandum to each of the twenty-one agency heads on April 18, 1973. This memorandum noted the need to focus on results and not just actions in the design and operation of federal programs and asked each agency head to identify those objectives he or she considered to be of presidential level importance during the coming fiscal year. Where an objective was part of a longer-term goal, the goal was also to be indicated.

Staff interactions. OMB was given the responsibility of coordinating the review of agency submissions before they were forwarded to the President. We looked for the following key features in each objective: its feasibility and achievability within budget constraints; its importance and consistency in terms of stated presidential policies; the extent of its measurability; and, above all, emphasis on accomplishments instead of merely activities.

With regard to the last point, we asked for a brief action plan showing both intermediate milestones and projected end dates for each objective. Specialists from the Domestic Council, the National Security Council, and other interested staff members from the Executive Office of the President were also asked to participate in these reviews.

Top-level management conferences. The objective-setting phase of the effort was brought to a close with a management conference, which was attended by the agency head and his or her key staff members. The purpose of these sessions was to hammer out a final agreement on the objectives before they were submitted to the President.

Presidential review and feedback. Once the President completed his review of the agency submissions, he personally communicated his thoughts to the agency head. In many instances, he noted areas of particular interest to him. In every case, he emphasized the need to be constantly on the alert for new initiatives that could be added to the list of objectives as the year unfolded.

A Variety of Objectives

Before discussing the operational phase of the effort, it might be desirable to briefly touch upon a few of the objectives that were established.

First of all, no constraints were placed on the types of objectives that could be submitted. Eventually, all objectives contribute to the delivery of needed services to the American public through the effective execution of federal programs. However, in some cases an objective would point to completing the necessary studies to define a new program or specify changes to an existing program. Or perhaps the study may have been concluded, but the objective was to complete the difficult task of working out acceptable legislation with Congress.

Finally, in many cases there are important administrative objectives that are keys to the operation of an entire department or a group of programs (such as a major reorganization). We did not want to preclude the submission of objectives in any of these areas if the agency head felt the effort was significant enough to bring to the President's attention. As a result, agencies focused on many different types of objectives. Generally, they can be divided into the four categories previously noted: policy formulation and program definition, legislative enactment, programmatic results, and administrative improvement. Some illustrations follow.

A Transportation Policy Statement

The various transportation systems of this country have evolved on an independent basis over the past one-hundred years. This has produced a rather fragmented set of policies and quasi policies depending on the mode (air, rail, water, or automotive). Both the President and the Congress have stressed the need for developing an integrated strategy that will help guide future decisions in this area.

For example, are current federal subsidies (encouragements) consistent with our long-term needs for moving goods and people from one location to another? What is the proper mix of economic regulation versus competitive pricing now and in the future? What are the proper roles of the federal, state, and local governments as well as the private sector? To what extent will other national priorities, such as the conservation of energy, be affected if the transportation systems now in the planning stage are implemented? Clearly, Transportation Secretary Claude S. Brinegar was correct when he designated the formulation of a national transportation policy statement as worthy of presidential concern for this fiscal year.

Federal Housing

We look back to the Housing Act of 1949 to find the original statement of our long-term goal in this area. It was repeated by President Nixon in his September 19, 1973 message to Congress on housing policy: "This Administration will not waver in its commitment to the objective of the Housing Act of 1949, 'a decent home and a suitable living environment for every American.' " The message actually contained a set of principles that came about through the completion of one of the presidential level objectives. It was initially submitted by James Lynn, Secretary of Housing and Urban Development, on May 3, 1973 in response to the President's memorandum.

The objective as finally approved called for the completion of a major study of federal housing policies and programs, and the development of options and recommendations for presidential consideration. The urgency of this effort stems from the lack of success of several housing programs in the past toward the achievement of the long-term goal. Unfortunately, many of these extremely costly, albeit well-intentioned, efforts had produced a result we were not pleased with—the designation of the federal government as the largest "slumlord" in the United States.

Trans-Alaskan Pipeline

The October 1973 outbreak of hostilities in the Middle East transformed our energy problem into an energy crisis almost overnight. However, well before that unfortunate event, Secretary of the Interior Rogers Morton had responded to the President's April memorandum with a significant, energy related legislative objective—the enactment of a bill that would permit the start of construction on the Trans-Alaskan pipeline from Prudhoe Bay in the north to the port of Valdez in the south.

His target date for enactment was September 1973, and although several difficult issues including those associated with conservation and the environment made the date unattainable, the legislation was eventually signed into law by the President on November 16, 1973. This significant step has opened the door to an increased supply of oil starting in 1977 that should eventually come to almost 2 million barrels a day.

Welfare Ineligibility and Overpayment

The welfare system in this country is in our view highly ineffective and inequitable. Our long-term goal is to replace the existing tangle of competing, overlapping programs with one program that will provide direct cash assistance to the individual who can then decide how he or she should use it to buy food, housing, clothing, or other essentials.

In the meantime, HEW Secretary Caspar Weinberger is committed to correcting deficiencies in the existing programs. One of these programs, Aid to Families with Dependent Children (AFDC), was selected by him as the subject for a solid programmatic objective. It consists of two major parts: to more accurately determine the extent of the ineligibility and overpayment rates, and to eventually reduce these rates to 3 percent and 5 percent, respectively. The first part has essentially been completed, and the results are even worse than we expected. Over 40 percent of the cases fall into the ineligible or incorrect payment categories at a net cost to the taxpayers of more than $1 billion per year.

The Operational Phase

Management Conferences

Objectives without results are meaningless and highly wasteful. The real payoff depends on the determination and competence of the line manager in working toward the objectives. Here again, the management conference plays an important role. Our main concerns in these sessions, which are generally held on a bimonthly basis with the agency head and his top people, are as follows:

◇ Is the line manager keeping his eye on the ball? Is he making progress toward the end result in keeping with his action plan?

◇ Are there major problems that should be brought to top management attention for resolution?

◇ Are there recent developments that may require the modification, deletion or addition of new objectives?

When the effort was first initiated with the agencies, many predicted that it would lead to a new snowstorm of bureaucratic paperwork. However, the emphasis is on a person-to-person dialog with a minimum amount of paperwork. Now written reports are required from the agencies, and personal contact is the primary means of communication at all organizational levels.

Use of the Objectives

Recognizing the usefulness of MBO in effectively running their operations, top officials are now setting objectives and then managing to achieve the desired results. Secretary of Agriculture Earl Butz is not "from Missouri." However, as those who know him will attest, he comes from the pragmatic "show me" school. He generally reserved judgment during the objective-setting phase, but, after a lively give-and-take review conference, he remarked enthusiastically: "Maybe we have something here. Maybe for the first time we will be able to coordinate positions and get concrete results."

There are also signs that the existence of objectives and action plans is helping new agency heads get on top of their operations more rapidly. For example, at the Environmental Protection Agency, the presidential level initiative fitted rather nicely into a previously developed MBO program.

On September 14, 1973, Russell Train was sworn in as the new administrator of EPA, and only thirty-five days later, a management conference was held to review progress on the agency's presidential objectives. He played an active leadership role in the discussions and noted that his ability to do so was directly related to "the excellent management process" that made it possible for him to focus on the material within a relatively short period of time.

Finally, there is no question that the existence of specific objectives has served the interests of the President. In many cases, a high priority objective such as National Health Insurance is the subject of a specific meeting between the President and an agency head. Presidential objectives are also discussed at Cabinet meetings and other broader-based sessions that may be scheduled with him as the need arises.

THE REAL CHALLENGE

We have come a long way in this first year. Thanks to a significant effort on the part of the agencies, which have worked long and hard to make our joint efforts a success, more than 200 presidential objectives have been defined and solid progress is being made toward their fulfillment. This approach to management is now fairly well accepted across the top levels of the government.

However, if we look back at our original mandate from the President, the real challenge still lies before us. The presidential level objectives are extremely important—but in this larger context they merely represent the tip of the iceberg. What the President really desires is fundamental and enduring reform of the way in which government executives approach their responsibilities. If we are to make a lasting contribution, we must make an impact on the infrastructure—the middle manager who is on the firing line every day and who in the aggregate can really change the way things are done. We want him to start thinking about what he is trying to accomplish for the American public. He is the one who must reach the conclusion that there is a better way to approach his job and serve the public's interests. Roy Ash has a simpler way of saying it: "We want to make managing for results a way of life." This means for all agency programs, not just those of presidential significance.

How should this be done? We think this question should largely be left up to each agency with only general guidance from us and the requirement by the President that it most certainly must be done. How to do it depends upon the agency's size and mission, the nature of its programs, the suitability and adaptability of its existing management techniques, and the like. General George Patton once said "Never tell people how to do things. Tell them what to do and they will surprise you with their ingenuity." We are confident that our surprises will be pleasant ones.

Part 2
PLANNING AND ANALYSIS

The Systems Approach— Tools and Techniques

WITHIN THE MANAGEMENT PROCESS, THE AREAS OF PLANNING AND SYSTEMS analysis have recently received increasing attention. As the saying goes, "every action has a reaction." There is no such thing as an absolutely independent activity within an organization. The systems approach to the management process takes these relationships and interdependencies into account and provides a valuable tool for the manager in a nonprofit setting.

	Government	Education	Health	Religious and Charitable	Associations and Others
New Tools and Techniques in University Administration Daniel H. Perlman		X			
A Systems Approach to Planning and Managing Programs for the Handicapped Robert Elkin			X		
Systematic Processes Applied to Health Care Planning Owen B. Hardy			X		
Break-Even Analysis for Higher Education L. Keith Larimore		X			
The Management of Congress Richard Bolling	X				
Model for Participation Howard L. Sampson		X			
Systems Planning Tomorrow's Hospitals Today William G. Akula and Jay A. Vora			X		
Strategic Planning in State Government Michael J. Howlett	X				

New Tools and Techniques in University Administration

Daniel H. Perlman

Large social organizations must balance growth in size and complexity with the development and implementation of new organizational and managerial techniques necessary to keep an organization functioning. The continuous efforts of large business organizations and government agencies to manage their increasingly complex activities illustrate this rule. Higher education is no exception.

During the 1960s higher education in America became a major enterprise. By 1970 enrollments had reached 8.5 million—more than doubling during the decade. These students are being taught by a third of a million faculty members at nearly 3,000 colleges and universities.

Although the rate of growth of higher education may have slowed somewhat recently and budgets at some institutions may have grown leaner, there will be no returning to the pastoral days of Mark Hopkins and the log. The very size and expense of higher education has put colleges and universities under increased pressure from many sources—trustees, coordinating boards, state legislatures, Washington agencies—to account more openly for their expenditures and to manage their operations more efficiently. Colleges and universities

Reprinted with permission from *Educational Record*, Winter 1974.

are being asked to adopt standard accounting policies and definitions so that academic and fiscal data from one institution or system can be compared with those from another. They are being told to justify or eliminate their high-cost programs and those of marginal significance. The problems these pressures create are compounded by other changes which have occurred in higher education in recent years. Faculty, administrators, trustees, and others reponsible for the governance of an institution or a system do not necessarily share, either among themselves or with each other, the same concept or model of higher education as a basis for cooperative action and decision making. Agreed-upon goals and shared priorities can no longer be taken for granted (if ever they could), but are themselves a goal which must be approached before other problems can be solved.

As a result of the internal pressure put on higher education by changes in governance, size, and rate of growth, as well as the external pressures for accountability and reduced costs, a variety of new administrative and managerial tools have been adapted for use in higher education from tools developed initially to administer large business organizations and federal agencies. They are an outgrowth of advances in computer science, organizational psychology, cost accounting, and other disciplines. These techniques are helping to maintain the balance between the organizational complexity of higher education and the structures, strategies, and skills needed to keep it functioning. Not all of the techniques have been accepted equally within higher education, nor has their value been generally accepted. Nevertheless, these techniques are making significant inroads into the way campuses are administered. Also, no managerial tool or technique will supplant balanced judgment and the ability to work with people as the most important elements in the administration of any enterprise. However, such tools may give the decision-maker better information on which to base his judgment or better skills with which to involve others in the organization's activities.

ADMINISTRATIVE TECHNIQUES

One of the leaders in the development of new administrative techniques for higher education is the National Center for Higher Education Management Systems (NCHEMS) in Boulder, Colorado. NCHEMS is supported primarily by contracts with the U.S. Department of Health, Education and Welfare and by grants from major foundations. Advances have also been made by various consulting groups including Rand Corporation, Systems Research Group, Peat, Marwick, Mitchell & Co., and Education and Economic Systems, Inc.*

* The advances made by these and other groups have been both in the development of new administrative tools and techniques (e.g., much of the early conceptual work in program budgeting

The administrative and managerial skills and tools being adopted by higher education include management information systems, program budgeting, modeling, management by objectives, and organization development.

Management Information Systems

The term management information system (MIS) refers to the processes and procedures by which raw data are organized into information useful for administrative decision making. Management information systems are commonly computer-based since the repetitive task of tabulating and aggregating large quantities of detailed information can be handled most efficiently by data-processing machines. Some information now being provided to administrators using computer-based management information systems is the same type of information formerly tabulated by hand at most institutions. (For example, administrators have always needed to know how many students are registered in each course.) Many other items of information available now were not generally available before because hand tabulation would have been too laborious to warrant their collection.

Information systems are designed to produce reports that aggregate and summarize individual data elements. In order to work, such systems require precise and accurate data of various kinds: For what courses did each student register? How many students are in each class? What courses does each faculty member teach? Where and when does each course meet? Computer programs are available that aggregate and array these discrete data elements to produce reports presumed to be useful to an administrator in reaching decisions or necessary for completing government reports.

Some of the kinds of information generated by a management information system might include:

♦ A comparative profile of admitted and rejected applicants by ability levels, schools and colleges previously attended, geographic origins.

♦ A comparative profile of admitted applicants who enroll and "no shows" (those who do not enroll) by such factors as date of application, school previously attended, income level, financial need, choice of major or academic-vocational goal.

♦ The numbers and percentages of enrolled students by various categories, such as program major, grade-point average, income level, ability level, age, credit hours completed, courses required for graduation.

♦ Student financial aid information including family income levels, sources of financial aid, average amount of university funds needed to supplement scholarship, and other student income sources.

was done by the Rand Corporation for the U.S. Department of Defense) and in their adaptation to higher education.

◆ Information about faculty, such as the faculty productivity rate (the total number of student credit hours "produced" by a faculty member during a year), as well as the numbers and percentages of faculty by various categories including terminal degrees held, tenure, years to retirement, salary levels by rank, department, seniority.

◆ Information about courses by size of enrollment, popularity of hours, frequency of offering during previous semesters, the extent to which courses are scheduled during the day and evening.

◆ Information about space including the number of hours each classroom is in use, the number of square feet available for various purposes, the extent to which small enrollment courses are being scheduled in small classrooms.

◆ Information about the costs per credit hour by department, per degree recipient by major.

Much of this type of information is already collected and tabulated—sometimes by hand, sometimes by computer—on most campuses. What characterizes a management information *system* is the consistency, quality, accessibility, compatibility, and continuity of the data and its aggregation and organization to answer administrative questions. An integrated management information system is necessary to implement other new administrative techniques and strategies.

Program Budgeting

A second administrative technique recently introduced to higher education is *program budgeting*, which establishes the program, rather than the department, as the important budgetary unit.* Program budgeting is primarily a tool for planning and resource allocation. It does not replace line-item departmental budgeting as a tool for expenditure control.

Program budgeting focuses on the outcome or products of higher education and their cost. For example, chief among the products of higher education are the degrees awarded in different majors or disciplines. Program budgeting is used to determine the per-degree cost of each program or "major" in which degrees are awarded. To determine the cost of a degree it is necessary to answer such questions as . . . . What courses are commonly chosen by students majoring in each discipline? What is the enrollment in these courses? What are the per-course salaries of the faculty members who teach these courses? and, What fraction of the general institutional expenditures (indirect costs or overhead) is consumed by, or should be allocated to, degree recipients in each area? A management information system that can provide these data is essential.

* Program budgeting is often referred to in the literature as PPBS (planning, programming, budgeting systems).

Appropriate Mixes

Once the cost of existing programs or majors has been determined, program budgeting draws attention to questions about the appropriate "mix" of various program elements that are cost related. These elements include the diversity of curricular offerings, the size of class sections, faculty workload, the balance of instructional modes (i.e., lecture, discussion, closed circuit transmission, team teaching, field research, clinical internship, the number and cost of required courses, staffing patterns and salary schedules, levels of support activities, and the balance of upper and lower division course offerings. One can see the financial impact of various "mixes" on each of an institution's degree programs simply by formulating instructional budgets for each program based on different assumptions and combinations.

Under program budgeting, direct program costs are arrived at by determining the costs of the credit hours produced by the various instructional departments for each degree program (e.g., the costs of the credit hours in history, literature, etc., taken by a student majoring in philosophy are included in direct costs). Indirect costs—the program's share of the general institutional and overhead costs—are also included in the total costs of each degree program. Indirect costs can be allocated to a department or program either on the basis of actual use (e.g., the pro-rated share of the costs of a computer service can be easily charged back to a program or department because the computer itself is able to maintain a detailed record of its use), or on the basis of a formula established by determining the number of credit hours produced by a program as a proportion of the total credit hours generated by the institution.

Program budgeting, by focusing on the ingredients and associated costs of instructional programs, leads to questions about the quality or "output" of programs in relation to costs. Such questions constitute cost-benefit analysis or "output accounting." The development of objective indexes of instructional quality is one of the least-studied areas of higher education: Are the differences in the cost of a degree between one institution and another related to measurable differences in quality? If not, what factors are?

Although program budgeting leads to many difficult and as yet unanswered questions, it is already a valuable technique for helping administrators make more rational decisions about allocation of resources.

Modeling

Modeling, cost simulation, or gaming is another new administrative technique. It is an attempt to predict and plan for the future by projecting what will happen over time to an institution operating under various assumptions. Once an institution has good program budget information, based on current and historical data that show the cost of every credit hour by discipline and level, it is helpful to project these data into the future to determine what would happen to the institution under different conditions. For example, if enrollment in a program increases by x students over the next y years, how many more full-time equivalent (FTE) faculty members would be needed if the faculty productivity ratio (the number of credit hours generated by the average faculty member) were to remain the same? * What are the costs or savings associated with lowering or raising the faculty productivity ratio by a given percent over a specified number of years? What are the probable effects on various departments of adding a new curricular program or of altering course requirements? What are the implications for classroom utilization of new degree modes, such as cooperative education, that involve off-campus work or instruction that is not classroom centered? When only one or two variables are manipulated, calculations of projected costs can be done by hand. However, when many variables are manipulated simultaneously, it is helpful to have a computer perform the calculations.

Common Capabilities

A number of fairly sophisticated cost-simulation models have been developed and are in use at various institutions:

◇ RRPM (Resource Requirements Prediction Model) developed by the National Center for Higher Education Management Systems, Boulder, Colorado.
◇ CAMPUS (Comprehensive Analytical Methods for Planning in University Systems) developed by Systems Research Group, Toronto, Canada.
◇ HELP/PLANTRAN (Higher Education Long-Range Planning/Planning Translator) developed by Midwest Research Institute, Kansas City, Missouri.
◇ SEARCH (System for Evaluating Alternative Resource Commitments in Higher Education) developed by Peat, Marwick, Mitchell & Co., New York City.
◇ EDANAL developed by the Inner City Fund, Washington, D.C.
◇ HEPS (Higher Education Planning Systems) developed by Education and Economic Systems, Inc., Boulder, Colorado.

These models have in common the capability to analyze the cost and resource implications of alternative assumptions, courses of action, and resource allocation decisions. They are also useful in projecting the costs and resources (faculty, classrooms, etc.) necessary to undertake new programs. All models operate on the basis of existing data or relationships combined with projections of the future made by people. Models simply manipulate variables

* An institution's faculty productivity ratio is determined by dividing the total number of student credit hours generated during the year by the FTE faculty.

that are fed into them; they cannot invent, intuit, or operate on hunch. Established trends, patterns, and relationships are projected to continue unless an alternative assumption is explicitly introduced into the calculations by the users. The determination of when, where, and how existing patterns may change is a matter of personal judgment. A model is simply a means to calculate the multiple effects of predicted changes in resource requirements.

All these models have been developed to estimate *cost* or to simulate the resource *requirements* for a college, university, or system. Models for the other half of the budget sheet—the income side—are also needed. Higher education is no longer in the favored position (if it ever was) of being able to expect that income will be provided in amounts fully equal to projected expenses. More often, expenditures must be adjusted to income. Therefore, a necessary ingredient of advance budgeting is an estimate of anticipated income. In many institutions estimating income is more vital to planning than cost estimation. The next development in college and university modeling should be a revenue-simulation model that takes into account the various categories of revenue of an institution and any changes that can be projected in the historical pattern.

Cost-simulation models may be a useful tool for demonstrating the magnitude of an institution's needs to a governing board or legislative body. A revenue-simulation model may be a more useful and realistic tool for an institution's long-range planning.

Management by Objectives

Whereas the techniques of management information systems, program budgeting, and modeling are all a means for working primarily with quantitative data, the techniques of "management by objectives" and "organization development" are primarily means for working more effectively with *people*. Management by objectives (MBO) involves procedures (many of which are already in use at well-managed institutions) that make explicit the goals and objectives of each major component of an institution and a timetable for their realization.

In a typical use of management by objectives each administrative officer of an institution formulates a series of specific behavioral objectives for himself and his department for the coming year. These objectives need not all be new tasks or projects, but might simply be a continuation of activities in operation prior to the adoption of MBO. The objectives are formulated to be compatible with the overall institutional goals and objectives stated usually by the president with the advice of a faculty or administrative planning committee or both. Each administrative officer works with the individual to whom he reports to reach agreement on the specific goals and objectives to be accomplished within the year. Also agreed upon are the priorities assigned to the objectives: the time schedule for their accomplishment; the resources needed to implement them; and the behavioral criteria for the objectives so an observer can determine whether or when the objectives are accomplished.

Accountability

When agreement is reached, the administrator is held accountable for the implementation of the objectives. Performance is measured at the end of the year by the extent to which an administrator has accomplished the previously established objectives.

MBO is not an inflexible tool and is not designed to force the accomplishment of an immutable list of hard-to-obtain objectives. If an objective proves too difficult, costly, or time-consuming to implement, or if it comes to seem less important than another objective that requires a new priority not previously anticipated, the administrator reevaluates his objectives with his supervisor and makes appropriate modifications. MBO will be working significantly if it helps administrators (1) clarify and make explicit institutional, divisional, and departmental objectives; (2) review these objectives to insure that they are compatible with the goals, mission, and objectives of the institution; (3) understand the importance of the objectives and the criteria by which their accomplishment can be judged.

A good institutional research office or management information system is an important component of a management by objectives system. If, for example, an objective of the academic unit of a college or university is to improve the quality of its degree programs in certain disciplines, then good measures must be found to assess the present level of quality and to monitor any changes. Or, if an institution's objective is to contain expenditures by reducing the cost per credit hour or by increasing the faculty productivity ratio, then good indexes of costs and productivity must be available to measure changes. Without sound data and good measures of what exists, many objectives become meaningless because their implementation cannot be assessed.

A technique sometimes used to increase the effectiveness of MBO and the motivation to attain the objectives is to relate the achievement of objectives to an administrator's compensation, possibly in the form of a merit raise for the successful and timely completion of high-priority objectives. However, some people question the appropriateness of this technique in a university setting.

Organization Development

Organization development is the professional application of the findings of such disciplines as psychology, sociology, and education to help an institution change. Organization development uses a variety of interpersonal techniques, such as information feedback, conflict management, sensitivity training, and confrontation meetings to bring about a planned change in an organization. Organization development is concerned with people—their attitudes, values, and relationships with others—and the interpersonal climate of an organization.

Organization development techniques generally are used by an individual (who frequently calls himself a "change agent") to bring about changes in the environment of an organization—away from a rigid, bureaucratic, secretive, suspicious, competitive, impersonal, mistrustful, and uncomfortable environment toward a more open, sharing, accepting, cooperative, and creative environment in which people feel psychologically "safe" to share their thoughts, feelings, and ideas and in which there is a greater congruence of personal and institutional goals. It is the contention of proponents of organization development that institutions and groups can be helped to move from rigidity to openness, and that an institution with an open and humanistic environment will function with better morale, less interpersonal or intergroup conflict, higher creativity and achievement, and greater success in organizational problem solving.

Openness and Flexibility

Like data-oriented management techniques, organization development grew out of theoretical work conducted at colleges and universities, but was applied in business and governmental settings before being used in the academic milieu. Because organization development techniques are designed to foster openness, flexibility, and understanding, they are most appropriately used with people whose responsibilities are primarily problem oriented rather than task oriented. College and university administrators are candidates by this criterion.

Since organization development techniques generally deal with people's feelings, their use may initially raise apprehension and anxiety, particularly if the techniques are not handled skillfully. Moreover, a danger exists that a naive or incompetent "change agent" may create situations in which people are encouraged to express feelings and fantasies that are inappropriate in a work setting and dysfunctional for the individuals involved. Some organization development activities, such as sensitivity training, are perhaps best used with people from various work settings who do not know each other and who are not likely to meet subsequently in professional capacities.

Despite the potential problems, organization development promises to be one of the most important of the new administrative techniques and strategies because its focus is on people and their interaction rather than on procedures, data, or dollars. Ultimately, in any organization, the problems of getting people to work together harmoniously, productively, and cooperatively toward the goals of the enterprise are more significant and more crucial than problems of any other type. Moreover, the mechanical problems of providing better data and manipulating them in interesting ways are easier to solve than problems involving people. Put another way, unless the individuals in an organization or an institution are working well together, it is difficult to implement any new system whether it is management information, program budgeting, or new curriculum.

Almost every administrator or manager needs a high level of interpersonal skill to be effective. Interpersonal skills are necessary to reduce or manage conflict, develop loyalty and morale, focus the institution's goals and set realistic objectives, resolve competing interests, and obtain the cooperation and consensus essential to the continuity of the organization and the attainment of common interests. Interpersonal skills are equally essential in conducting collective bargaining or other negotiations. The skills of working with people are harder to teach than the quantitative methods of accounting and business management; they are not like legal or economic principles and are not easily codified. For this reason, interpersonal skills frequently have been left out of administrative training programs and curricula. Administrators and managers have had to develop these skills "naturally" or as a by-product of their other experiences. Those who develop them tend to become more successful. Perhaps one of the values of organization development, therefore, will be the emergence of a curriculum (i.e., educational experiences) by which individuals can acquire the interpersonal skills necessary in administration.

A CRITICAL EVALUATION

Management information systems, program budgeting, modeling, management by objectives, and organization development are a few of the more important administrative tools being adopted by colleges and universities, and coordinating boards, to manage the vast higher education enterprise. The successful use of these techniques in business and government has made them appear promising to higher education. Other techniques and procedures have also been borrowed from business and government including collective bargaining, coordinated planning, cost-benefit analysis, and output accounting (the measurement of the products of higher education).

Educators should not adopt these techniques uncritically or expect them to substitute for sound judgment or compensate for an unstable or immature personality. There is little hard evidence that more data or "better" data have actually enabled administrators to make better decisions than they otherwise would. It is undoubtedly easier to justify to others a decision supported by objective rather than intuitive data, but the decision may be the same in either case.

JUDGMENT NEEDED

These new techniques have seductive appeal for the universal hope for easy solutions to difficult problems. No management information system eliminates the need to exercise judgment. Computers and data do not make decisions or arrive at conclusions: they merely present evidence that must be interpreted and evaluated. The need to weigh alternatives, balance consequences, and reason out conclusions cannot be suspended or abrogated.

Two related problems must be guarded against by anyone establishing or using MIS or program budgeting. One is the tendency to accumulate too many data; the other is the tendency to collect the wrong kinds of data. In establishing or working with an information system it is often compelling to acquire as much information as possible about as many elements as possible. Acquiring too many data is a tendency to which inquisitive academicians and methodical systems analysts are particularly prone. Sometimes the tendency is a reaction to a previously existing situation in which few hard data about anything seemed to be available. But one can easily develop too many data, which can be distracting, confusing, conflicting, and dysfunctional, especially when the data are presented in cumbersome and voluminous computer printouts. There is a principle of parsimony with regard to the utility of information in managerial and administrative decision making: an administrator should acquire the *least* amount of data necessary to reach a sound decision. The tendency to acquire more should be resisted. The demands on the time of a college or university president preclude his studying long reports or analyzing tables of data. The essential information must be distilled, summarized, and presented without distractions.

FOCUS ON THE IMPORTANT

A comparable problem exists when the wrong kind of information is collected. It is not uncommon for institutional researchers to collect and quantify that which can be easily counted, rather than what is most important to know. As a result, no one can achieve precise information about the irrelevant and little information about the important. It may well be that the important questions cannot be answered, but an administrator should not be confused into thinking that he has all the data. For example, a conceptual or theoretical analysis of an administrative problem that takes no account of the charactertistics of the people involved is incomplete and inadequate. The important aspects of people—their personalities, temperaments, strengths, and weaknesses—cannot be easily quantified, but they must be part of an administrator's judgment about the total situation. No array of data, however precise, will eliminate the need to consider the nonquantifiable personal, social, and political factors in arriving at decisions; nor will it reduce the importance of considering the impact of proposed decisions on the people affected by them. Weighing the impact of decisions on people is one of the most difficult aspects of administration, and it cannot be delegated to a computer.

A misconception related to others about the new administrative techniques—that the computer or the office of institutional research will take over the hard decisions, that more information is always desirable and likely to lead to better decisions, that the quantifiable data are the important data—is that any of the administrative techniques is likely to save money in the short run. All of the techniques cost money to implement. When that money has to come out of this year's or next year's already overstrained budget, it may appear too high a price to pay. The value of such techniques to an institution is realized over the long run. The savings these techniques may bring about are almost never line-item reductions in the budget, but are the larger, though less tangible, savings of avoiding costly mistakes and making better decisions. Unfortunately, not every college and university can afford to invest in the long run.

Although these cautionary remarks relate primarily to misuses of and misconceptions about the quantitative techniques (MIS, program budgeting, and modeling), there is also a caveat with regard to the use of management by objectives and organization development—if these techniques are used without discretion and expertise, they may be tools for exploitation and manipulation rather than administrative leadership. If misused in this manner, the techniques will backfire, resulting in a less effective work environment.

Clearly, all of the new management techniques will not be implemented on every campus, nor should they be. However, many administrators may find some or all of the techniques helpful in equipping them to do a better job of managing the people and resources of their institution. As long as the techniques are not regarded as panaceas, they may have a significant impact on college and university administration.

A Systems Approach to Planning and Managing Programs for the Handicapped

Robert Elkin

Everyone has had the experience, at one time or another, of reaching out instinctively to aid a handicapped person—it is a basic human characteristic. The act of helping satisfies essential human, personal needs, but it also serves important economic aims of our society, since many handicapped persons can become contributing members of society if they receive appropriate services. For many of the handicapped we can provide a choice as to whether they will live their lives as burdens or as contributors to society. In this article, however, we shall set aside our personal motivations for serving the handicapped and concentrate instead on the discipline of what we may call a systems approach to measuring what handicapped individuals need as well as the costs and benefits of different ways of helping.

Reprinted with permission of the author and Peat, Marwick, Mitchell & Co. from *Management Controls*, August 1974.

INTERRELATED ELEMENTS

Systems are composed of interrelated elements. Hence, the fact that the impact of a decision reverberates on many elements of the system must be recognized and analyzed. For example, a decision by the legislature to cut the budget for services to families of the handicapped may have a major impact on all the services, both for children and adults. This could lengthen a stay in institutional care and possibly decrease the effectiveness of outpatient care. Or a school board may decide, for example, to restrict funds for facilities for special education classes, with the result that children from these classes must be combined with other classes serving children with less severe problems, perhaps reading difficulties. This situation could mean that the children with reading problems fall behind, and the seriously handicapped children also fail to progress.

DEFINING THE AREA OF CONCERN

In delimiting the areas within which we are going to work, we need to draw certain boundaries. Careful attention to these boundaries is an essential aspect of the systems approach. Thus, we must define whether we will be dealing with handicapped children as well as handicapped adults. We need to decide whether we will be concerned with mental as well as physical problems. To what depth will our service system go in dealing with special problems of retardation, psychosis, developmental disabilities, or the autistic child? Will our system include work with parents?

   As we think about a total service system we need to be concerned with all of its functions including planning, mobilizing resources, outreach or informing patients, direct service provision or purchase of care, aftercare, and evaluation of the services. In addition to this, will our system include research, the building of facilities, etc.? Unless decisions are made early as to the focus of a particular program, the subsequent decisions tend to be diffuse and ineffective.

STATING THE OBJECTIVES

One of the most serious problems facing the management of programs for the handicapped is the fuzziness with which objectives are often stated. This can be a serious obstacle to applying the systems approach in the management of these programs.

   This problem can be illustrated in programs for the handicapped by different philosophies of prevention, treatment, rehabilitation, and maintenance. Each of these four very sound goals carries with it a different set of activities, costs, and implications for the patient. One statement of the goal of rehabilitation is that it aims to help the client obtain his highest potential, economically, vocationally, personally, and socially. This is an extremely broad statement of goal which would need to be broken down into clearer statements of objectives in order to properly plan or evaluate programs for the handicapped.

Adding to the difficulty is the dichotomy between the employment objectives of many of the national rehabilitation efforts and other nonemployment objectives. The latter may include helping persons live more meaningful lives, learning to care for themselves so that other family members are free to work, or simply learning to dress themselves. These nonemployment goals appear to be the most difficult to state clearly enough to provide a basis for a disciplined evaluation.

As these objectives become known and clearly stated, they can drastically affect the area of concern, the target group being served, and many other aspects of the systems framework for decision-making, particularly that of identifying the alternatives.

IDENTIFYING AND ASSESSING ALTERNATIVES

An important attribute of the systems approach is the determination and assessment of alternative ways of reaching the objectives of the system. For example, consideration of alternatives to institutionalization of the handicapped is a major concern. An evaluation of the costs and benefits of community-based care compared to institutional care means that the total community-based system must be identified, including its costs. While it is generally believed that community-based services are not only professionally better for individuals but also less costly, we need to examine this concept more carefully by including all of the resources required for quality services.

Part of the issue in this analysis will be the question of cost to whom. Certainly it would be less costly to a state if individuals were taken out of state institutions and put into local counties where county and voluntary sources shared the burden. It will be important in these analyses to examine total costs—to the community as well as to the state.

There are still other complications. The measurement of benefits of a better lifestyle (for example, for retardates who can work in a sheltered workshop) is extremely difficult. In addition, the effects of a program on the total family must be considered. In other words, benefits to individuals cannot really be assessed separately from the family and the community.

In reaching for the solution to a problem and identifying the best way of doing something, a number of choices are available to the planners. For each alternative, a cost (or requirement for resources) can be identified and a level of relative effectiveness in reaching the objectives of the system can be assessed. This conscious identification of alternative ways to reach objectives, and the use of methods to quantify the cost and effectiveness of as many alternatives as possible, are essential attributes of the systems approach. The search for the preferred way of accomplishing an objective, moreover, is based on the concept that resources are always scarce in relation to needs. The established way of doing something, therefore, must be assessed as one alternative rather than as a sacred cow. These alternatives, however, must be contained within the broad boundaries of the area of concern and its objectives.

This view of alternative ways of reaching an objective is an essential aspect of such systems-related activities as cost/benefit analysis and the planning, programming, and budgeting system (PPBS).

INTEGRATION OF SUBSYSTEMS

In any systems approach, a series of subsystems can be identified and should be dealt with. This enables the planner and manager to break down a large and complex task into smaller tasks. Thus, we may envision a program for the handicapped as including a workshop, a day care center, a series of social services and psychological treatment services, work with parents, aftercare, and referrals from and to other agencies.

It is essential that a common language be established among the many professionals involved which will permit communication between the subsystems. Careful attention must be given to "interface," or the way in which the subsystems feed into each other. For example, if a workshop for the retarded has rigid limits on the hours of operation, it may mean that a family member will be forced to curtail his time available for employment in order to be at home when the retarded person returns from the workshop. This limitation imposed by the workshop, perhaps caused by limited funds, has a ripple effect upon the ability of another family member to get out of the home and find employment.

There are also many external environmental factors to be considered. To a large extent, these may provide the most significant constraints upon the entire system. For example, the agency may have to meet the standards required by city, county, state, and federal agencies, as well as voluntary agency standard-setting groups. A particular type of medical care which is required may be lacking in a community. There may be no funds for financing supportive services for the handicapped individual or his family.

In studying the subsystems of a given system, a theoretical framework or model used as a point of departure would usually include:

◇ Inputs, or what is put into the system.
◇ Outputs, or what the system produces.
◇ Processing, or what is needed to convert inputs into desired outputs.
◇ Control, or some arrangement for supervising or monitoring the operations of the system.
◇ Feedback, or transmission of information to maintain the system.

DATA FLOW

In order to tie together the various subsystems, it is essential that information be available to monitor and control activities. This assumes that objectives have been clearly stated at the inception so that the manager can monitor activities and accomplishments against objectives. With respect to assessment of programs for the handicapped, a number of problems exist. For example, there is the problem of how to weight the difficulty of a particular patient or patient situation. Another is how to measure the effectiveness of rehabilitation efforts. Complicating the latter is the period of time over which rehabilitation extends, and the difficulty in maintaining statistics when agencies must report on an annual or shorter period.

Rehabilitation may also involve many agencies, and information is therefore needed from a number of different sources. But perhaps the most basic problem is the fact that rehabilitation is a process and, much like counseling in other social services, can be directed to a multitude of objectives and a multitude of target groups. This means that the ability to obtain data must be based upon prior development of improved concepts of measuring effectiveness and meeting objectives.

ORGANIZATIONAL ARRANGEMENTS

The contributions of systems organization to the delivery of service is one of great potential significance in assessing the many programs for the handicapped provided by specialized agencies and government departments and bureaus. In addition, the sources of funds are multiple. Current financing of the programs for specialized purposes tends to splinter the organizational basis of the program. From a practical point of view, therefore, an organizational arrangement on a project basis may be necessary in order to cut across the myriad organizational lines. Although such a project organization would be inefficient, it may be the best that many local communities and states can develop at the present time.

SYSTEMS ANALYSIS

Systems analysis is an application of the systems approach in a disciplined framework in which a variety of specialized techniques may be brought to bear on some problem. The following observations will help to clarify what is meant by the term:

◆ Systems analysis is characterized by the objective way in which the elements of a situation are assessed as an aid for decision-making.

◆ Decisions concerning programs for the handicapped must be related to relevant political, social, and economic factors.

◆ Specialized resources and technology—especially the computer, telecommunications, operations research, and cost/benefit analysis—are used by systems analysts.

It is possible to apply the concept of systems analysis without a computer, but it is unlikely that computer applications can be successful without the use of systems analysis.

CONCLUSION

The idea of a "management information system"—which may be viewed as the capstone of the systems approach—is beginning to be explored in organizations for the handicapped. Sound, timely information for decision-making is a basic need in managing any program. In management information systems we are concerned with specifying information that is required to make planning and operational decisions to monitor the productivity of an organization, and to meet external requirements for information. To the systems analyst who sees an entire organization as a system, procedures for acquiring and transmitting information appear as subsystems rather than as independent and duplicating processes. Attention is given to future requirements for information in addition to current uses. Furthermore, when the system is optimally designed, data are collected once at their source, and then stored in such a way that they can be retrieved efficiently for a variety of purposes. And finally, information systems require definitions of boundaries of services, statements of objectives, and appropriate statistics for measuring productivity or progress toward objectives.

It should be emphasized, however, that no system of automation will resolve many of the conceptual problems that have endured for years in aid to the handicapped. The pressure to move toward resolution of these long-term problems in the management of programs is a healthy pressure and should be responded to actively. At the same time, the partnership with systems analysts provides a new resource. The systems approach may well constitute the tool needed to clarify thinking and to establish a framework within which better decisions can be made and operations managed more efficiently. What better gift can be given to the handicapped?

Systematic Processes Applied to Health Care Planning

Owen B. Hardy

Among subjects now receiving serious attention in the health care field is planning, and particularly long-range planning. Because of a fortunate combination of factors or circumstances, the importance of anticipating needs beyond the immediate future and devising schemes of action to meet them is becoming widely recognized and appreciated by both voluntary and governmental officials. That the health care rendered in this nation can be improved materially through proper and adequate planning is to be little doubted, and optimistic hopes are certainly warranted as one views the planning activity being carried forward at national, regional, and local levels.

REACTING TO DEMAND

Until a few years ago, only a very small percentage of hospitals or related health institutions possessed a long-range plan of any sort, and physical expan-

Reprinted with permission from *Hospital and Health Services Administration* (formerly *Hospital Administration*), the quarterly journal of the American College of Hospital Administrators, Winter 1971.

sion programs, as well as the provision of new services, resulted, typically, from demonstrated demand. This situation accrued somewhat directly from the absence of a perceived need for planning but perhaps in some measure also from the lack of planning skills among those in positions of leadership in the health care field. Even yet, the term planning itself remains ill-defined, and concepts of planning methodology vary widely.

The interest being currently evinced in formal health care planning centers around the almost simultaneous progressive evolution of four key factors:

1. Health care has been rapidly ascending in the priority of importance among our nationally held values; there is a heightened interest in all its aspects.

2. Financial assistance by the U.S. Public Health Service for the formation and operation of areawide planning councils, plus more recent federal legislation which features comprehensive regional health planning, has focused increasing attention on long-range planning. Rather than unwarranted meddling in the affairs of our so-called voluntary health system, such federal actions are coming to be recognized as justifiable and necessary inasmuch as research and experience over the past twenty years have shown rather conclusively that planning by the single hospital (or the lack of it) with disregard to the plans of others will result in wasted resources, and/or serious omissions in the provision of optimum health care to a total population.

3. Resources required for the efficient delivery of modern scientific health care greatly exceed those needed for rendering the services of a few years ago, with regard to both quality and quantity, as well as complexity. Thereby, their marshaling requires a considerable period of time, exclusive of that time required for proper planning. For example, from six to eight years are now generally necessary to plan, build, and open a new hospital. This span of years, per se, forces resort to techniques of long-range planning.

4. There is, in spite of a seeming internecine ideological and semantic warfare among management experts, a greater sophistication than ever before among administrators and governing board members with regard to management itself. Undoubtedly, this is due in large part to educational assemblies, institutes, and seminars being conducted among top echelon health care personnel, as well as an increasing number of persons who hold advanced degrees entering the field.

GROWING STIMULUS

Small likelihood seems to exist that the causative relationship of any of these factors to planning will decrease in importance. Indeed, each of them will probably provide a greater stimulus to planning in the immediate years ahead than ever before.

While planning is certainly carried forward independently of formal organizations, most recognized conceptual views of the process have been set forth in management literature. Unquestionably, planning is a part of management and stands as one of the most important responsibilities of managers. Considering then that management, under which planning is usually subsumed, remains so indiscriminately perceived, it is small wonder that either the dilettante or serious student of planning becomes easily confused when reviewing current opinions about the subject.

"THE MANAGEMENT THEORY JUNGLE"

Professor Harold Koontz has succinctly and forceably drawn attention to the utter and widespread confusion with regard to concepts of management in his widely noted paper "The Management Theory Jungle." [1] This insightful dissertation has gained a great deal of recognition, but it has brought little fruitful agreement concerning management, or planning, theory. Social, physical, and biological scientists, as well as practicing managers, consultants, and a variety of armchair strategists continue to thrash about in a dense conceptual and semantic fog which enshrouds the whole field of inquiry into all management processes; thus one can merely grope for pillars of substantive principle. While regrettable, this is not to say that this situation might have been entirely avoided, for management, as a separate discipline, is indeed in early formative stages.

There are as many ways to plan as there are ways to think or to make decisions, and this being so, men indulge in all of them. As a result, bad or ill-conceived plans are sometimes evolved. The very fact that choices present themselves to the mind throughout the planning process brings into being the constant possibility of error and mistake. *Thus, when one considers on the one hand that an incorrect plan may be worse than no plan at all and on the other that health planning now involves both billions of dollars and the very physical and mental well-being of our nation's populace, the importance of employing the best known planning methodology and techniques draws into sharp focus.*

TWO-PRONGED PURPOSE

The purposes of this paper are (1) to set forth a meaningful concept of proper planning and trace its genesis in brief manner, more or less from the academic viewpoint, and (2) to present the notion that the systems approach represents a methodology by which optimum health care planning can be carried forward at any level of cognizance and at any point in time. This approach has been used effectively in solving highly complex problems in many diverse fields, and its adaptation to health care planning seems to be clearly indicated.

Planning in its broadest sense has been accorded a variety of definitions, and there still exists considerable disagreement with regard to its scope within the overall management process and among the various actions undertaken by managers. Most authorities agree, however, that it invariably involves the future and that it is basically a process wherein decision making plays a vital role.

A MAJORITY OPINION

A careful review of management literature reveals that Newman and Summer give planning a definition which embraces the key aspects of what might be called a majority opinion. This definition states:

> The process of planning covers a wide range of activities, all the way from initially sensing that something needs doing to firmly deciding who does what when. Planning is much broader than compiling and analyzing information, or dreaming up ideas of what might be done. It is more than logic or imagination or judgment. It is a combination of all these that culminates in a decision—a decision about what should be done.[2]

One immediately concludes that the crux of these statements revolves around the point that the various activities as cited culminate in actual decisions about what should be done. Further, one could conclude that a plan *is* a decision or, usually, a group of decisions about actions to be undertaken. This latter point neither means that the decisions must be nor will be implemented; certainly, plans can be revised, altered, or discarded, as they should be from time to time, in view of changing circumstances. However, it does mean that any given or described course of action remains in the realm of suggestions, recommendations, or alternatives unless officially adopted as a guide for action; it means that a plan, in reality, is composed of consummated decisions.

STANDING AND SINGLE-USE PLANS

Traditionally, there have been two broad categories of plans cited as being involved in any organized effort, either in the health care field or elsewhere. The first of these is called standing plans and includes policies, standard methods, standard operating procedures, and/or rules and regulations. Such plans are geared to guide actions which are generally repetitive in nature, and they form a base for the making of additional decisions necessary to ongoing operations. The second of these categories has been regarded as comprising what are commonly designated as single-use plans; examples are programs, schedules, and special methods, all of which are designed for unique circumstances.[3] And, it is to this category of single-use plans that long-range health care planning has usually been relegated. However, a new trend is emerging, called systems planning, which cuts across the traditional planning categories and embraces the delineation of operational processes at various levels of cognizance. Depending on the level of cognizance and the component group of interrelated actions involved in the accomplishment of respective, proximate objectives, a given process may be called a system or a subsystem.

The term long-range planning has been employed variously, and, per se, implies a meaning which is relative. In the context of this paper, it is arbitrarily construed to mean the formulation of decisions having to do with actions which will be executed over a considerable period of time and which will be either directly or indirectly integrated into defined operational processes. Usually, depending on present-day constraints, periods from about five to thirty years are involved in typical long-range health care planning.

The long-range planning process, as cited, is in complete harmony with the previously noted broad definition of planning enunciated by Newman and Summer. Additionally, the construction outlined clearly includes long-range forecasting and image making, both of which are often mistakenly called long-range planning.

Because decision making can be applied to mere selections or choices, not pertaining to future courses of action, not all decision making can be called planning. On the other hand, all concrete planning definitely involves decision making, and whether or not planning is regarded as being synonymous with decision making depends entirely on the scope of activities accorded the decision-making process. Some authorities view decision making as a rather simple and uncomplicated process of choice; others regard it as an essentially sterile, deductive process. An appreciable number espouse two types of decision making, intuitive and rational, and describe distinct and separate processes by which both are accomplished.

A UNITING METHODOLOGY

For proper long-range planning, a process is required which will allow thousands (if need be) of subordinate, supporting decisions to be correctly made, interrelated, and built into the key decisions comprising an overall plan; as well, a combined intuitive-rational, deductive-inductive process is needed, and the systems approach clearly constitutes a methodology which unites the necessary elements.

Reasons for the sudden, widespread application of the systems approach to the solution of complex problems of diverse nature would seem to include these points: (1) Formal education has become more scientifically oriented in recent years. (2) Statistics, as a branch of applied mathematics and a distinct body of knowledge, has been expanded widely in both theoretical and practical use since World War II. (3) The computer has reduced to seconds the long periods of time formerly required for various manual computations, detailed data analyses, and the operation of simulation models, thus allowing experimentation to be carried out and conclusions reached within reasonable time periods. (4) The employment of the team concept in problem solving requires that some methodology be followed for effort coordination, and considering the scientific disciplines usually involved, it was inevitable that a scientific approach, such as the systems approach, would be taken.

The genesis of the systems approach lies in the scientific method, but it is also closely akin to the reflective thought process, as well as most of the decision-making processes which have been prolifically described by management authorities during the past few years. Without derogation to the systems approach, rather than being a brilliant discovery by a new and brighter generation, its generally recognized steps constitute purely and simply a refinement and extension of methodology which has been extant for many years, and the chief acclaim due its proponents lies in their deliberate adaptation of its methodology to the solution of complex problems of great diversity, exclusive of those primarily involved with experimentation, or actual research.

GALILEO, BACON, AND JOHN DEWEY

The scientific method, the progenitor of the systems approach, was used by Galileo (1564–1642), and Bacon (1561–1626) enunciated much of its process. In the nineteenth century many writers elucidated upon the basic methodology as it was used by a host of scientific investigators. Today, the scientific method is employed world-wide and is recognized as that process, par excellence, which has thrust mankind into the atomic age and to the frontiers of space. Briefly, the scientific method encompasses the following steps: (1) Define the problem to be investigated, (2) obtain pertinent facts (observation), (3) formulate hypotheses, (4) test the hypotheses (experiment), (5) construct a theory on the basis of the hypothesis which seems best, and (6) submit the theory to proof through wider testing, either by experiment or in the real world.

The reflective thought process, first described by the philosopher John Dewey in 1910 and given further elaboration in 1933, has been widely used as a decision-making technique. As a heuristic approach to education, the reflective thought process has encountered considerable criticism in recent years, but its validity as a tool for problem solving continues to generate acclaim, and Dewey's statement that "It converts action that is merely appetitive, blind, and impulsive into intelligent action" [4] seems to be, on the whole, merited.

Reflective thought, as opposed to the mind's stream of consciousness, mere beliefs, and daydreams, was seen by Dewey [5] as being composed of five essential phases, which he described as:

◇ *Suggestions,* in which the mind leaps forward to a possible solution.
◇ An intellectualization of the difficulty or perplexity that has been *felt* (directly experienced) into a *problem* to be solved, a question for which the answer must be sought.
◇ The use of one suggestion after another as a leading idea, or *hypothesis,* to initiate and guide observation and other operations in collection of factual material.
◇ The mental elaboration of the idea or supposition as an idea or supposition (*reasoning* in the sense in which reasoning is a part, not the whole, of inference).
◇ Testing the hypothesis by overt or imaginative action.

That Dewey connected the reflective thought process to planning is clearly contained in the following statement:

. . . It has been suggested that reflective thinking involves a look into the future, a forecast, an anticipation, or a prediction, and this should be listed as a sixth aspect, or phase. As a matter of fact, every intellectual suggestion or idea is anticipatory of some possible future experience, while the final solution gives a definite set toward the future.[5]

AN EXPLOSION OF INTEREST

In recent years decision-making processes have received widespread attention. A brief review of volumes listed under the general heading of decision making in the Library of Congress reveals some five volumes published prior to 1940, twelve in the years 1940–1949, fifteen during the period 1950–1959, and about 130 in 1960 and subsequent years to date. This explosion of interest in decision making reflects the importance currently being attached to obtaining the highest possible percentage of correct solutions to problems and to determining optimum courses of action under given circumstances (planning), not only in business enterprises, but in many other unrelated endeavors.

Concisely stated, the rational decision-making process is usually regarded as containing four steps, or phases: (1) diagnosing the problem and defining the mission, objective, or goals; (2) determining and setting forth alternative solutions or courses of action; (3) analyzing and testing the relative feasibility of each of the alternative solutions or courses of action, and (4) selecting the most feasible plan.

The *creative* decision-making process, though frequently described apart from rational decision making is, in reality, an elaboration upon the initial steps of the rational process. For example, Newman and Summer enumerate five stages in the creative process and provide the following explanations [6]:

> Although no two people's minds work exactly alike, the testimony of inventors and great scientists indicates that the creative process is likely to follow these stages:
>
> 1. *Saturation:* becoming thoroughly familiar with a problem, its setting, and, more broadly, with activities and ideas akin to the problem.
>
> 2. *Deliberation:* mulling over these ideas, analyzing them, challenging them, rearranging them, thinking of them from several viewpoints.
>
> 3. *Incubation:* relaxing, turning off the conscious and purposeful search, forgetting the frustrations of unproductive labor, letting the subconscious mind work.
>
> 4. *Illumination:* a bright idea strikes, a bit crazy, perhaps, but new and fresh and full of promise; you sense that it might be the answer.
>
> 5. *Accommodation:* clarifying the idea, seeing whether it fits the requirements of the problem as it did on first thought, reframing and adapting it, putting it on paper, getting other people's reaction to it.

PART OF THE CREATIVE PROCESS

Certainly all of these stages will ensue in the *individual mind* (provided creative ability is present) as the steps of the rational process are pursued; thus, that the rational process is exclusive of the creative process constitutes a fallacy of the first order.

The similarity of the systems approach to the scientific method, the reflective thought process, and the decision-making processes, as discussed, will be distinctly noted as following discussions are perused.

The concept of the systems approach is characterized by three basic aspects. These are: (1) problem solving is tackled according to a deliberate methodology (the steps of the systems approach, subsequently described), (2) the problem is usually analyzed as a total process, and conclusions drawn are utilized in the decision making inherent to planning, and (3) an interdisciplinary team is employed in the problem solving task, rather than an individual.

Figure 1 shows the steps of the systems approach arranged in classical operative positions within the complete planning process. It should be stressed that none of the steps are discrete; each is shown discretely merely as a guide to establish order in the process and as a checkpoint to assure that no short circuits are inadvertently made. The diagram, by feedback loops, denotes the inherent iterative nature of the process, both between certain steps and within the process as a whole.

SYSTEMS DESIGN AND PLANNING

Whereas the systems approach is admirably adapted to providing solutions to many varied problems, its efficacy in the design of operational systems has been widely demonstrated, thus lending validity to the name it bears. With regard to the case in point, if the objective of planning is to determine, identify, describe, and adopt a future ongoing activity or process the plan evolved will be essentially a system design. Thus, systems design and planning became one; and, most generally, a long-range health care plan, at any level of cognizance, will be a designed system of health care. If it is not, the plan should be carefully reevaluated for deficiencies.

The analysis or design, or both, of a system centers on definitions of who (if humans are involved), when, what, where, and how. This is a point seldom clearly outlined in the now considerable body of literature pertaining to systems analysis and engineering, but it is basic to any correct understanding of systems, and especially open systems, such as are found in the health care field. Figure 2 portrays the basic concept of an open system, as described by Optner,[7] and introduces, additionally, the descriptive parameters inherent to the process.

The same definitions which are integral to a system as a process are also integral to a complete plan. Although physical models; mathematical, diagrammatical, and/or statistical models; flow diagrams; PERT charts; narrative description, and so forth, may each be used as descriptive techniques (and when appropriate as developmental and testing techniques) the whole concept of system and plan is grounded in this simply conceptual context.

Figure 3 shows the steps within the systems approach as they can be adapted to long-range health care planning, at national, regional, or local levels.

Step 4, the development of alternatives in terms of who, when, what, where, and how, begins the delineation of a future system which will finally emerge as the output of the total cycle.

Figure 1. Steps within systems approach.

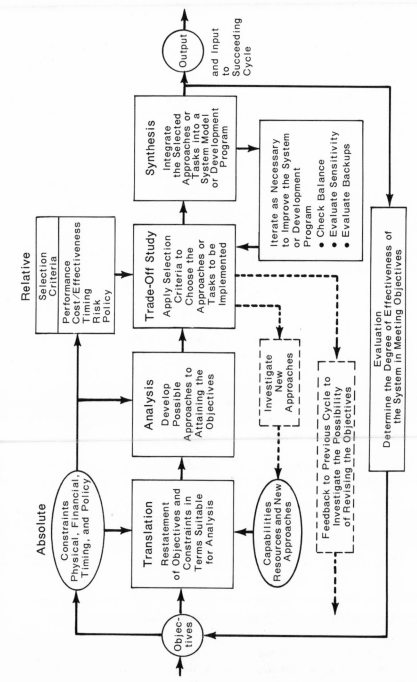

Figure 2. Descriptive parameters of open systems.

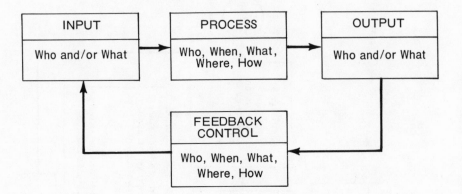

IMPLICATIONS FOR HEALTH CARE PLANNERS

In examining the systems approach as depicted in both Figures 1 and 3, it is obvious that the output will be a designed system, and just as clearly the output will be a plan. Surely, the proved efficacy of the systems approach in systems design has important implications for planners in the health care field.

The construction of alternative courses of action in planning (through step IV, analysis, in the systems approach) is brought about by both deductive and inductive processes, but emphasis is upon induction—the making of inferences and, narrowly, the formulation of hypotheses. For best results in this phase of the total planning process, creativeness, keen insight, intuition, and high intellectual capability are required. Because even near exhaustive examination or testing of all *possible* courses of action (in most cases these would be multitudinous) would not be feasible from the standpoint of cost and time, usually only a limited number of alternatives are constructed for consideration. Thus, it is highly important that experienced persons capable of somewhat complex psychological activity be here employed to reduce to a minumum errors which will require needless effort for discovery in later steps and force the reformulation of additional alternatives. Of course, barring the disproving of a fallacious plan, activities could be directed on a wrong course and cause irreparable setbacks in the procurement of optimum goals.

"NO NATURAL CHECKS TO WRONG BELIEFS"

Of equal importance, however, is the requirement for professional competency in the application of selection criteria, the employment of deductive processes,

Figure 3. Steps in the systems approach.

STEPS		LONG-RANGE HEALTH CARE PLANNING (any level of cognizance)
I	Objectives	Establish the broad objectives.
II	Constraints	Set forth the constraints: Existing needs and demands Planning at other levels Present levels of care Projected needs and demands Manpower Existing facilities Financial Demographic Population characteristics Timing Existing policy
III	Translation	Restate refined objectives in consideration of constraints.
IV	Analysis	Develop possible approaches to attaining the objectives, with each approach being stated in terms of: Who When What Where How
V	Selection criteria	Set forth the criteria for the selection of an approach: Total cost Performance or results Cost/effectiveness Timing Risk Policy Avoidance of untoward consequences Flexibility
VI	Trade-off and synthesis	Apply selection criteria to the possible approaches. Integrate the selected approach or approaches into a system model or development program.
VII	Cycle output	After final testing and evaluation, specify and adopt the plan.

SOURCE: Re-entry systems department, General Electric Company; Gordon A. Friesen, International, Incorporated.

and/or the implementation of experimental or statistical testing with regard to the alternative courses of action established through inference. Although the monuments to intuitive geniuses are many, history has tended to forget many plausible schemes and tenets which, through a failure to substantiate the utterances of supposed great minds, gained favor and, in some cases, actually deterred the advancement of civilization and scientific inquiry for considerable time periods. Thus, the suggested courses of action must be subjected to the cold and impersonal light of factual evidence and real constraints. Dewey has said ". . . there are no natural checks to wrong beliefs" [8] and "Superstition is as natural as science." [9] Unquestionably, these opinions represent reality.

Throughout the entire planning process as shown, the avoidance of prejudging solutions must be given strict adherence, and objectivity is demanded insofar as processes employed are concerned; especially is objectivity important in the comparison and evaluation of alternative courses of action. Just as the true scientist, the planner must provide for dispassionate examinations and comparisons, and although many writers broadly deny that true objectivity exists, the proving of scientific fact and the discard of false notions through the ages, and notably in our own age, stand in direct refutation. That none of us is or can be objective all of the time and that most of us are seldom objective does not alter the fact that some of us, at least on occasion, can deliberately commit ourselves to processes of at least nearly complete objectivity, even with regard to aspects of the human personality and psyche. So it must be and can be in later phases of the planning process, here exemplified by the systems approach.

OBJECTIVE OF THE TEAM APPROACH

Inasmuch as views of the future can only be entertained mentally (though expressed in words or figures) the framework of the planning process must necessarily be a mental framework, and regarding the systems approach as such, the conceptual diagram shown in Figure 4 will be found useful.

Figure 4. The systems approach to planning viewed as a thought process.

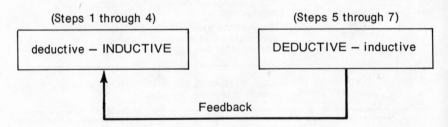

Whereas this diagram is based on an individual mental process (an interindividual process being impossible) there is no reason why each individual member of the planning team cannot be aware of and internalize this vital concept of the overall endeavor. In fact, the whole objective of a team approach is to bring the broader knowledge of a number of individuals to bear on a given problem in the coordinated manner of a single mind, seeking a solution through a reflective process (described by Dewey) that is completely inherent to the systems approach.

FEWER ERRORS

Even cursory contemplation of planning in the manner presented leads one to the belief that the process will be best implemented by a team rather than an individual. Certainly it is true, as Herbert Simon has observed, that "It is impossible for the behavior of a single isolated individual to reach any high degree of rationality." [10] The tasks involved far surpass the limits of the knowledge and skills of any one person, and there are man-hours entailed in any complicated plan or system formulation which would almost certainly extend beyond required deadlines if undertaken by a single workman, even though he possessed the requisite skills. Additionally, authoritative evidence seems to indicate that error occurrence will be smaller with a number of persons engaged in the process rather than an individual. Under controlled laboratory conditions, where the ability of individuals was compared to that of small groups in solving complex problems involving a series of steps, all of which had to be correct before the right answer was obtained, Shaw found that groups seemed assured of a much larger proportion of correct solutions than individuals. [11]

Although one or two persons might carry the bulk of the work load in only moderately complicated long-range health care planning, even here there exists a great need to draw on the skills of such individuals as statisticians, physicians, architects, and experienced management personnel. For major planning, at least eight to ten disciplines should be readily available to make their special and unique contributions.

OUTSTANDING KEEN INSIGHT NOT PRECLUDED

Although the systems approach to planning indicates rather clearly the desirability for the use of a team rather than an individual, this approach in no way precludes or thwarts the use of the keen insight and outstanding intellectuality which one or more outstanding members of the team may possess. In most instances a penetrating individual mental grasp of the total planning problem is needed. As well, an acute awareness of the resource requirements of the planning endeavor itself plus a knowledge of the psychological aspects of group behavior should be held by the group leadership. These capabilities, employed correctly, can greatly enhance the total effort, while at the same time the advantages of in-depth talent afforded only by an interdisciplinary team will be retained.

AN ORDERLY UNDERTAKING

As would be suspected, the systems approach, per se, provides an excellent vehicle for the organization of planning work, and considering the dearth of management expertise among specialists this attribute proves to be invaluable in many instances. With little difficulty, the leadership of the team can segment and assign the operative jobs integral to the process and outline a logical work flow. In such a manner the planning process becomes an orderly, rather than a haphazard, undertaking.

An increasing number of scientific and technological discoveries within the general field of health care promise to force continuing reevaluations and reformulations of plans by the providers of both preventive and curative care. This consideration, plus the fact that long-range planning must necessarily be a continuing process to account fully for changing resources and needs, indicates that planners will come to be placed on a retainer basis by many health care organizations and agencies, and where the range of planning problems is both broad and complicated, permanent planning departments will probably be organized. The latter instances will likely include governmental planning, at least at the higher echelons, as well as the planning functions of voluntary bodies operating large health care complexes. The ongoing activities of such departments will actually constitute a subsystem of the larger health care system.

TREND ALREADY APPARENT

Thus, the expected volume, breadth, and complexity of health care planning in the immediate years ahead all strongly indicate that a sizable portion of the work will be performed by teams of experts utilizing the systems approach. In fact, the trend is already apparent as hospital consulting firms and the systems engineering divisions of several large corporations tool up for major efforts in this specialized area.

Such teams, regardless of their relationship to the health care system being served, will specify raw data required, supervise its accumulation, assemble it in interpretable form, ascertain its implications through the systems approach, consider alternative solutions, test the alternatives, synthesize an optimum solution, and present recommendations to the implementing authorities. After study and adoption, a plan will have been born and, most likely, the plan will look to the evolvement of a health care system which, except in the case of the national level, will always be a part of a larger system.

AVOIDING TANGENTIAL COURSES

Although the systems approach to planning may not be a panacea, its widespread proper use will better assure those who deliver health services that makeshift expediency, tangential courses of action, and boxed corners will be avoided. And at the same time, change, when warranted, will be a sought-after and accepted product rather than a traumatic experience dictated by factors over which little or no control is held.

The very fact, however, that a plan constitutes a definite control mechanism may lead some to fear that through such planning activities as have been outlined here control may be taken from the hands of traditional health care professionals and volunteer laymen only to be vested in "outsiders" manipulating esoteric computers and mysterious formulas and possessed of no real concern for the welfare of the patient or the future of the individual health care institution. On the contrary, knowledgeable use of the systems approach to planning as an additional tool in the instrumentation available to health care authorities will permit them to control the future of their institutions and their profession with far greater precision than has ever been the case before. Beyond this, they will be able to increase the efficiency of their delivery system and narrow the gap both qualitatively and quantitatively between existing systems and optimum systems in the present-day context of science and technology.

REFERENCES

1. Harold Koontz, "The Management Theory Jungle," *Journal of American Medicine,* Dec. 1961.
2. William H. Newman and Charles E. Summer, Jr., *The Process of Management* (Englewood Cliffs, N.J.: Prentice-Hall, 1964).

94 PLANNING AND ANALYSIS

3. Ibid., pp. 391–436.
4. John Dewey, *How We Think* (Boston: D.C. Heath, 1933).
5. Ibid., p. 117.
6. Newman and Summer, p. 280.
7. Stanford L. Optner, *Systems Analysis for Business and Industrial Problem Solving* (Englewood Cliffs, N.J.: Prentice-Hall, 1965).
8. Dewey, p. 23.
9. Ibid., p. 24.
10. Herbert A. Simon, *Administrative Behavior* (New York: Macmillan, 1957).
11. Marjorie E. Shaw, "A Comparison of Individuals and Small Groups in the Rational Solution of Complex Problems," *American Journal of Psychology,* July 1932.

Break-Even Analysis
for Higher Education

L. Keith Larimore

In the field of educational administration, most methods of analysis employed for internal managerial control, or for justification purposes, emphasize either costs or revenues. Analytical methods which do tie costs and revenues together are generally too sophisticated and the resulting data are therefore difficult to explain. This situation is becoming more and more serious since the demand for the services of colleges and universities has been negatively affected by tight money, reluctant taxpayers, population trends, and a number of other demand depressing factors.

With regard to the relationship between the institution as the seller and the potential student as the buyer, a "buyer's market" is rapidly developing. This buyer's market has manifested itself in stable or declining enrollments following a decade of rapid expansion in physical facilities, curricula, and faculty size. In short, many colleges and universities have geared up for an unending growth in demand for their services only to find that the demand is shrinking. Thus, large numbers of institutions are left with excess capacity accompanied by declining enrollments—a situation which plays havoc with productivity and

Reprinted with permission from *Management Accounting,* September 1974.

costs. Instead of virtually receiving a blank check from legislators who are now interested in trimming the fat from appropriations for higher education, college administrators are asked to justify objectively and quantitatively not only proposed new programs but also the existing programs and curriculum.

Top level administrators are thus caught on the horns of a dilemma in that they have almost constant pressure from above and below. The pressure from above comes from legislators and boards of control demanding more economical operation of the institution with orders to hold the line on, or even cut costs. The pressure from below comes from faculty members who typically want to add courses and programs to the curriculum.* The resulting cost-revenue squeeze simply means that college administrators must do a more effective job of applying or adapting the available tools of management to their financial operations.

The objective in this article is to provide an effective yet easily understood method of analyzing costs and revenues together, whether the purpose be for curriculum decisions, resource allocation, costs and productivity analysis, or management effectiveness. The proposed method is nothing more or less than an adaptation and application to college and university operations of a simple management tool known as "break-even analysis."† If properly employed, the method aids the administrator to determine precisely that level of activity (enrollments) which will generate sufficient revenues to just cover the costs of operations. In addition, the magnitude of the losses or excesses associated with other levels of activity is also indicated. However, the process of generating the needed input data should not exclude the generation of other information which is not specifically needed for break-even analysis.

REVENUES

Revenues may come from any one of a great many sources. However, for the most part, the revenues generated will depend on levels of enrollment. For

* Many of these proposals are based on "pet" interests and are, more often than not, in addition to existing programs and courses which in themselves may not be justifiable in terms of enrollments or the costs and revenues associated with them. Some of these existing "financial losers" are necessary for a sound and complete academic program and should be carried by the more profitable courses. However, even if such financial losers are not crucial to the overall curriculum, it is very difficult to remove such programs or courses for at least two reasons. First, the quantitative data upon which the courses were determined to be losers are not adequate to support such a determination, or such data are not easily understood by the cross-section faculty usually involved in the decision to drop courses or programs from the curriculum. Second, the welfare of the personnel who would be negatively affected by the elimination of programs or courses becomes a major consideration.

† Break-even analysis can be presented in the form of tables, formulas, or charts and graphs. The graphic illustrations are generally accepted as the most informative and most readily understood.

most public colleges and universities, tuition and governmental appropriations (based on full-time equivalent enrollments) are the major sources of revenue. Therefore, revenues will increase as enrollments increase, and decrease as enrollments decrease. The relationship between enrollments and revenues is for all practical purposes assumed to be linear.

COSTS

As in industry, most costs will fall into two categories—fixed costs and variable costs. Fixed costs are generally overhead costs which do not change as the level of activity changes. Some examples of fixed costs would be top level administrators' salaries, maintenance costs, and building and grounds expenses. Such costs are very broad and general in that they are difficult to associate with any academic area but represent necessary services for every phase of the institution. Variable costs, on the other hand, are those costs which vary directly with the level of activity. Faculty salaries and testing supplies are among examples of variable costs. As enrollments increase the expenditures on these items will increase or vary within limits. It is important for the reader to realize that many such variable costs appear to be fixed within a budget or contract period. However, these variable costs do and should change with the level of activity from period to period.

COLLECTING BUDGET COSTS INFORMATION

It is suggested that the break-even approach be applied to the smallest subdivisions of the institution's total academic program for which budgets and enrollment data are available. It is also suggested that the time frame for the analysis include past as well as current budget periods. The budget data for the entire institution should be broken down by colleges, divisions, and departments. The more budget information can be broken down, the more meaningful the results will be.

A useful format for collecting budget information is shown in Exhibit 1. The column heads are for the most part self-explanatory. However, a question may be asked with regard to what budget items to include in the Department

However, the reader is reminded that break-even analysis is only a tool of management and not a "cure-all." The method should be used in conjunction with other more traditional measures of productivity and performance in an effort to improve the quality of decisions required of college and university administrators.

Exhibit 1. Budget costs information.

Responsibility center	Dept. budget	Dept. salaries	Total dept. variable costs	Allocated overhead (fixed costs)	Total dept. costs	Credit hours taught	Costs per credit hours taught (actual dollars)		
							Var.	Fixed	Total
College of X									
Division A	$20	$120	$140	$40	$180	5,000	$28.00	$ 8.00	$36.00
Dept 1	$ 5	$ 45	$ 50	$10	$ 60	2,000	$25.00	$ 5.00	$30.00
Dept 2	$15	$ 75	$ 90	$30	$120	3,000	$30.00	$10.00	$40.00
Division B	$25	$130	$155	$50	$205	5,500	$28.18	$ 9.09	$37.27
Dept 1	$10	$ 50	$ 60	$15	$ 75	2,500	$24.00	$ 6.00	$30.00
Dept 2	$15	$ 80	$ 95	$35	$130	3,000	$31.67	$11.67	$43.34
College of Y									
Division A	$18	$115	$133	$35	$168	4,000	$33.25	$ 8.75	$42.00
Dept 1	$12	$ 80	$ 92	$20	$112	3,000	$30.67	$ 6.67	$37.34
Dept 2	$ 6	$ 35	$ 41	$15	$ 56	1,000	$41.00	$15.00	$56.00
Division B	$22	$124	$146	$45	$191	6,000	$24.33	$ 7.50	$31.83
Dept 1	$ 8	$ 54	$ 62	$15	$ 77	2,000	$31.00	$ 7.50	$38.50
Dept 2	$14	$ 70	$ 84	$30	$114	4,000	$21.00	$ 7.50	$28.50

budget column. The recommendation here is to include the total known budget of the individual responsibility center even though an amount for equipment and other capital expenditures will be counted. A one time expenditure for a building, a computer, or a comparable item should obviously not be included. This then assumes that all the amounts included are recurring from budget period to budget period and are not a disproportionate amount of the total budget.

The main point is that the analysis be consistent from one responsibility center to another. The argument is well taken that a microscope, for example, may have a useful life of more than a year and should therefore not be charged to a single year's expenses. However, a portion of the microscope's life will be consumed during the current period, and since depreciation accounts are generally not maintained in college and university accounting systems, it is suggested that the entire cost of such recurring equipment expenditures be charged to current operations. A further justification for handling such expenditures in this manner is that depreciation costs for investments in physical plant and facilities will not be charged to the various responsibility centers, thus resulting in an understatement of fixed costs to some extent. The important point again is that the analysis be consistent from one responsibility center to another.

If salaries are not included in the department budgets, the contracted amounts for faculty and other personnel are simply listed in the department salaries column. Thus, departmental administrative salaries which are clearly related to a single department as well as various clerical salaries are also included. Other administrative costs, not associated with a specific department, should be allocated on a credit-hour basis. The allocation would depend on the relationship which total credit hours taught in the department bears to the total credit hours taught by the organizational unit to which such costs can be specifically tied. For example, the salary of the dean of the college of arts and sciences should be allocated to the various departments of that college, and should be based on the relationship which the credit hours taught by the individual departments bear to the credit hours taught by the entire college of arts and sciences. This amount should be included in the column labeled Allocated overhead.

Allocated overhead includes other fixed cost items such as salaries of the president and other top level or staff administrators in addition to expenditures which are vital to the institution but which cannot be clearly tied to a specific department or responsibility center. These costs should also be allocated among the various departments on the basis of the number of credit hours taught by the individual department relative to the number of credit hours taught by the entire institution.

The column Total department costs is simply a summation of the Department budget, Department salaries, and Allocated overhead.

Credit hours taught are, of course, available from historical schedules and enrollment information. Knowing the credit hours taught, cost per credit hour taught can be obtained by dividing total department costs by credit hours taught. Once the cost per credit hour taught for a particular department is determined, the cost of offering a class in that department can be closely approximated.

For all practical purposes, the cost of the class remains fairly constant regardless of enrollment, once resources have been committed to a given course offering. Certainly more students require more supplies, but the cost difference in most cases is not material. Therefore, the cost side of the analysis represented by the variable cost, the fixed cost, and the total cost, in Exhibit 2, are constant for the contract period.

Exhibit 2. Break-even analysis for a typical three-hour course.

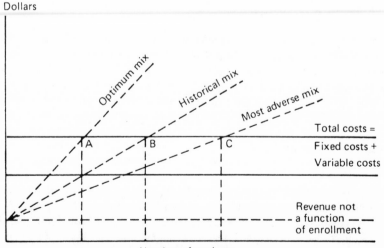

REVENUE DETERMINATION

The revenues that are important for this analysis are those which are closely correlated with enrollments. Major sources of such revenues are tuition and state or federal appropriations based on full-time-equivalent (FTE) students. The FTE is determined by dividing the number of student credit hours by the criteria for full-time designation. For example, assume the attendance criterion for one FTE student is 24 hours per year, or 12 hours per semester. Thus, a three-hour course with eight students enrolled would result in 24 student credit hours divided by the 12 hours per semester criterion. The number of full-time-equivalent students sitting in that class in that semester is two. The revenue associated with the course would be the governmental appropriation per FTE student for the semester multiplied by two plus the tuition per credit hour multiplied by 24.

Another way of handling this situation is to divide the annual appropriation per FTE student by the annual criterion for FTE designation. The resulting amount is the appropriation per student credit hour. This value, when added to the tuition rate and then multiplied by the number of hours in the course in question, provides the revenue per student enrolled. The revenue per student enrolled is recommended here because this is the manner in which costs have been defined to this point. Enrollment then becomes a common denominator, allowing the costs and revenues to be analyzed simultaneously.

It should be emphasized that revenue per student enrolled will vary in most institutions depending on whether the students are resident, nonresident, graduate, upper division, lower division, and so on. The recommendation here is to calculate the revenue per student enrolled under the optimum revenue mix, the most adverse revenue mix, and the actual revenue mix through time. These values can then be illustrated as shown in Exhibit 2.

In some junior colleges, additional governmental aid is often received when certain vocational or technical programs are offered. If this aid can be expressed on (or converted to) a per course basis this amount would be added as a fixed revenue amount in Exhibit 2. The sloped revenue lines would then intersect the vertical axis rather than the origin.

BREAK-EVEN POINTS

With the revenue data superimposed over the cost information, the break-even points under a number of circumstances can be determined. The points A, B, and C represent break-even points under different revenue conditions and provide the basis for review and control of operations. The level of enrollment

68509

which is associated with the most realistic revenue situation is the key at this point. Classes with consistent historical enrollments below the break-even level can easily be "red flagged" for appropriate action, whether it be reductions in sections offered or elimination from the curriculum. However, it is advisable to allow courses or programs to continue for a short time (possibly more than one contract period) even though enrollments are not sufficient to reach the break-even point, provided variable costs are being covered by current enrollment levels. If variable costs are not being covered, immediate corrective action will be required.

Classes with consistent historical enrollments above the break-even point can be readily identified also. The net revenues generated by such classes are measured by the vertical difference between the appropriate revenue curve and the cost level. A trend of growing enrollments beyond the break-even point would probably justify plans for the allocation of additional resources. The reallocation of resources need not result in increases in total expenditures but may necessitate intra-and/or interdisciplinary transfers of resources from low-demand nonessential courses or programs to growth areas of the institution.

CONCLUSION

The adaptation of break-even analysis for use by college and university administrators, while not a cure-all, can be a valuable management tool in coping with the buyer's market that now exists in higher education.

The Management of Congress

Richard Bolling

It is time that active legislators and experienced persons knowledgeable in public administration pool their observations and talents to produce better management for the legislative branches of our national and state governments. Legislators have tolerated chaos, and public administrators have apparently ignored the unique and perplexing management problems in the legislative branches.

In the 93rd Congress, I chaired the Select Committee on Committees of the House of Representatives; our task was to make recommendations to the House on how best we could reform ourselves in order to do a better job. Our bipartisan Committee—five Democrats and five Republicans—unanimously reported a reform proposal more than a year ago, but the history of the disposition of the controversial recommendations in that proposal is not yet complete. At the moment some are already part of the working machinery of the House—the preorganization of the 94th Congress before Christmas 1974 is an example. Other parts have been rejected for the time being—such as single committee ju-

Reprinted with permission of the author and publisher from the September/October 1975 issue of *Public Administration Review*, bimonthly journal of the American Society for Public Administration.

risdiction for certain critically important subjects like energy. From my experience as chairman of this Select Committee and my 26 years service in the Congress, I would like to address this article to problems dealing with three important aspects of national legislative management (the first two of which the Select Committee did not consider at great length):

◇ The logistical support of basic services, buildings, and equipment needed to make the legislative branch function.
◇ An information and analysis system which supplies basic facts about issues with which the legislature must deal.
◇ A system to make possible coherent policy formulation by legislators given proper logistical support and adequate information.

LOGISTICS SUPPORT

The United States legislative branch has an infrastructure of thousands of people who maintain its buildings and grounds; who provide police and security protection; who supply telephones, telegraph lines, and equipment; who operate duplicating, assembly, wrapping, and mailing services; who handle payrolls and accounting and purchasing; who run one of the greatest printing plants in the world; who manage botanical gardens; who provide parking and vehicle management; who protect health and operate eating facilities. Much of this complex operation is accepted without a great deal of thought as to its requirements for systematic planning and management. Several separate institutions provide these many services, with only limited coordination provided at the time of annual appropriations.

As one reviews this large array of services, he or she is aware that many are performed well, some can be lavish, some are haphazard, and few are consistently exposed to any rigorous cost-effectiveness test. In general these services are provided with a promptness and quality comparable to services available to the White House, cabinet members, and the judiciary. When members of Congress want something, they are in a position to attract the undivided attention of those who work directly for their branch, since they control the funding that provides these services. Most of these services are necessary to the efficient functioning of the members, and I would submit that their availability on a par with the other two branches of government is entirely appropriate.

But despite all the money spent and all the expedited services this money buys, one can still develop an impressive list of basic shortcomings and inadequacies. For example, traditionally, there has been no long-range, coordinated planning of work load and of staff size linked to land acquisition and building construction.

Members' individual office staffs are as unique as the members themselves. The philosophy has been much the same as the philosophy governing election of the member—as long as the person and his or her work is acceptable, uniform standards among individual members' offices of hours worked, leave time, qualifications, and so on are not required. Each member is given a staff allowance to use very much as he pleases within certain parameters prescribed by law and regulations. Detailing the parameters is not important to this discussion, but what is important is to point out that they do allow a great deal of latitude for each member, much like those of a small business. The system is not "neat." Staff members have even less guaranteed tenure than the members themselves, and both the employees and the system can and have been abused. But to propose a uniform civil service type system as a more effective way to assist a member to fulfill his responsibilities would be an unthinking oversimplification of the nature of legislative staff work. This latitude, however, does not have to preclude some coordinated planning for adequate space to house increases in the number of staff personnel required to keep up with increasing work loads.

A day's inspection of House members' offices and locations of support activities may demonstrate bizarre allocations of space in the three House office buildings and ingenious solutions developed to cram people into space that mock all research and experience about efficient working environments. Administration of the logistics support for the legislative branch not only lacks sufficient orderly central planning, but it also has a special element of capriciousness. Parts of the system are given broad supervision by committees whose chairmen can exploit their control of the systems they oversee for their own in-house political advantage, rather than to serve the interests of efficiency or equality of treatment to all legitimate users.

It is not easy to construct a management system that is both responsive to the users and fair. For example, if elaborately detailed rules are written to govern all supporting services, the bureaucracy created in most instances tends to become remote from the need of the users. Procedures become complex and all responses slow down in the flood of paper work and authorizations required. But a system that shortcuts these problems has a way of playing favorites. And any system of support that meets everybody's needs immediately and completely has a cost that is impractically high.

Throughout much of government, those serving the public or carrying out some assigned public mission find themselves having to shape their activities and timetables to the convenience of those who provide them with logistics services, rather than the logical reverse of this. Congress probably has escaped this problem better than most. But it does pay the price in return that many services are provided promptly and abundantly to those in favor with the committee overseers, and such services are often inadequate to those in disfavor. Services are not consistently tied to any concept of overall congressional need in the business of legislation and of oversight.

These are some of the problems which must be addressed in developing superior management of logistical services for the legislative branch.

INFORMATION AND ANALYSIS SYSTEM

There is little uniformity in the way the 535 members of the House and Senate do their work, although the basic functions are fairly universal. Most members are conscientious and are concerned about the several missions they undertake—to legislate, to serve constituents, to oversee the results of past legislation, and to get re-elected. To function well, they must have information. Some go about this very objectively and in an organized, intellectual way. Others have informal ways of sensing, for example, how constituents and other members feel. We really do not know enough about the total population of members to be able to say how they receive, select, and process the information on which they base their actions and decisions.

Information will always be partial, often imprecise and difficult to interpret. But within the limits of reality, information should be accurate, complete, timely, digested, either bias-free or clearly identifiable as to its slant, relevant to the requestor's needs, and either coordinated with other information or relatable to it. A great deal of what Congress receives falls far short of the ideal.

Congress is flooded with more information than it can absorb. The daily mail delivers more reports, letters, studies, analyses than any staff, let alone the member himself, can absorb. The sheer volume makes much of the information unuseable. It is too bulky to store and it is not indexed for retrieval. There are usually no facilities to test its validity. The growth of the business of government has required the establishment of staffs in member offices, with committees, and in such other legislative branch organizations as the Congressional Research Service, the General Accounting Office, the Office of Technology Assessment, the Congressional Budget Office, the House Information Systems Office, the Offices of Legislative Counsel, and others. There is considerable expense in bringing about this growth, and heavy use is made of these services. But can we answer whether they are used effectively or that these services have ever been designed realistically?

An example in point is the Congressional Research Service. Despite its rapid growth in recent years, it is still swamped with work ranging from answering members' constituent requests to in-depth analysis of national issues. Rational decisions need to be made about the best use of CRS capabilities, and some meaningful priorities should be established; otherwise it will simply continue to grow as appropriation and space considerations of the moment allow.

The same kinds of questions can be posed about the much larger General Accounting Office. GAO products are often thorough, but are limited by the way the original questions are framed and by the long time from when the question is asked to when the reply is finally reviewed and printed products are made available. The Office of Technology Assessment has yet to prove itself. A few warning signs suggest it is being asked to support conclusions already reached by powerful requestors and, if this is true, its credibility as a source of objective advice will be destroyed.

The questions and comments mentioned here merely open the door to a host of issues surrounding the administration of an effective information and analysis system for the Congress. Until we increase our understanding of how the whole population of legislators gathers information, assimilates it, and judges it, we cannot design a better system which they would use, and which would serve them better. For example, if computer terminals were placed in every office, at high expense, would most offices use the terminals to tap into databanks elsewhere, and if they did, would they understand and use wisely the information made available to them?

Today we have a system of information that just grew from a variety of legislative actions, which show the effects of lacking any rational, coordinated planning. Perhaps some order could be brought to the present chaos. But immediately the crucial question would be, what kind of central control? There are dangers that such control could be biased, self-serving, parochial in outlook, and/or unimaginative. It could put a stranglehold on the independence of other members if it were run by some powerful committee chairman. With information and its processing so essential to the Congress, planning its operation and control is one of the most challenging and difficult problems faced by Congress, although it may lack the public appeal and political benefits of some current substantive issues.

The lines between information collection, summarization, analysis, and application are blurred, and the activities are a continuum. At one end the activity is perhaps fairly neutral and nonpolitical, whether clerical or professional. At some point as one moves to application there are judgments introduced which properly must be conditioned by ideology and political objective. Ultimately this becomes the task of the legislator himself. But can he receive staff and institutional support in phases of this process without losing vital control, and without being screened away from insights important to him? Can a staff member in a supposedly neutral support role give the legislator strong views growing out of his "expertise" without becoming a special pleader, or destroying the neutrality of his support institution? All of these are issues deserving of close and continuing consideration.

I cannot emphasize too strongly the need for better information and the absolute requirement that the member—not the staff—ultimately receive this information in a way that enables him or her to make rational decisions. The democratic process demands nothing less.

COHERENT POLICY FORMULATION AND EXECUTION

Let us assume that the legislative branch puts its house in order, equips itself adequately with the logistics support it needs, and has an effective information and analysis service. This will still be for naught if the members do not pull together to debate and construct rational, interactive, and consistent legislative programs. Congress, like the rest of the American government structure, operates with a system of checks and balances, designed to insure that issues are thought through before action is taken. The adversary process is supposed to apply in hearings, in markups, and in floor debate. At times the processes seem very cumbersome while they are protecting us from haste. When we look at problems from several points of view, we also often end up with fragmented and contradictory results. Note the inconsistencies of what we do in energy, taxes, transportation, health, foreign policy, military policy, the environment, and so on. A simple example: we legislate tobacco crop supports one place, and support antismoking measures somewhere else.

When policy is made on an entirely centralized basis it becomes dictatorship. We already have rivalry, and often antagonism, between the legislative and executive branches of government, and the checks and balances within the process, while delaying prompt action, provide some protections. If Congress were more like the executive branch would we like the results more? Our two major national parties are disparate collections of ideologies and regional or economic interests. Yet the Congress operates on the basis of a majority and minority party which, of course, often leads to strange coalitions on specific issues before the Congress. Some people have suggested that instead of Democrats and Republicans there should be a trading of party memberships until we end up with a Liberal and a Conservative Party. This is a recommendation that misreads the nature of American politics. Most people think of themselves as centrists and do not want to see the country polarized by ideology or economic group. We have learned many methods in the Congress for arriving at workable accommodations and compromises.

All of this is appropriate to thinking about policy formulation and execution in the Congress. It brings us back to the advantages and the costs of each of the conditions we have seen in the past when a speaker, or the caucus, or the committee chairmen were the dominant source of power in the Congress.

My own leanings have been toward stronger leadership in the House, but a leadership responsive to the party caucuses, both leading the caucuses and being influenced by them. I view this as a better compromise for achieving coherent policy formulation than struggling along on only a few cylinders—as often happens when individual chairmen become almost untouchable because of seniority. Sometimes these chairmen are very good. However, they are sometimes owned by special interests or are senile and there is no coordination of their policies except as the rules require a few hours of debate on the floor after months or even years of desultory or slanted considerations of issues back in the committees or subcommittees.

I have discussed the issues of legislative administration in rather general terms and without detailed reference to the recent endeavors of the House Select Committee on Committees. Our bipartisan committee came up with a report which dealt with a number of problems of jurisdictional substance and of organization and parliamentary procedure in a reasonably synoptic fashion. Not every provision pleased every one of the ten members of the committee and, through the caucus, another proposal was substituted for the reported version of the resolution. This so-called Hansen Committee version was further modified in a floor debate that occupied part of the time of the House for two weeks before it was adopted. The end product was less comprehensive and balanced than the committee version, but it did begin some processes of change. It is too early to judge how pleased we shall be with these reforms. The history of past reforms is that they create new excesses and imbalances which in turn need correction. Reform is a never-ending process, not only to adjust and fine tune revised rules, but to meet changed conditions in the society at large.

We have before us a field of great importance to study and understand. I am convinced that we can significantly improve the systems needed to support the functioning of the American legislature. It is important that these systems be improved because the legislative process must effectively deal with increasingly complex problems.

Model
for Participation

Howard L. Sampson

A major problem confronting administrators in schools is presenting change in a manner that can be understood and accepted by those affected. The Administrative Services Division was concerned with ascertaining if systems management theory is a viable concept to use in gaining acceptance of change in the Madison, Wisconsin Public Schools. It was anticipated that a systems management model would assist administrators to overcome feelings of insecurity and threats by becoming involved in planning and decision making of systems projects.

Every system has a boundary that encompasses its parts and through which input–output exchanges are made with adjacent systems. These are adaptive exchanges through which the various systems mobilize resources and energies to its various parts and integrate these parts into a working whole.[1]

The systems concept must include the human aspect. People determine the systems goals and objectives; in addition the necessary steps needed to implement solutions are taken by the people. Although people organize themselves

Reprinted with permission from the *Journal of Systems Management*, Jan. 1974, pp. 30–34.

into groups, they are interdependent beings requiring responsibility, cooperative action, and competition. Competition is cooperation against, and is common when satisfiers are scarce. Complementary cooperation exists when all parties share in both rights and responsibilities to produce an optimum satisfactory relationship.[2]

A conscientious effort to install proposed changes will smooth eventual acceptance, regardless of the amount of actual participation. Efforts to gain acceptance should begin early in the planning phase and continue indefinitely. If acceptance can be gained early in the planning stage, the emotional commitment of administrators will be channeled in the implementation of changes resulting in pride of ownership.[3]

Madison Public Schools' top management personnel realize long-range planning is an important factor in determining the future position of the school district.

Long-range planning, though, has not always been a factor in acquiring the services of the Systems and Computer Services Departments. Many administrators have viewed these services as a necessary evil and have failed to realize their potential benefits. The design, development, and ultimate implementation of the systems management model which began in 1970 and continues at the present time was accomplished to inform administrators about the available services.

THE SYSTEMS MANAGEMENT MODEL

The nucleus of the systems management model is the Management Information Systems Coordinating Committee. All Directors are included on the committee with the manager of Systems Services serving as chairman. The committee meets on a monthly basis at the request of the Systems Services Department to accomplish the following objectives:

◊ Establish a communication medium to share effective procedures from individual schools throughout the Madison Public Schools.
◊ Provide a legitimate vehicle for planning, implementing, and evaluating new systems.
◊ Provide a better means of understanding mutual practices and procedures throughout the Madison Public Schools.
◊ Act as a decision-making group for the establishment of systems project priorities and policy formulation.

Most recommendations to the Management Information Systems Coordinating Committee are submitted by three working subcommittees. The subcommittees are: (1) Elementary School Data Processing Committee, (2) Middle School Data Processing Committee, and (3) High School Data Processing

Committee. Each subcommittee investigates and makes recommendations to improve its respective instructional levels. A subcommittee consists of four members with respective chairmen serving on the Management Information Systems Coordinating Committee to ensure representation when policy and decisions are enacted.

Special task forces are created by the Management Information Systems Coordinating Committee, including appropriate professional staff, to research and develop recommendations for resolving problems or improving given situations, or both. The functions of the special task forces are similar to the subcommittee functions; however, the task forces are eliminated after completing their delegated tasks.

Few organizations have been or are now involved in future systems planning. A lack of systems and procedures function knowledge and interest by top management tends to develop systems by the "bottom-to-top" method. This method of developing systems requires that the lowest manager determine systems needs and requirements and then force the needs up the organizational ladder for additional requirements. The result is the development of a majority of systems with narrow scope and little chance of being integrated into larger systems.

Two requirements were necessary for the systems management model to become functional. First, administrators must be committed to a logical systematic approach for considering management systems, theories, and ideas. Second, administrators must make a concerted effort to plan, analyze, design, implement, and evaluate systems projects deemed appropriate for the Madison Public Schools.

The systems management model, shown in Figure 1. is a principle and not a cure-all. Management must make the model part of their philosophy to be successful in implementing and stabilizing this type of management. Considerable patience and a change in thinking is required from all participants. An ability to develop an opinion regarding proper systems development and planning must be learned by participation. The following three elements are needed to change long-held attitudes and build an effective participation environment: (1) time, (2) education, and (3) continuous follow-up. It was felt that the systems management model would provide an opportunity for administrators to grow, develop, and contribute their talents.

THE MANAGEMENT STUDY

Subsequently, a study was undertaken to ascertain whether or not systems management was a viable concept to use in gaining acceptance of change within the Madison Public Schools.

Figure 1. A model for applying systems management theory to the
administration of change within Madison public schools.

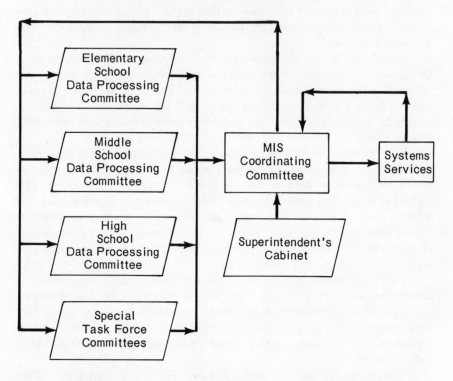

The independent variable of this study was the extent to which participating administrators involved in selected systems projects have participated. It
was necessary to know to what extent this variable was related to the success of
systems projects undertaken utilizing the systems management model. A participation scale was developed to determine how participating administrators involved in systems projects would react. This scale provided a measure of their
perceived participation. The results of the participation scale were compared
with the selected dependent variable of this study in order to determine if a
relationship existed and to what degree.

The dependent variable of this study was defined as the perceived effectiveness of the MIS Coordinating Committee, as viewed by participants of systems projects undertaken utilizing the systems management model. Effectiveness was selected as the dependent variable for two reasons. First, it has
been a classic problem in the study of organization. Second, effectiveness,
partly because it is a classic problem, has been highly researched. The determi-
nates for perceived effectiveness were predicted to be confirmed from the following two constructs: (1) planning, and (2) decision-making. These constructs

were expected to emerge from the clustering of data obtained from the survey of participants of four systems projects undertaken utilizing the systems management model.

DESCRIPTION OF THE STUDY INSTRUMENTS

As noted previously, the perceived effectiveness of the MIS Coordinating Committee was theorized to be dependent upon the interrelated effects of participating administrators involved in systems projects. Further, the determinants of the perceived effectiveness postulated in the study were planning and decision-making.

As there were no instruments available which would adequately gather the required data to investigate the problem defined within this study, two instruments were constructed. The first instrument included belief statements which reflected the ideal role of the MIS Coordinating Committee.

Belief statements were written that would relate to each construct for the ideal and real roles of the MIS Coordinating Committee. Although the ideal belief statements were standard on each instrument, the real statements were developed relevant to each of the four systems projects and the MIS Coordinating Committee. To identify belief statements, the author drew on both his experience as a director of administrative services and his discussions with business associates and members of the faculty in Educational Administration at the University of Wisconsin.

On both instruments, the statements were scaled with a Likert Scale, modified to provide four responses instead of five. The four responses were: "Definitely Agree," "Probably Agree," "Probably Disagree," and "Definitely Disagree." "Probably Agree" and "Probably Disagree" were defined for respondents to mean "you agree more than you disagree," and conversely. The elimination of the "Uncertain" or "Don't Know" category, usually part of a Likert Scale, was thought necessary to prevent respondents from avoiding statements perceived as socially sensitive. Support for this decision was provided by Nunnally [4] and Lang.[5] They found that the neutral category influences response styles, since there was evidence that some respondents tend to use that category more than others.

SYSTEMS PROJECTS

Selected systems projects for this study included the Elementary School Attendance System, the Middle School Class Scheduling System, the High School

Annual Questionnaire System, and the Budgetary Accounting System. With the exception of the Budgetary Accounting System, which was developed through a special task force, the systems projects were developed through each of the Elementary, Middle, and High School Data Processing Committees. Finally, all the systems projects selected for the study were developed in agreement with the MIS Coordinating Committee.

The total population surveyed in this study was 53. The Elementary School Attendance System had seven elementary principals as participants: The Middle School Class Scheduling System had ten middle school principals as participants; the High School Annual Questionnaire System had four high school principals and 16 assistant principals as participants; and the Budgetary Accounting System had two assistant directors and three accountants as participants. In addition, the 11 members of the MIS Coordinating Committee were surveyed, completing the population selected for this study.

COLLECTION OF THE DATA

Both the pilot instrument and the target instrument were distributed to administrators at scheduled meetings. At each meeting the administrators completed an instrument and returned it to this investigator. The data collection was composed of two phases. In the first phase, the instrument concerning the ideal role of the MIS Coordinating Committee and personal data were presented. The second phase consisted of presenting the questionnaire concerning the real role of the MIS Coordinating Committee and the participation scale.

One hundred percent of the respondents returned the pilot instruments at a series of meetings held over a two-week period. A follow-up was not administered, since the investigator felt that this would be a satisfactory response with which to examine the structure of the questionnaires. In the target study, 52 of 53 administrators in the population returned the questionnaires at a series of meetings held over a four-week period. The return not obtained was an administrator who had ceased to be employed by the school system between the time the systems projects defined in this study were completed (1971–72 school year) and the time the target instruments were administered (October 1972).

To answer the general and ancillary hypotheses posed in the study, a correlational analysis was conducted in order to determine the relationship between the ideal and real item subscores. PROGRAM STATJOB DSTAT2, [6] a descriptive statistics computer program prepared by the Academic Computing Center, The University of Wisconsin—Madison, examined the strength of the correlation between the two variables in each of the hypotheses. The degree of relationship, the extent to which two sets of measures vary in unison, was commonly expressed by means of the correlation coefficient.

A perceived effectiveness score was determined to be the difference between the ideal and real item subscores for each construct. The measurement of the resulting effectiveness scores was considered proportionally more significant as the amount of the difference between ideal and real item subscores for each construct declined. Also, these scores were correlated with the results of the participation scale. The purpose of this analysis was to determine if a relationship existed and to what degree.

FINDINGS AND CONCLUSIONS

The major conclusion drawn from this study is that the systems management model was perceived as an effective means for bringing about change by those involved. However, there is evidence that the respondents were somewhat less likely to feel that the ideal role of the MIS Coordinating Committee was being implemented as ideally as perceived. Further, there is evidence that variability in the perception of effectiveness among respondents was attributed to the independent variable of participation. The implication of this finding is that if administrators place a greater emphasis on participating in the design, development, and evaluation of systems projects, the perceived effectiveness of the systems management model will be improved. These findings would seem to be concurrent with findings and speculations cited earlier.

Thus, it might be speculated that the systems management model provided a basis for dialogue wherein individuals could explore each other's needs and through a process of compromise establish cooperative alliances in meeting individual, group, and organizational goals. It might be speculated, too, that the systems management model provided a basis for congruence between the informal and formal organization acknowledging the awareness of political thinking in making decisions regarding change. If such a climate exists, it can be suggested that the establishment of project groups resulted with the creation of synergistic relationships which produced total effects greater than the sums of their effects had they been taken independently.

Also there is evidence that the goals and objectives of the MIS Coordinating Committee and the other project groups were somewhat in congruence. Furthermore, there appears to be a significant relationship between the perceived effectiveness of the MIS Coordinating Committee among project groups and the independent variable of participation. By implication, this suggested that the measure of participation appeared more positive when the formal organization was decentralized and there was a sharing of authority in planning and decision-making. Thus, it might be speculated that increased participation influenced the effectiveness of the systems management model. Conversely, a lack of participation might be speculated to have resulted with disagreement and fragmentation among individuals.

Other findings suggested that the MIS Coordinating Committee had a better perception of themselves regarding perceived effectiveness than did the other project groups. By implication this suggested that a sense of integration of functions and activities had been established within the organization. Thus, it might be speculated that a climate was established for a team management approach for undertaking change in a more effective and efficient manner. Subsequently, it might be speculated, too, that the group approach to change provided a basis for consensus and thus, a means for decreasing conflict among individuals through negotiation.

SUMMARY

The intent of this study has been twofold: (1) to determine the perceived effectiveness of the systems management approach to change, and (2) to determine whether there is a relationship between the perceived effectiveness of the systems management approach to change and the degree of involvement by participants. While findings provided evidence that the systems management model reflected positive results, the magnitude of the problem will not become apparent, however, until considerably more research has been devoted to documenting the concept theoretically and empirically. In conclusion, it is hoped that this study has made an early contribution to that documentation and will have made a far more important contribution if it serves as a catalyst for additional research.

REFERENCES

1. Lloyd L. Byars, "A Philosophy of Systems Management," *Journal of Systems Management,* July 1971, pp. 38–41.
2. D. M. Hall, *Management of Human Systems,* pp. 4–8 (Cleveland, Ohio: Association for Systems Management, 1971).
3. Warren G. Bennis, Kenneth D. Benne, and Robert Chin, *The Planning of Change,* pp. 193–194 (New York: Holt, Rinehart and Winston, 1961).

4. Jim C. Nunnally, *Psychometric Theory*, pp. 521–522 (New York: McGraw-Hill, 1967).
5. Gerhard Lang, "Motives in Selecting Elementary and Secondary School Teaching," *Journal of Experimental Education*, Sept. 1960, pp. 101–104.
6. PROGRAM STATJOB: DSTAT2 (Madison, Wisconsin: University of Wisconsin—Madison, Academic Computing Center, 1972).

Systems Planning
Tomorrow's Hospitals Today

William G. Akula
Jay A. Vora

With the basic goals of hospitals in process of change are hospitals ready and prepared to "control their own destiny"? A systems planning approach is developed to facilitate coping with the continuing changes in the socioeconomic and technological environment relevant to health care.

The nature and direction of the hospitals' goals are dependent upon the impact from the technological developments, from the social changes in values and attitudes toward medical care, and from the shifting allocations of economic resources.

Crichton's book [1] describes some recent technical advances performed at the Massachusetts General Hospital for five specific patients. For example, there is one individual "whose nearly severed hand is re-attached by a team of surgeons in a six-hour operation. . . ."

Within the next 30 years, some developments with possible consequences for hospitals were forecasted by Helmer et al. [2]

> Demonstration of non-surgical techniques by which the sex of babies may be chosen with 90 percent certainty . . . might result in: Creation of legislation and

Reprinted with permission from *Managerial Planning*, January/February 1972.

incentive designed to guarantee a socially desirable ratio of males to females. . . . Decrease in family size, since parents will no longer have to 'keep trying for a boy'! Simulation of placenta, making extrauterine development possible . . . might result in: Changes in family structure, particularly in women's attitudes toward mothering. Pregnancy becoming virtually nonexistent.

From Representative Griffiths' pending bill for a comprehensive National Health Insurance there is a demand for "health care for *all* Americans." According to Rep. Griffiths [3]:

The cost of a major illness is such that 9 out of 10 Americans are medically indigent right now—unable to pay the high cost of care without severe economic sacrifice . . . an estimate that puts the cost of a single coronary, within the next three years, at $16,000. This, in itself, is a heart stopper.

Consumer price index for medical care in this country has ascended from 73.4 in 1950 to 145.0 in 1968, a rise of 97.5 percent. The overall price index, for the same period, increased from 83.8 to 121.2, a rise of 43 percent. The cost of health as a percentage of total consumption in this country has shifted from 4.6 percent in 1950 to 6.9 percent in 1967. In dollar terms the cost of medical care has increased from 8.8 billion in 1950 to 34.0 billion in 1967.[4]

The goals of hospitals included, in the past, providing "care for the sick"—yet, what about those who cannot afford to go to hospitals or who do not know they need health care? Are the goals to be redefined to provide care to every citizen at any location for any kind of disease or injury? Are the goals going to include preventative as well as curative measures? Are the goals going to include the environmental conditions and health education requirements of a community as a respondent or as an initiator?

Hospital policy-makers concerned with such goal-oriented questions can be assisted by systems planning in order to:

◇ Cope with ambiguity and uncertainty resulting from the accelerated change rate of internal and external innovations.
◇ Provide time priorities with which to transform the pending changes and demands on hospitals into opportunities.
◇ Focus on preventative as well as curative aspects of health care.
◇ Relate explicitly the socioeconomic and technical changes over time to the reformulation of alternate goals and to the devising of means for achieving them.
◇ Establish specific sequence of actions that should be taken over the intervening years to achieve a subset of goals for each period.
◇ Allocate resources—physical, human, and monetary—to gain adaptability against rising costs and natural resources waste due to advances in technology, in organizational concepts, and in economic developments.

WHAT IS SYSTEMS PLANNING?

A systems planning concept identifies various components of a set, explicitly analyzes the relationships among those components, facilitates synthesizing them into a coherent whole in order to formulate periodic goals which integrate into long-range goals, and establishes a sequence of actions for achieving these goals in a highly dynamic environment. This environment encompasses exponential growth in technological advances as well as legal, political, and socioeconomic developments.

The three dimensions of this systems planning model consist of (1) planning time interval, (2) levels of planning, and (3) variables related to planning. The time dimension is measured in years, The length of the planning interval must be determined by (1) the time it takes to prepare for the decision, plus (2) the time it takes to implement it in light of (3) the time when implementation must be completed.[5] For this presentation, one to two years represents "short-range" planning, three to four years is "medium-range," and five years or more is considered as "long-range."

The ascending levels of planning follow prevailing stratification along the lines of departmental unit; divisional unit; individual institution; groups of institutions (regional and statewide); and national representation. The international planning level could be incorporated into an extended version of the systems planning model. The omission of the international level from the expository model does not underestimate the meaningful contributions from world health organizations.[6]

The variables considered relevant to planning are (1) goal specifications, (2) physical facilities, (3) human organizations, and (4) monetary. The goals are dynamic—that is, they are changeable or vary for different time periods and for different levels of planning. Furthermore, the four planning variables considered are not exhaustive, as other relevant variables may be added to this system.

CONCEPTUAL FRAMEWORK OF SYSTEMS PLANNING

The relationships among the various components of this system and their synthesis are facilitated by explicitly identifying relevant components of the systems planning set in a conceptual framework, as shown in Figure 1. Also, the interdependencies among those components are graphically portrayed in Figure 1 by three intersecting flow-patterned ellipses.

Each cube of the model represents a nucleus of the planning set. This model displays 120 planning nuclei: *six* planning time intervals times *five* levels

Figure 1. Conceptual framework of systems planning.

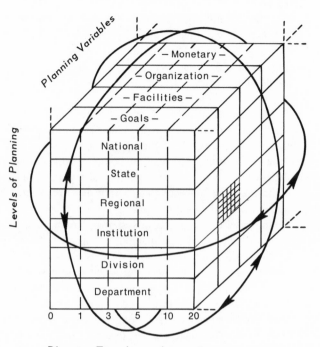

Planning Time Interval (years)

of planning times *four* variables. The shaded cube of Figure 1 represents one specific nucleus—for example, the long-range (10–20 years) facilities planning of one hospital. For this single set shaded nucleus, the number of possible relationships with other nuclei of the planning set that could influence its systems planning can reach the magnitude of thousands and beyond. A recent study that deals with a long-range facility planning system for ancillary departments in hospitals indicates the feasibility of computing and summarizing the significant relationships.[7]

HOW SYSTEMS PLANNING DIFFERS FROM OTHER PLANNING CONCEPTS

Systems planning resembles some features of current planning concepts and techniques—for example, Gantt charting, PERT (Program Evaluation and Review Technique), long-range planning, and so forth—but differs substantially in the way goal specifications, planning variables, and time dimensions are dynamically integrated.

Gantt charting for several decades has been used in industry for devising current timetables (schedules) that graphically project, track, and highlight given milestones (subgoals) for a "here and now" time reference point.[8] The schedule resulting from this relatively rigid and precise planning usually covers time intervals of less than one year and the goals are generally irrevocably fixed. Systems planning is *not* scheduling.

PERT, and allied concepts such as Critical Path Method, represent refinement, sophistication, and an extension of the Gantt planning concept.[9] The refinement, in the main, is the result of the application of network theory, the sophistication is the result of the statistical method of estimating the duration of the time interval between the start and completion of a planned milestone, and the extension of the planning time coverage is not day-to-day but short-range and medium-range (meaning beyond one year). The PERT planning, however, is based on achieving *fixed* or *given* goals. Systems planning is *not* PERT.

"In its broadest sense, long-range planning is an attempt by an organization to establish rational direction and control over its own destiny."[10] An organization is engaged in long-range planning when it selects and defines its goals and objectives and determines the means required for achieving these objectives within a stated period of time; five years ahead is usually regarded as the minimum time period to qualify as "long-range" planning. Long-range planning does not formalize or make explicit the short-range or medium-range planning of goals. In time perspective, long-range planning tends to be one-dimensional—dealing exclusively with the goals of five years and beyond. Furthermore, it does not require relating and planning for each and every relevant planning variable as is the case with systems planning. Systems planning is *not* long-range planning.

In summary, systems planning is not really "new"—in some of its analytical aspects, it does resemble current planning techniques. However, in its synthesis (integration or coordination) of short-range, medium-range, and long-range goal formulation or organizational units, systems planning represents a different, difficult, and dynamic concept. Systems planning requires making explicit the environmental constraints with which to relate and plan for *all* the relevant planning variables rather than concentrating on only one of these variables.

We believe this conceptual framework of systems planning, when empirically tested, will yield evidence to support it as a necessary and worthwhile effort with which to "control one's own destiny" within mutually acceptable goals from different organizational levels and with changing perceptions of tomorrow's and today's hospitals.

REFERENCES

1. M. Crichton, *Five Patients* (New York: Knopf, 1970).
2. O. Helmer, T. J. Gordon, S. Enger, P. de Brigard, and R. Rochbert, "Development of Long Range Methods for Connecticut: A Summary" (The Institute for the Future, Menlo Park, California).
3. M. W. Griffiths (Rep.-Mich.), "Health Care for All Americans," *The American Federationist*, April 1970, pp. 20–24.
4. *Statistical Abstract of the United States, 1969* (Washington, D.C.: United States Government Printing Office, 1969), pp. 314–345.
5. F. K. Warren, *Long Range Planning* (Englewood Cliffs, N.J.: Prentice-Hall, 1966).
6. R. R. Puffer and G. W. Griffith, *Patterns of Urban Mortality*, World Health Organization, Pan American Health Organization, Scientific Publication No. 151, Sept. 1967.
7. J. A. Vora, Long Range Facility Planning System for Ancillary Developments in Hospitals, Ph.D. Thesis, New York: Rensselaer Polytechnic Institute, Oct. 1969.
8. H. Koontz and G. O'Donnell, *Principles of Management*, pp. 681–686 (New York: McGraw-Hill Book Co., 1968).
9. G. N. Stilian, *PERT: A New Management Planning and Control Technique*, pp. 147–148 (New York: American Management Association, 1962).
10. A. E. Emech, "Long Range Planning for Colleges and Universities," Unpublished report prepared for Rensselaer Polytechnic Institute, May 1969.

Strategic Planning in State Government

Michael J. Howlett

During the early months after I had assumed the position of Secretary of State of Illinois, I began to question the very manageability of the office. The office had more than 4,000 employees, and we were engaged in providing as diverse a range of services as exists in any single governmental unit. For example, I serve as the State Librarian as well as the State Archivist; the office distributes annually some seven million vehicle licenses, titles about three million vehicles a year, and issues more than two million drivers' licenses a year; and is installing the biggest nonmilitary computer system ever equipped by the second largest computer manufacturer.

The fact there had been little or no formal planning before was, at one and the same time, a matter for concern and evidence of an opportunity. Just why hadn't the office been subjected to formal planning? Was not the strategic planning of the business world applicable here?

We decided that it would be worth the risks to find out. For one thing, if the office were to be managed in a more effective manner, something other than the customary ways of operating was necessary. For another, the payoffs

Reprinted with permission from *Managerial Planning*, November/December 1975.

could be considerable. If successful, we would not only be able to manage better the wide-ranging activities of the office, but we would also be better prepared to respond to new citizen needs as well as the changing politics in Illinois and the increased regimen which has followed the advent in 1967 of annual sessions of the Legislature.

We would also go a long way toward realizing my campaign promise to do more to serve the public at a lower cost of operation as well as toward bringing about a human commitment within the work force which could assure the continuing receptivity to change that I desired. In short, our endeavor to employ strategic planning techniques in the Office of the Secretary of State was undertaken to realize a higher level of cost-benefit results and to do so in terms of both facilitating the personal growth of the key employees of the office and becoming more responsive to the will of the citizens through their elected legislators.

Though some substantial changes in the operations had recently been consciously instituted, most of the wide-ranging activities of the office had emerged simply in reaction to external influences. Moreover, we recognized that there were significant differences between a public agency and a business organization. For these and other reasons, we decided to design our own planning system, selecting the components and giving form to them in a gradual manner.

We would not create overnight a total planning system. We would develop the system over a period of time, discovering gaps, testing its acceptance with operating administrators—proceeding over a two-year period to firm up and expand the system, trying always to remain fully sensitive to the developing capability of the administrators who had to play the critical role in the planning. We could and would take advantage of the experience of others, but the design of our planning system would be fixed on the basis of the present and potential capability of the people who had to make it work.

THE BEGINNINGS

The first step was the employment of a professional planning specialist. With his help, the senior administrators proceeded to define the beginnings of the system. We agreed that a number of results from our early efforts would be critical, if the planning was to have any long-term viability. These included the following:

1. The definition of organizational missions or purposes on the basis of legislative intent and the policies of the office.

2. In accordance with these missions, the development of key organizational objectives for each major area of operating responsibility.

3. Involvement of all key managers in the determination of these objectives, striving for objectives that not only offer a sense of challenge to the operating units but are also relevant to the office's overall aims.

4. Participation in the planning process by operating employees to the fullest degree to which they are or can be helped to become meaningfully involved.

5. Officewide coordination of the planning so as to assure a reasonable determination of overall priorities insofar as any recommendations had to be made to the Legislature and existing resources allocated for the entire office.

6. Results readily assessed by those within the office as well as by outside agencies engaged in performance evaluation.

EARLY PLANNING CONSIDERATIONS

I wanted only a small central staff of "professional planners." Their role would be to facilitate widespread participation on a continuing basis as well as to provide the means for bringing together all the subordinate planning in a meaningful as well as more easily managed manner. They were to be guided by a number of considerations. In retrospect, these seem to have eased their work and led to a number of early successes.

First, it was felt to be important to minimize any interference with the planning which was already taking place below the central management level. The concerns of the central planning department were stated in such a way that those administrators who felt a need to continue their individual planning could do so and, indeed, be helped to do so by the central planners. This consideration was a particularly critical factor in the two departments where formal planning geared to federal grants had been going on for some time.

Second, the professional planners were determined that the administrators would not view the planning system as imposed upon them. They tried hard to gain the administrators' acceptance of the need for *some* planning at the officewide level and to help the administrators to see themselves as making this central planning possible.

Third, the planners decided to risk the disadvantages which would come from asking the administrators to participate in an incomplete and seemingly fragmented system. The planners preferred to make good on their promise to minimize the administrators' frustrations in doing the planning as well as to involve them in determining the nature and scope of the planning system.

It was agreed that the system would be developed and implemented over a period of two years, quite in contrast to situations where a complete, highly explicit planning system is introduced within a very short time. Only after the lapse of two years would all the parameters of our planning system exist. Then, and only then, would we make an overall analysis of our progress so as to come up with improvements and gain the maximum advantage from formal planning.

I might say here that taking two years to develop the total system involves a political risk as well as a human one. There is a real possibility that others will look at the partial results and misinterpret them because of the absence of a total rationale and framework. We expect that much of this risk will be offset by careful explanation of our reasons for proceeding in this manner. Frankly, even if it isn't, taking one step at a time was the best way to gain the full cooperation of the key administrators, and without it, we believe we would have little or nothing to show for our planning efforts.

Fourth, the planners introduced the central planning process by engaging the administrators in the planning, rather than by asking them to participate in a formal training program. The planners emphasized that there would always be an entry cost to the administrators' engaging in formal planning. Moreover, there would be decided benefits from paying the price early rather than waiting to learn and then trying to put their learning into practice.

Fifth, the planners allowed for the individual administrators to exercise their own leadership styles. They did not expect each administrator to plan in the same manner. If one wanted to do the planning for his department with only a few assisting him, the planners tried to help him do just that. On the other hand, if an administrator wanted to stimulate widespread participation among his own managers, the planners supported him by helping him to organize the participation as well as by meeting with any of his subordinate managers who wanted their help.

Sixth, the planners concentrated upon producing reasonable results just as soon as possible and using these as a tentative "model" for the subsequent efforts. An example of this purposeful gradualism is their preparation of a "working draft" of one department's mission statements which they then shared with others. This first set of missions had the impact of sustaining the initial excitement in the planning and reinforced each administrator's sense of accomplishment and participation in a new, broader effort than had heretofore been present. Each had the feedback that earlier work (sometimes his own, sometimes another's) was being seen and reacted to by others.

Seventh, and somewhat complementary to the previous consideration, the planners sought to dramatize tangible results at the end of each stage. The "finished products" were not stored until the completion of the entire system. Just as soon as all organizational units had completed one step in the process (to theirs and the planners' satisfaction), the results were published.

Eighth, the initial thrust was explicitly focused on the planning of organizational activity, as contrasted with the emphasis upon individual performance which is common in management-by-objectives programs. The planning was done in terms of *organizational* missions, *organizational* objectives, and *organizational* programs. Our primary need was to better manage the office. So, why not do this first? Moreover, such an approach would be far less threatening to individual managers and would, if successful, provide much learning which could benefit later efforts to set personal objectives.

Ninth, because of the decided lack of management-oriented data, the planning specialists directed a good part of their efforts to urging administrators throughout the office to do more to capture and analyze facts about their operations. They provided staff support, both directly through their own particular expertise and in cooperation with the data-processing organization.

The first step taken to increase awareness of our expectations that managers throughout the office were to play a greater part in effecting change was the institution of a management newsletter prepared by the planning staff. It was entitled, "From the Desk of Secretary Howlett." Twice a month, this newsletter disseminates reports of operating changes and items of general management interest to all supervisory and administrative personnel.

The planning specialists also assisted administrators in establishing systems for reporting production and manpower utilization. A special team of college students serving internships with the office was organized to prepare uniform statements in a playscript format of all operating procedures. In addition, a listing of all services provided to the public was prepared. It identifies the nature of some 250 different services, the annual volume, and the usual time period required to provide the services. All legislative provisions which affect one or more of the organizational units of the office have also been identified and made part of our total management data base.

Another element in this data base was the Key Event Calendar intended to provide ready identification of all major recurring commitments. The latter is already proving most helpful in assuring a minimum of conflict in setting new deadlines as well as in assuring effective coordination between the central planning efforts and the operating demands upon the various organizational units. Moreover, the Communications Department has benefited by being better able to anticipate departmental requests for external and internal publications and news releases.

The merits of a tenth consideration made early by the planning specialists are being reviewed at the present time. It had been decided that there would be no attempt to relate the planning system to the externally imposed budgeting process until after the entire system was operational. While this separation could magnify the incompleteness of the planning effort as well as create unresolved conflicts in resource allocation, the faster start thereby possible was expected to produce the offsetting benefit of easing the administrators' entry into formal planning.

The recent demands of the outside agencies for including a program orientation in our state's fiscal budgeting may require that we move much faster toward a full articulation in our planning and budgeting. Hopefully, the knowledge that these pressures are coming from outside will minimize the adverse effects of having to deal earlier than expected with a more complex system.

The impact of these early considerations can be seen in the very design of the system as well as in the continuing approach taken by the central planning staff. The conceptual design has admittedly evolved as we have learned more about individual and organizational capacities and the prevailing attitudes toward strategic planning. A broad outline of the planning process (see Exhibit 1 for a recent version) was distributed to all senior administrators as well as those to whom they delegated staff responsibilities for planning. Similarly, these key

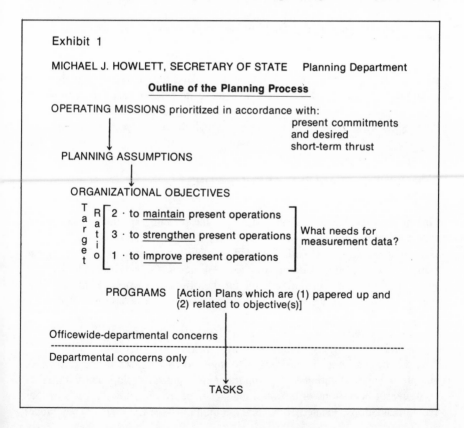

Exhibit 1

MICHAEL J. HOWLETT, SECRETARY OF STATE   Planning Department

Outline of the Planning Process

OPERATING MISSIONS prioritized in accordance with:
present commitments and desired short-term thrust

PLANNING ASSUMPTIONS

ORGANIZATIONAL OBJECTIVES

Target Ratio
2 · to maintain present operations
3 · to strengthen present operations
1 · to improve present operations
What needs for measurement data?

PROGRAMS   [Action Plans which are (1) papered up and (2) related to objective(s)]

Officewide-departmental concerns
Departmental concerns only

TASKS

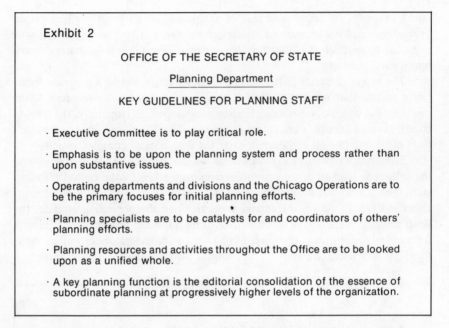

Exhibit 2

OFFICE OF THE SECRETARY OF STATE

Planning Department

KEY GUIDELINES FOR PLANNING STAFF

· Executive Committee is to play critical role.

· Emphasis is to be upon the planning system and process rather than upon substantive issues.

· Operating departments and divisions and the Chicago Operations are to be the primary focuses for initial planning efforts.

· Planning specialists are to be catalysts for and coordinators of others' planning efforts.

· Planning resources and activities throughout the Office are to be looked upon as a unified whole.

· A key planning function is the editorial consolidation of the essence of subordinate planning at progressively higher levels of the organization.

persons received a copy of the guidelines prepared for the central planning staff (Exhibit 2). With the dissemination of these items, our preparatory stage for strategic planning was at an end. Let us now turn to a description of the actual documents which have been developed through the use of the planning system.

OFFICEWIDE PLANNING ASSUMPTIONS

One of the first things requested of me by the planning specialists was to provide a set of assumptions which would indicate my estimates of probable future developments. I agreed with the need to clearly express and gain the understanding of key administrators of these estimates. Only then could I expect them to join together in setting plans for the office as a whole. Even their stating of organizational missions was to be put off until these assumptions were in hand.

In formulating these assumptions, I enlisted the help of the department heads and the central staff directors who make up our Executive Committee. Each of these administrators suggested items to be included in the general assumptions, either treating a very important anticipated development within their own area of operations or a central management concern. On the basis of their recommendations, I stated 16 general assumptions (see Exhibit 3). They ranged

Exhibit 3   OFFICE OF THE SECRETARY OF STATE
                    Department of Planning

GENERAL ASSUMPTIONS TO GUIDE DEPARTMENTAL PLANNING

It is impossible to plan without a tentative hypothesis regarding probable developments. For managers to plan together, they must share the same estimate of future occurrences. Their critical need is for assumptions which are clearly expressed and understood to be accepted by higher management and their peers as the foundation for their planning.

An assumption is NOT a prediction or forecast—it is a temporary estimate or hypothesis regarding a very important anticipated development. When there occurs a significant deviation in an assumption, it must immediately be changed and all plans based on the premise must be reviewed.

Administration

1. Officewide planning and coordination will be principally sought through the strengthening of the Executive Committee, assisted by the Planning Department of the Executive Office and planning staffs reporting to Executive Assistants and major Divisional Managers.

2. Responsible decision making will take place at increasingly lower levels.

3. Every rule and regulation and/or amendments thereto will have the approval of the Commercial Department prior to the initial filing of same.

4. Every legal document (contracts, leases, etc.) will have the approval of the Commercial Department prior to being submitted to the Secretary for his approval.

Fiscal Budgeting

5. For Fiscal '75, planning will take place within the budget constraints of turning back __% of the approved operating budget.

6. For Fiscal '76, planning will take place within the office-wide constraint of the total Fiscal '75 appropriations, except for new programs and any substantial increases in transactions (as separately justified).

Personnel Management

7. Some 2.3% of the Office's Personal Services FY '75 Budget (Regular Positions) will be spent for personnel development: training, attendance at technical and professional workshops and meetings, and reimbursement for related educational expenses. Personnel development can involve charges to all major line items (e.g., personal services, contractual, equipment, commodities) insofar as they relate to the learning and growth of employees.

8. Much greater consideration will be given to identifying meritorious employee performance and rewarding it by monetary and non-monetary means.

9. Of all job placements above the entry level, at least __% of them will be made by promotion from within.

10. The number of regular positions will be decreased to ____ by October 1, 1974.

11. Increased attention will be given to developing the Office of the Secretary of State as a highly desirable place of employment, concentrating on its being viewed as a total career opportunity.

Project Management

12. The Honeywell Computer System will be operational by April 1, 1975.

13. Effective integration of Regititle Division will be of highest priority with reorganization completed by Oct. 1, 1974, and use of a computer-printed title by Feb. 1, 1975.

14. The Photo Drivers License Program will be of highest priority, with issuance of photo-licenses to begin on January 1, 1976.

Facilities Management

15. Personnel of the Regititle, Commercial, General Accounting, Buildings & Grounds, Fiscal Control, Accounting Revenue, Personnel, Securities, and Management Information Services will be more functionally realigned in the Centennial Building by November 1, 1974.

16. The Honeywell Computer System will be housed in The Computer Center on Dirksen Parkway by April 1, 1975.

from the emphasis that I sought to place upon strengthening the work of the Executive Committee as the key unit in officewide planning and coordination to assumptions about the current fiscal year's budget and the contemplated preparation of appropriations requests for the next fiscal year.

There was a general emphasis on the importance of the human resources of the office. Five different assumptions in particular addressed key aspects of the management of the office's personnel, including the proportion of job placements above the entry level which would be made by promotion from within and the desired decrease in total employment so as to follow through on my campaign promise to eliminate the deadwood from the office and achieve maximum efficiency in our operations.

Another area addressed in these general assumptions was the establishment of key project priorities through which I intended to minimize conflicts in resource allocation as well as invite maximum cooperation in their realization. Three such projects were identified in the assumptions: (1) the conversion to a larger and more complex computer system, (2) the effective integration of two previously separate organizational units so as to provide better and more efficient services in all matters having to do with the registration and titling of vehicles, and (3) the revamping of the process for issuing drivers' licenses.

STATING ORGANIZATIONAL MISSIONS

The administrators of all major organizational units were then asked to search their operations in order to answer the fundamental question, "Why does the organization exist; what purpose does it serve?" They were to look into, but also go beyond the existing statutes and policies. The resulting missions were to be as few in number but yet as comprehensive as we could make them. They were to be listed in order of approximate priority, based upon both the current emphasis and the desired short-term thrusts.

The psychological reinforcement which came from the formal publication of these mission statements was greater than expected (see Exhibit 4). In their simplicity they communicated much. There were ninety-one statements, each of them worded in a uniform manner. Each was written in a similarly crisp language with an emphasis upon fundamental purposes. They were attractively published in a single brochure entitled, "The Mission of the Secretary of State." I included a formal acknowledgment of my appreciation for the efforts extended in preparing them and affirmed my desire that the mission statements serve as the principal focus for all subsequent planning. Copies were not only distributed to all senior and middle managers, but a reduced reproduction was given to all other employees.

Exhibit 4

MICHAEL J. HOWLETT, SECRETARY OF STATE   Planning Department

THE OBJECTIVES OF Regititle Division

In seeking to fulfill its mission . . .

1. To collect revenue as a condition of titling and registration for all vehicles other than those for which the Commercial and Farm Truck Division has specific responsibility.
2. To provide acceptable unique instruments as evidence of ownership and vehicle registration.
3. To assure proper titling and registering of vehicles.
4. To serve the users of information regarding ownership and registration of vehicles.

the following objectives have been set for the remainder of Fiscal Year 1975:

Objectives to Maintain Operations

By June 30, 1975, the direct salary cost per letter produced by the Correspondence Unit will be maintained at the current level of $__ (year to date).

Objectives to Strengthen Operations

By June 30, 1975, the processing time, from mail receipt at work processing center to receipt by Data Processing, will be decreased from current level of __ days to __ days.

By June 30, 1975, the processing time, from Data Processing release to internal files, will be decreased from current level of __ weeks to __ weeks.

By June 30, 1975, the methods of handling current categories of "Go-back" letters will be altered resulting in a 10% reduction in mailed correspondence—a reduction of 2,000 letters per month from the current level of 20,000 at an estimated cost savings of $__ per month (i.e., $__ per letter).

By June 30, 1975, the distribution of forms to the public will be tightened in such a way that the total purchase quantity for the year will be reduced from __ million to __ million (a reduction of approximately 50%).

Objectives to Improve Operations

By June 30, 1975, the time taken for release of I.D. card from the work processing center to issuance of a plate to the public will be reduced from __ days to __ days.

By June 30, 1975, the time for release of the application from the work processing center to the issuance of a title will be reduced from __ days to __ days.

By June 30, 1975, the average processing time for routine title applications will be reduced from the current __ week average to __ working days.

SETTING ORGANIZATIONAL OBJECTIVES

Once the organizational missions were identified, the planning staff moved on to assist in the preparation of organizational objectives. Again, just as in the case of the mission statements, there was a maximum effort to assure the administrators that, though the planning staff envisioned the objectives as precise and key parts of the total planning system, broad participation in designing both the form and the substance of the objectives was desired. At the outset, it was emphasized that the objectives were to be related to the missions in terms which would leave no doubt that the realization of the objectives would contribute to the realization of the stated missions or purposes of their various organizational units.

The objectives were to indicate the desired results believed to be possible from the utilization of allocated resources. The setting of meaningful objectives for each key result area was described as the best means for realizing an organizational unit's mission. The process was also to serve as a meaningful opportunity for the administrators' exercise of personal leadership and more effective monitoring of their operations. The objectives were to include not only those areas in which the administrator sought change and innovation but also where he sought conditions which reflected his intention to maintain continuing operations (see Exhibit 5). Our limited resources meant that all objectives could not be equally attractive. In order to minimize conflict in allocating them, we needed to limit at the outset the degree of change which could be expected during any particular time period.

The planning staff set forth these expectations by stressing that each organization might beneficially project a different emphasis, one particular to its current and historical situation. The administrators were encouraged to establish

---

Exhibit 5

MICHAEL J. HOWLETT, SECRETARY OF STATE   Planning Department

THE MISSION OF COMMUNICATIONS

1. To educate those who are served by the Secretary of State in regard to their rights and responsibilities as applicable to the missions of the Office.

2. To stimulate and take advantage of expressions of citizen attitudes and thoughts concerning the activities and plans of the Secretary of State.

3. To coordinate and support the internal communications efforts of all other departments of the Office of the Secretary of State.

4. To inform the public regarding the activities and plans of the Secretary of State, both directly and through the public media.

5. To inform the public regarding the nature and operation of the Capitol Complex.

their own emphases, but to specifically include among their objectives three different, though complementary aims: the maintenance, strengthening, *and* improvement of their present operations.

Each of their objectives would thus be distinguishable on the basis of the degree to which the administrators were seeking to *change* present operations. They were to set more objectives which projected a strengthening of their operations than those which sought an improvement in them. As a general guide, on the basis of stating six objectives, an administrator might well include two of the maintenance type (i.e., those whereby the organization attempts to reinforce and protect present levels of organizational performance), three of the strengthening type (i.e., those whereby it seeks to solve existing problems in fulfilling the organizational mission, shore up deficiencies, or eliminate a major obstacle), and one aimed at improving the present operations (i.e., those whereby it is endeavoring to achieve a major departure from existing operations).

PREPARING PROGRAM STATEMENTS

At the time of this writing, we are engaged in the first round of setting organizational objectives for the remaining months of the fiscal year. Once these are completed, we intend to direct our energies to preparing uniform statements for all new and major continuing programs. These statements will be carefully documented in terms of both the benefits sought and the resources required. They will, as an essential ingredient, be related in very definite terms to the realization of already projected objectives. Indeed, I intend that no new program will be approved without full justification in terms of the proposing unit's current missions and organizational objectives.

ACTION PLANS—A SHORT-TERM FOCUS

Concerned as we were with the early demonstration of tangible results from the planning effort, we decided not to wait for the completion of the organizational objectives in order to bring about a centrally-directed momentum in planning departmental programs. We needed to know just as soon as possible what projects were in process or under consideration throughout the office. We needed, too, to establish early a clear perspective of the role that my Deputy Secretary was to play in the management of the office. We wanted also to provide an early learning opportunity for the administrators in terms of the scope and depth that was anticipated for the entire planning cycle. We needed to emphasize that it was not sufficient to plan; the administrators had to secure and use feedback about the progress they were making in realizing their plans as well as deal with others' reviews of their planning efforts and the results that they had attained.

The planning staff therefore proceeded to "capture" in a systematic way the existing planning. They requested the administrators to identify all projects which were either underway or under consideration, regardless of their purpose or magnitude. They asked that they be told about all projects currently active, whether or not their superiors had authorized the project or the project had been consciously related to the realization of a specified objective. The primary aim was simply to gather the diverse bits of information together in a common format so as to facilitate the Deputy Secretary's efforts in coordinating and expediting their decision making.

Beyond realizing this primary aim in capturing some 250 projects in a single data base, we have gained online experience in timely confronting action to plan (thus, the terminology of "action plans") as well as the valuable discipline of working under an officewide focus upon departmental planning. As a result, the administrators have concrete evidence that they no longer can isolate themselves from the overall direction of the office or raise planning issues in a sporadic, unorganized manner. All of this, of course, is occurring far sooner than would have been possible if we had waited for the year-end review of accomplishments against the objectives and the more formal program statements, i.e., the continuing elements in our planning system.

For the first time, as a result of the detailed classification of the action plans in process and under consideration, we know just how many projects are currently being addressed by our administrators. Though the numbers are themselves impressive, far more significant is the information that has resulted as to just what kinds of projects are being attempted, the expected impact of the projects, and the anticipated completion or decision dates. As a result of summaries prepared from the data about these action plans, for example, we know for the first time that there are over one hundred plans in process or under consideration which are expected to lead to the improvement of internal services and nearly as many expected to contribute to the improvement of external services.

Furthermore, we know that while the number of action plans expected to be completed or decided upon during each of the various months of the current fiscal year range from three to twenty-seven, there are more than 50 action plans that will extend beyond the current fiscal year. We also have learned that the projects are of many different kinds though more than 90 of them involve the planning and control of operations, some 17 of them involve fiscal matters, and four of them are addressing issues of social responsibility.

A very important result of capturing the action plans is the identification of the demands the organizational units are making upon one another. We know for the first time, for example, that one of the divisions within the Motor Vehicle Department has underway or under consideration six action plans that require the cooperation of the Personnel Department, five plans that involve other operating departments, one with which they are working with the State Library, and one whereby they are receiving support from the Central Planning Department. In the absence of these findings, we are convinced that far more interdepartmental conflicts would have arisen, to say nothing of delays in completion or decision.

THE VALUE OF STRATEGIC PLANNING

Introducing strategic planning into an organization is always a most complex and difficult task. This is particularly so where the emphasis is on achieving substantial involvement of line administrators who have had little or no experience in formal planning. When it is a public agency which is the arena for the strategic planning, the task is even more risky.

Although I cannot say that we have been wholly successful to date, I am satisfied that there have been some notable results. We are making strides in producing plans which are seen by the operating managers themselves as having a practical, results-oriented nature. A number have told me of dramatic examples of just how helpful the planning has been to them. Indeed, we have seen signs of a healthy competition developing in their efforts to produce planning data and documents better than those of their peers.

The key to our early successes, in my opinion, has been our determination to keep the planning process just as simple as it can be. We have profited much from gearing our efforts to the learning curve of the users, rather than to any arbitrary perfection of the instruments. Our emphasis upon gradualism and expeditious publication of tangible results has made it far more certain that the exercise is a real one.

We conclude that strategic planning *is* possible in state government. And, just as important, strategic planning *does* make a government agency (at least, the Illinois Office of the Secretary of State) a more manageable organization. One state official outside my office phrased it well when, after receiving "The Mission" brochure, he wrote, "With the development of these missions, the framework now exists . . . from which a meaningful and responsive total program for planning and management can be attained."

Part 3

MANAGEMENT BY OBJECTIVES

A Practical Approach

MANAGEMENT BY OBJECTIVES—OR MBO, AS IT IS MORE COMMONLY CALLED—
is an approach to the management process that has been successfully applied in
a variety of organizations and sectors. Today, in most industries, the MBO
concept is well known and, as can be seen from this selection of articles, is currently being applied in many nonprofit organizations.

	Government	Education	Health	Religious and Charitable	Associations and Others
Applying Management by Objectives to Nonprofit Organizations Dale D. McConkey	X	X	X	X	X
Management by Objectives for Schools Thorne Hacker		X			
MBO in Church Organizations Dale D. McConkey				X	
Tailoring MBO to Hospitals Herbert H. Hand and A. Thomas Hollingsworth			X		
A Study of Management by Objectives in a Professional Organization Y. K. Shetty and Howard M. Carlisle		X			
The Future: Its Challenge and Its Promise Dale D. McConkey	X	X	X	X	X

Applying
Management by Objectives
to Nonprofit Organizations

Dale D. McConkey

Management of nonprofit organizations has no landed right to be inefficient, to ignore managerial productivity, to ignore the profit motive, or to fail to evaluate new or revised approaches to management as these approaches develop. A manager is a manager regardless of the product or service with which he deals. Nor should these managers be immune from strict accountability to those whom they serve and from those on whom they depend for their funds and support.

Nonprofit organizations, too, must earn a profit by operating with a high sense of priority and as efficiently and effectively as possible. While the nature of their profits may bear different labels, the profit motive must be present if they are to avoid drifting into practices which are economically and socially wasteful and which raise major questions about their reason for being.

The magnitude of the mandate to maximize "profits" is emphasized by the huge amounts of capital often entrusted to nonprofit entities. A profit-oriented business with only five or ten million dollars must observe the best in management practices if it is to stay in business and continue to earn the trust of its owners. It has no leeway to practice sloppy management. In contrast,

Reprinted by permission of the publisher from *S.A.M. Advanced Management Journal,* January 1973, © 1973 by S.A.M., a division of American Management Associations.

many nonprofit organizations frequently have hundreds of millions of dollars entrusted to them. Their mandate to maximize profits can be no less!

The profit motive is present in both a profit and nonprofit organization. A business makes profits depending on the way it manages the resources (assets) entrusted to it. Business profits are enhanced in one or both of two ways: (1) by realizing a *higher* return on the *same* amount of assets, and (2) by realizing the *same* or better return on a *lesser* amount of assets.

Nonprofit organizations have the same mission, as illustrated by the following ways used to realize a higher return on resources:

⬦ Increased productivity from present employees.
⬦ Improved patient care from present staff (in hospitals).
⬦ Increased quality and/or quantity of teaching from present staff.
⬦ Lower overhead costs of fund raising.
⬦ More effective crime prevention through improved law enforcement techniques.
⬦ Improved state of defense readiness by replacing troops with electronic or space hardware.
⬦ Better distribution of relief and disaster funds.
⬦ Greater results from volunteer workers.
⬦ Lowering the administrative costs of operating the organization.
⬦ Reducing wasted effort and/or wastes in the utilization of any assets.
⬦ Blending together of the efforts of all personnel to achieve an overall effectiveness which is greater than the sum of the individual efforts.

An increasingly higher priority is being placed on managing nonprofit organizations so as to achieve what Peter Drucker has referred to as the prime duty of a manager, namely, to produce economically significant results. This upgrading of priorities results in large part from the dramatic changes taking place in the mix of organizations comprising our economy. Increasingly, the swing is proportionately away from manufacturing-type organizations to service types—including nonprofit groups. Most informed observers believe, with considerable justification, that we are rapidly approaching a service-oriented economy which will overshadow the manufacturing sector in terms of numbers and their impact. Thus, nonprofit organizations now are and will continue to be challenged to adopt the more effective approaches for managing their resources.

The question that plagues most managers, administrators, and executive personnel of nonprofit organizations bent on effective performance is not whether they should increase their ''profits,'' but how the improvement can be brought about—what means, methods, or tools are available to them.

One of the means being used with increasing success for improving effectiveness of both the organization and the individuals in these entities is Management by Objectives (or MBO or Management by Results, as it also is termed). Although MBO developed and has realized its major success in businesses operating for profit, the preponderance of the MBO system is equally applicable and beneficial to the nonprofit organization. Subsequent portions of this article will illustrate actual examples of successful MBO applications in various nonprofit organizations.

MBO DEFINED

A simple yet comprehensive definition of the MBO system of managing includes several major provisions:

1. MBO is a systems approach to managing an organization—any organization. It is not a technique, just another program, or a narrow area of the process of managing. Above all, it goes far beyond mere budgeting even though it does encompass budgets in one form or another.

2. Those accountable for directing the organization first determine where they want to take the organization or what they want it to achieve during a particular period (establishing the overall objectives and priorities).

3. Requiring, permitting, and encouraging *all* key managerial and administrative personnel to contribute their maximum to achieving the overall objectives.

4. Blending and balancing the planned achievements (results) of all key personnel to promote and realize the greater total results for the organization as a whole.

5. Providing a control mechanism to monitor progress compared to objectives and feed the results back to those accountable at all levels.

TESTING FOR APPLICABILITY

In light of the fact that MBO developed in an environment of profit-oriented business organizations, an examination should be made of the system's applicability and value to the nonprofit organizations before any decision is made to adopt it. Both writers and practicing managers in nonprofit entities have raised major questions concerning the system's value in the absence of the profit motive.

The subject matter contained in the following questions will serve as an audit checklist for helping determine the applicability of MBO to nonprofit organizations. The questions cover the major aspects of organizing and managing an operation. Also, they exert the major impact on MBO and, in turn, MBO exerts a major impact on them:

1. Does the organization have a mission to perform? Is there a valid reason for it to exist?
2. Does management have assets (money, people, plant and equipment) entrusted to it?
3. Is management accountable to some person or authority for a return on the assets?
4. Can priorities be established for accomplishing the mission?
5. Can the operation be planned?
6. Does management believe it must manage effectively even though the organization is a nonprofit one?
7. Can accountabilities of key personnel be pinpointed?
8. Can the efforts of all key personnel be coordinated into a whole?
9. Can necessary controls and feedback be established?
10. Is it possible to evaluate the performance of key personnel?
11. Is a system of positive and negative rewards possible?
12. Are the main functions of a manager (planning, organizing, directing, etc.) the same regardless of the type of organization?
13. Is management receptive to improved methods of operating?

The applicability and value of MBO to a nonprofit organization is directly correlated to the number of affirmative answers to the above questions. Use of these questions as tests of the wisdom of applying MBO to profit-oriented entities has been well validated by about twenty years of successsful practice in every type, size, and category of business entity, both in the United States and abroad. Increasingly the same tests are proving their validity when applied to nonprofit groups.

Naturally, the degree of conviction with which the questions can be answered with a "yes" will vary with any limitations which may be imposed by the nature of the nonprofit organization, especially its locus of authority and its policies or regulations.

POSSIBLE LIMITATIONS

Limitations on the value of MBO to the nonprofit sector can be real or imagined, or both. They are real when an organization's managers can do nothing to change them, for example, the compensation of federal civil service employees is established by Congress. The manager of a civil service organization cannot vary the compensation policy even though he could motivate better performance among his subordinates if he had the requisite authority.

The limitations, even if they do exist in fact, are imagined if they can be changed by the manager, for example, the false assumption that there is no way for a fund raising organization to motivate volunteer workers to meet their targets.

Possible limitations, again in varying degrees, probably do exist in some nonprofit organizations. For example, a government or quasi-government organization may well have several constraints which would detract from realizing the full benefit of MBO that could be realized by a profit-oriented firm. These are shown in the accompanying list.

Nature of Limitation	Impact of Limitation
1. Many decision making areas are preempted by law, rules, and regulations.	Less flexibility for making profit-oriented decisions. Tends to "level" all key personnel—less opportunity to prove individual mettle.
2. Less opportunity to participate in setting objectives.	Lowered managerial motivation—lack of opportunity to determine own accountability and destiny.
3. Many forms of rewards and recognition are set by law.	Less flexibility to reward the outstanding performer over the mediocre one.
4. Emphasis on seniority rather than merit.	Tends to protect the inefficient and impede the efficient.
5. Performance measurement often lacking—emphasis on effort rather than output.	The achievement-oriented manager suffers. He demands results-oriented measurement.

A goverment organization was deliberately selected for this example because governmental units are more frequently cited as having so many limitations that MBO cannot be successfully applied. Now, let's go back to these limitations and assume that they do in fact exist to a considerable degree. Does their existence destroy the value of MBO? Or, does their existence merely limit the benefit and spotlight matters which, if changed, will increase the benefits? It is submitted that such limitations do not destroy the value of MBO but merely limit realizing its full potential.

Management of most nonprofit organizations is starving for better management methods and much of its hunger is being caused by increasing pressures from users of its services and those who finance its endeavors. Given this situation, even half a loaf of bread—possibly in the form of an MBO system whose full impact cannot be realized immediately because of the limitations—would appear eminently better than continuing to waste away as the hunger remains insatiated.

At the same time, MBO will help to quickly spot the limitations so that all possible action can be taken to eliminate or minimize them. In the absence of MBO the limitations are destined to continue, often without recognition of their impact on the progress of the organization. Concurrently, the organization's valuable resources continue to be dissipated. It often is said that much of the solving of a problem results from properly identifying and defining it; one of the chief virtues of MBO is its ability to highlight "sacred cows" and other impediments to increased effectiveness.

MBO IN PRACTICE

Today, MBO is making rapid strides in nonprofit organizations. While its progress has not been as dramatic or widespread as is true with business firms, it is becoming increasingly difficult to find a category of nonprofit organization in which MBO has not been successfully applied.

The examples illustrated in the following paragraphs of nonprofit organizations now practicing MBO were selected to show the wide range and diversity of the entities which have adopted and are practicing MBO.

Schools

By virtue of their sheer weight of numbers and the importance of their end product—education—schools represent an area of prime concern with respect to first determining what their objectives should be and then coordinating all efforts to achieve these ends. Undoubtedly, this concern and the increasing burden on the taxpayer, have caused the rather sudden surge of interest in applying MBO to schools. Probably no other category of nonprofit organization is receiving more MBO attention than are schools.

Dr. Donald W. Shebuski, Superintendent of Schools of Holt, Michigan, is one of those most active in applying MBO to schools. He summarizes his experience as follows:

"School administrators have long endorsed the concept of a management team. Recently, however, a managerial strategy, known as Management by Objectives, has assisted scientific-management minded administrators to operationalize this team approach in education. Management by Objectives is a method of participation and involvement of supervision and subordinates whereby decisions are reached and results explicated. Management at every level in schools has a continuing responsibility to improve the organization of the work under its supervision. It is accountable for the successful outcome of the team effort at any given level of responsibility.

"The key word in the MBO approach is improve. A primary responsibility of a school administrator is to improve the work of the people he supervises; to improve the product (students); and to improve the team effort that makes the organization successful. Through successful accomplishment of the above, he also improves himself.

"Accomplishment of an accountability concept for schools means that we must explicate clearly defined goals, and have developed a management plan whereby goals can be reached in measurable ways.

"MBO is not a panacea for all of education's many problems, nor is it an attempt to turn schools into a mechanized factory-like process. It is a procedure in which scarce resources (people and dollars) can be allocated to accomplish established goals, and then account for the degree to which goals and objectives have been reached.

"Educational administrators have a great challenge before them as they face the durable concerns for accountability in education. At this point, educators are compelled to translate the educational process, which up until now has been considered an art, into a viable, scientific procedure. Management by Objectives processes are proving to be a successful approach in this endeavor."

The Management Institute of the University of Wisconsin—Extension, Madison, was one of the earliest university groups to adopt MBO. Its Director, Professor Norman C. Allhiser, traces his experience with MBO:

"Before adopting MBO, the Institute had made good progress in a number of key areas:

◊ Staff members were dedicated to the principles and concepts of adult education.
◊ Subject matter was problem-oriented and practical.
◊ Institute meetings were limited to thirty participants, and small group sessions within each group were utilized.
◊ Resource leaders used directed discussion techniques for maximum involvement.
◊ The Institute was beginning to expand its activities and was developing an out-of-state following.

"However, weaknesses existed in our organizational structure. Valid description covering the accountabilities of faculty members had not been developed; quality of programs varied; the selection of speakers and resource leaders was erratic; programs were canceled; deadlines were missed; administration tended to be rather loose; and the evaluation of faculty and programming was extremely difficult.

"The need to improve the department's own management was apparent and in the early 1960s the Management Institute adopted the MBO concept. Emphasis was placed on improving and measuring the quality of the faculty and programming in a manner which encouraged the blending of individual efforts into a total team effort.

"The original MBO application was improved each year and now has culminated in a much more sophisticated approach. A long- and short-range planning meeting is held each year with active staff involvement. Overall objectives are established for that year, followed by the development of performance standards (objectives) for faculty members. These standards emphasize quality, quantity, and innovation and clarify individual accountability in the areas of programming, administration, self-development, teaching, services, innovation, and results achieved.

"Each member of the faculty prepares a 'planning guide' in which he spells out how he is going to achieve his objectives. Periodic conferences are held to discuss progress on objectives and plans.

"Our experience with MBO can be summarized in a number of ways. The number of our programs has increased more than sevenfold and enrollments by more than thirty times, although quality continues to be emphasized over quantity. MBO has helped us build this quality into our product. Greater decentralization for broader statewide service also has accompanied the growth. We believe MBO has helped us achieve and retain a leading reputation among the oldest and largest university-type programs. The Institute has weathered several 'recessions' and continues to grow even though some of its 'competitors' have suffered serious setbacks."

Another excellent example of a successful MBO application in schools is Harper College in Palatine, Illinois. A wide range of MBO applications has been made at this college.

Government Laboratory*

The U.S. Forest Products Laboratory located in Madison, Wisconsin, has recently completed a review of its first year of introducing Management by Objectives for its research management. The results are gratifying although there are many opportunities for continued expansion and improvement.

* This summary was prepared by Professor Fred C. Schwarz, University of Wisconsin, Madison, who served as a consultant during the installation. It is used here with his permission as well as that of the management of U.S. Forest Products Laboratory.

Although project management in research requires goals and has been using them for many years, it was decided that Management by Objectives had some additional benefits which would be useful for all Forest Products Research managers. The system was launched by first indoctrinating the top management group. Following this meeting, sessions were conducted for all project leaders and key scientists.

The mission of the Laboratory was reviewed at the beginning of each session which was "to conduct research leading to greater social and economic benefits for the people of the United States, and of the world, through the better utilization of their timber resources." The broad areas of concern of the Laboratory were also reexamined during the sessions. Then each individual prepared objectives within the scope of his or her responsibilities consistent with the mission and within the following areas of concern:

The properties and behavior of wood and wood constituents
Timber supply and utilization
Efficiency in processing and use
Better housing for the 70s
The environment
The rural economy
Protection of wood in use
Consumer interests

Areas of improved management which the top management team has identified as a result of applying Management by Objectives include:

◆ Clearer understanding of what is expected of research teams, project leaders, and individuals.

◆ Specific connection between budget allocations and results accomplished on projects.

◆ Increased involvement of entire staff in developing specific objectives to accomplish Laboratory mission.

◆ The management team is Managing by Objectives.

◆ The management team now has a common language and there has been a demonstrated ability to attack a problem and approach it with a more positive management attitude than before.

Canadian Post Office

MBO was applied to the Canadian Post Office in January of 1970 beginning with a "pilot" project in the Ontario Region, one of the four large regions into which the postal system is divided. Subsequently, it was decided to extend MBO to all four regions and the headquarters of the system.

Several factors lay behind the decision to adopt MBO. The Canadian Post Office employed up to 50,000 people annually and was known as "the sleeping giant." Costs and deficits had mounted. Mail service, vital to both commerce and citizens, had been deteriorating. Increasing difficulty was being encountered in attracting competent personnel for key managerial positions.

A package of eight interrelated management programs was designed for the total planned change. The basis of these programs was the application of MBO, especially true delegation from the Regional Manager to the District Manager to the Area Manager (the lowest level of management).

The experience gained in the pilot project leading up to the decision to adopt MBO for the total postal system included:

1. True delegation of accountabilities had taken place.

2. Management in the Ontario Region was becoming stronger and more professional than the management at headquarters.

3. The potential for systemwide application was so encouraging that the decision was made to waive the two year trial period planned originally for the pilot project and to accelerate the systemwide adoption.

Management of the Canadian Post Office doesn't kid itself into believing that MBO is a panacea. A turnaround the size of this giant will take time. There is no quick, magic cure. However, they feel that now the organization has an approach which is sufficiently flexible to meet the dynamics of work even in the Post Office.[1]

Hospitals

Plagued as they are with labor costs which frequently average 70 to 80 percent of total operating cost, hospitals represent a fertile field for any management approach which promotes increased effectiveness. It seems only natural that hospitals have turned to MBO as a way of alleviating their plight.

Prior to assuming his present position as administrator of a large nonprofit hospital in Ottawa, Garry D. Cardiff [2] played a significant role in applying MBO to another nonprofit hospital. In the following paragraphs, Cardiff summarizes the experience with MBO after three years:

1. Regardless of the effort put forth, enthusiasm and utilization of MBO is cyclic.

2. Only about 60 percent of those that started the program are still successfully using the approach. However, in light of factors such as background, personal limitations, and other organizational circumstances, this percentage seems acceptable to us.

3. The greatest enemy of an MBO program in a nonprofit organization is apathy. With the recent advent of "global budgeting," perhaps realistic incentive programs will be devised in a way that successful MBO performances can be rewarded in more tangible terms.

4. Many projects that "should be done" are done because of MBO. Procrastination generally is the result of lack of commitment.

5. The contribution to communications both horizontally and vertically has been immeasurable.

6. Contribution of MBO to our budgeting process has been equally rewarding.

7. Since MBO is an essential ingredient of writing and executing a long-range plan, the program will no doubt continue to prove invaluable, as we are currently in the primary stages of formulating such a plan.

8. On balance, the benefits we have gained far outweigh expenditures of time and money. Management by Objectives is an interesting theory and a worthwhile practice.

Volunteer Organizations

Volunteer organizations are considered among the more difficult when applying MBO. However, the fact that an MBO application is possible is illustrated by the highlights of the experience of a large volunteer organization which, at this stage of development of its program, chooses to remain anonymous.

It operates nationally from a central headquarters, through regions, to local areas headed by a local manager who is the lowest level of management. Managers of all of these levels are paid professionals. Managers of the local areas are the real guts of the organization as they are accountable for the fund raising, motivating volunteers to carry out the bulk of the organization's work in the area, and directing the local programs for effectiveness.

Strict standards of accountability have been established for each of the area managers. Their primary accountabilities are:

Program quantity
Program quality
Financial stability
Public relations
Internal relations

Each of these accountabilities is assigned a weight or value which reflects its importance to the manager's overall effectiveness. Commendably, quality is weighted proportionate to quantity.

Next, each of the accountabilities is defined in terms of standards of performance required. For example, the "program quantity" objective is spelled out in terms of the population size of the area, the percentage of the population represented by the age group which the organization seeks to bring into its program, the number of eligibles who do actually participate in the program, and the percentage of total potential which this number represents. Program "quality" is defined and measured by factors such as the number of participants who stay in the program and how this compares with medians which have been established.

The application now has endured several years of experience and those to whom the organization is accountable are pleased with the results. The program emphasizes participation of all managers in setting their goals, strict accountability, measuring of performance and feedback to the managers, and maximizing the benefits provided for all funds raised.

Municipal Organizations

Often a nonprofit organization has functions and operations which are identical with those existing in a profit oriented one. The more common of these include purchasing, personnel, finance, administration, operations, and public relations. Organizations like municipal governments often have suborganizations which are almost exact duplicates of profit making organizations, for example, the Port Authority of cities like Boston and New York. Madison, Wisconsin, has nine "enterprise funds" which include: water utility, sewer utility, airport authority, bus utility, parking utility, golf courses, ice arena, concessions, and cemeteries. These funds are run on a consumer reimbursement basis in which costs are paid by the users. Each of these constitutes a minibusiness within the municipal government.

Certainly, these types of organizations readily lend themselves to applying MBO and applications are well underway in several instances.

Other Applications

The handful of examples described in the preceding paragraphs should not mislead the reader into believing the examples constitute the bulk of nonprofit organizations to which MBO has been applied. In the absence of space limitations, the number of examples could be expanded considerably. For example, MBO has been applied in the U.S. Navy Supply Systems Command and in the Mayor's office of the city of Sapporo, Japan—where in only one area, the tax division, major efficiencies have been realized in better methods of collecting taxes with substantial reductions in personnel. Nursing homes, churches, and child care centers all have embraced MBO as have many other nonprofit organizations. Based on experience to date, it appears only logical that nonprofit applications will continue and accelerate.

CONCLUSION

In essence, MBO is a systematic approach to achieving desired ends. When viewed in this, its true perspective, it appears obvious that it has considerable value when applied to nonprofit organizations. Those who would hold otherwise place themselves in the untenable position of advocating that the desired end, for example, quality education, should be approached by hit or miss methods. Nonprofit organizations have no landed right to assume this unique position.

Nonprofit organizations are not unique. They, like all organizations, have an objective to achieve, namely, to provide the highest quality product or service consistent with the funds available. They have assets entrusted to them— people, capital, and plant and equipment. They serve in a stewardship capacity to those upon whom they depend for their continued existence. Managers of these organizations have no inherent right to waste any of these assets or to violate their stewardship. They must be held accountable for results.

Highly successful MBO applications have been made in every conceivable type of organization—profit and nonprofit, the private and public sectors, large and small organizations, organizations in the United States, Canada, Europe, Japan, and elsewhere. These include hospitals, schools, police departments, nursing homes, defense departments, municipal-government units, and agencies of the federal government.

Over twenty years of MBO experience has demonstrated value and applicability of MBO to all types of organizations. The nonprofit sector is no exception. This same experience has demonstrated that MBO can be applied to these organizations only if they insist on and meet the same demands the system imposes on other categories of organizations and endeavors. As a minimum these include:

♦ The selection of highly competent managers, administrators, and professionals in all key positions.

♦ In-depth training in the complete MBO system before any attempt is made to apply it.

♦ Allowing the three to four years required to make a successful installation.

♦ Substituting maximum participation from all personnel for the sometimes autocratic and despotic ideas of a few.

♦ A complete tailoring or adapting of the MBO system to the individual problems or conditions that exist in the individual entity to which it is applied.

◆ The removal, or diminishing, by legislative or executive action of many of the impediments which act as limitations on the ability of MBO to achieve the full potential of which it is capable—limitations such as emphasizing effort rather than results, provisions which protect the ineffective personnel, practices which stifle individual initiative and permit flexible decision making, and systems which fail to provide recognition and rewards.

◆ A constant reexamination of the system after installation to improve it and render it responsive to the changing conditions in the environment in which it is being practiced.

MBO cannot be blamed for any failure to meet these exhaustive and exhausting demands. Any failure must be placed squarely upon the shoulders of the real culprits—the persons who fail to meet the demands imposed by the system.

REFERENCES

1. This summary of experience is adapted largely from "Business Planning in the Canadian Post Office," by P. J. Chartrand: *Canadian Personnel and Industrial Relations Journal,* Oct. 1971, pp. 17–22. Used with permission.
2. Garry D. Cardiff, "Management by Objectives—It Will Work in a Hospital Setting," *Hospital Administration in Canada,* Nov. 1970, pp. 23–26.

Management by Objectives for Schools

Thorne Hacker

School officials are becoming increasingly concerned with the quality of services their systems provide. Desire to clarify and more effectively fulfill their mission has caused administrators to look beyond education for examples of practices able to focus objectives and integrate efforts toward their attainment. The attention of some large school systems [1] has been drawn to the management by objectives (MBO) technology currently popular in business.

Educators enjoy certain advantages in turning to an established set of practices. As borrowers, they are able to benefit from previous efforts at working the kinks out of MBO. On the other hand, they risk assuming that this technology comes to them trouble free. To the contrary, MBO contains inherent tendencies creating pitfalls for the unwary and confronts the administrator with a number of difficult choices.

MBO has been described as an outgrowth of rational management theory as advocated by Frederick Taylor and his disciples. The technology's initial

Reprinted with permission of the author and publisher: Thorne Hacker, "Management by Objectives for Schools," *Administrator's Notebook,* Vol XX, No. 3 (Nov. 1971). The *Administrator's Notebook* is published by the Midwest Administration Center of the University of Chicago.

formulation is attributed to Peter Drucker, whose statement is contained in his 1954 publication, *The Practice of Management*. Its core features are relatively few. Management is guided by the specification of sets of objectives for positions within an organization. These goals are sufficiently concrete to make their attainment evident. Thus the technology permits effective expenditure of resources and evaluation of individual performances in terms of goal attainment. Other elements have become attached to this core representing choices to be made upon implementation rather than necessary parts of the package. Two options are participation of the employee in setting his own goals and an incentive system based upon payment by results.

INHERENT PROBLEMS

MBO programs typically measure performance exclusively in terms of goal attainment. The employee is considered to have performed well to the extent that he fulfills the objectives targeted for him. This emphasis upon hitting the target frequently results in the setting of trivial goals. Such objectives are especially likely to result when the program calls for goals to be negotiated by the employee and his superior. Under such conditions, it is patently irrational for the subordinate to maximize his risks by accepting challenging goals. His interests, instead, dictate a strategy of negotiating for easily attained and therefore, in all probability, insignificant objectives. Incentive to set challenging goals is lacking, for such objectives increase chances of failure when performance is judged solely by goal attainment.

Emphasis on goal attainment also influences the kinds of goals which are set. The desire to determine readily whether a target has been hit results in the setting of easily quantified goals. For example, a principal may have as an objective an improved relationship with his faculty, but for purposes of measurement this goal is equated with the number of faculty meetings he holds during the year. In this fashion the concern for hitting the target results in the substitution of a trivial goal for a significant one.

Payment by results reinforces the tendency of MBO programs to produce trivial goals. The desire to incorporate an incentive system results in an emphasis on goal attainment rather than broader criteria of success. Target hitting is an unequivocal criterion by which to judge what constitutes rewardable performance: the target objective has either been reached or it has not. Broader criteria of praiseworthy performance, on the other hand, lack this mechanical precision. The desire for complaint free programs accounts for the frequency with which MBO plans incorporate target-hitting criteria and quantitative goals.

STEPS TOWARD SOLUTIONS

The tendency of MBO programs to produce trivial objectives can be partially counteracted by reducing emphasis on goal attainment. Basing performance appraisal on a variety of criteria, rather than solely on hitting the target, frees the employee to experiment with more meaningful objectives. One additional criterion is the employee's ability to formulate goals that are both realistic and significant. Furthermore, taking into account the relative difficulties presented by various goals provides incentive to set challenging objectives. Another criterion is the effectiveness with which resources are employed in moving toward a goal regardless of whether it is attained. A major consideration is the employee's skill at analyzing those factors that intervene between planned and actual performance, for this capacity for intelligent review of past performance is the key to improved performance in the future. Attention to the entire process of setting and pursuing goals and of analyzing factors affecting progress toward them combats the myopia resulting from exclusive focus on goal attainment. This broader perspective encompasses a wide range of skills and looks to the quality of goals rather than emphasizing attainment of a goal regardless of its worth.

The tendency toward trivial goals which results from setting easily quantified objectives can be checked through development of criteria reflecting worthwhile goals which cannot be easily quantified. The need is for instruments able to satisfy canons of objectivity without reducing high quality goals to the trivial. Consider a case in which a principal's goal is to produce a system for managing student discipline capable of satisfying students and parents and of withstanding scrutiny by the courts. Attainment of this objective can be assessed in terms of the presence or absence of mechanisms contributing to an adequate due process procedure for students. Although the elements of an adequate procedure may vary with the school, a list of specific features might resemble the following:

1. The accused student shall be informed of the charges against him and of the evidence on which they are based.
2. He shall be permitted to testify in his own behalf and to call witnesses.
3. The appropriate administrator shall state to both the student and the complainant his evaluation of the facts of the case, his disposition of the incident, and the reasons for his decision.
4. The student shall be informed as to how his case can be appealed.[2]

Such criteria are one way to objectify performance appraisal without reducing standards to the easily quantified and often trivial components of an employee's behavior.

SIGNIFICANT GOALS

Reduced reliance on easily quantified goals and reduced emphasis upon goal attainment open the way to serious consideration of worthwhile objectives; that is, objectives which are both significant and appropriate.

One criterion of significance can be stated as follows: the significance of an objective increases the more closely it approximates the organization's top priority goals. Since the major goals of the entire organization provide the context that determines what is significant for that organization, they are necessary reference points for judging the worth of subordinate objectives within the organization. Objectives which contribute to fulfilling the organization's major goals are more significant for the organization than objectives whose attainment contributes little to this end.

However, the application of this criterion is not trouble free. Goals for the entire organization may be implicit or imprecisely formulated and therefore inadequately guide the setting of subordinate goals. Furthermore, even when these goals are clearly stated, the relative importance of subordinate objectives as related to top priority goals may not be evident. For instance, in light of a school system's general goal of providing for the development of the whole child, how does one rank the relative significance of an expanded athletic program, hiring a school nurse, and employing an arts and crafts teacher? A third area of difficulty stems from shifting priorities among goals. Altered circumstances can result in goal shifts at the highest organizational levels or in adjustments of the relative capacities of subordinate objectives to contribute to the attainment of major goals. Either kind of change affects the relative significance of subordinate goals. For instance, a bond election required to finance an enriched instructional program may cause a successful athletic program or an attractive commencement to gain significance, for they become means of marshaling public support for the election.

As this criterion applies only to objectives subordinate to the goals of the entire organization, it leaves open the matter of how the significance of these overall goals can be judged. A reference point beyond the organization in its present state is required in order to judge the significance of such goals. The concept of progress, understood as the step by step approximation of an ideal state, provides a context for these judgments.[3] In these terms, an organizational goal is more significant the more closely it approximates that organization's ideal. This ideal need not be attainable; the notion of progress requires only that it be approximated more and more closely. The concept is analogous to a mathematical series, like:

$$\frac{1}{2}, \; \frac{3}{4}, \; \frac{7}{8}, \; \frac{15}{16}, \; \ldots \; ,$$

although each number is greater than its predecessor, the series will never reach its "limit," the number 1.

This second criterion of significance is a necessary adjunct to judging subordinate objectives through reference to the organization's top priority goals. Without its application to overall organizational goals, reference to top priority goals permits ranking of subordinate objectives but does not guarantee their ultimate worth. This guarantee requires a standard for assessing the significance of top priority goals which incorporates an organizational ideal. In this way, the problem of significance becomes a matter of progress rather than maintenance.

APPROPRIATE OBJECTIVES

The fit between the set of objectives under consideration and other objectives within the organization constitutes one criterion of appropriateness. An organization embodies many sets of objectives forming a hierarchy running from the most general and often implicit goals of the entire organization to specific targets of individual members.[4] An appropriate set of objectives for a given position is one which is compatible with more general and more specific goals at higher and lower organization levels. In the case of a principal attempting to extract himself from a time-devouring commitment to an extremely small and phlegmatic PTA chapter simultaneously with the launching of a district-wide campaign to increase community involvement with schools, the principal's objective is inconsistent with a higher level goal and is hence inappropriate. An appropriate objective in this instance is kindling interest in the PTA by holding forth the promise of greater parental involvement in the school and using this group to fulfill this promise. By this criterion, a goal's appropriateness is increased in proportion to its degree of compatibility with goals at other organizational levels as judged on a continuum running from opposed to contributory, and in proportion to the number of levels taken into account.

A second criterion of appropriateness is the feasibility of goals in view of internal and external resources and constraints. An appropriate goal reflects awareness of the realities within an organization and is adjusted in light of available resources. The employee is one locus of crucial resources and constraints which often receive inadequate attention. The widespread business practice of employee participation in goal formulation and encouragement of candor between an employee and his superior helps ensure the availability of information sufficient to determine the feasibility of goals.

Additionally, feasibility depend on factors beyond the organization capable of affecting the pursuit of goals. Some school MBO plans have incorporated mechanisms intended to guarantee consideration of external factors. The Chicago Performance Appraisal Plan, for example, stipulates that an administrator must involve community groups in the goal-setting process.[5]

Attention to present internal and external resources and constraints is, however, an inadequate basis for judging feasibility. Assessing the feasibility of objectives to be met in the future requires attention to emerging realities both within and beyond the organization. Without an orientation to the future, energy is expended on problems rather than opportunties and on yesterday's problems at that.

The question of whether objectives are best established for individuals or groups is an additional aspect of the problem of formulating appropriate goals. The prevailing tendency is to set goals for individuals; nonetheless, concern with integration of effort argues for group goals. The question, however, is not whether all objectives ought to be set for groups or for individuals, but how to determine which objectives are appropriate for groups and which for individuals. The demands made by goals and the capabilities of employees are primary considerations in making this determination. If pursuing a goal requires resources beyond those of an individual, then it is appropriate to set the goal for a group which has the required resources. When an individual's resources are sufficient to attain a goal, it may be appropriately set for him.

A glance at an elementary school principal's duties as they presently stand reveals that some are contingent upon the efforts of other staff members while some are solely his responsibility. Clearly he often operates within a power network,[6] his performance relative to a particular goal depending upon the efforts of others. His attempts to improve instruction are necessarily mediated by his teaching staff. His ability to supply his staff with desired materials depends on resource decisions made beyond his school. Accordingly, goals related to instruction and the acquisition of supplies are appropriately set for groups. On the other hand, objectives concerned with classroom visitation and evaluation of teachers, chairing faculty meetings, and providing disciplinary support for his teachers are presently duties for which a principal is considered to have adequate resources, and hence are appropriately set for him alone.

The difficulties of establishing appropriate and significant objectives are many. Yet, their presence serves to highlight rather than diminish the importance of developing workable criteria by which the worth of goals can be judged. Without these, any MBO program is doomed to become another paper consuming routine, valued by no one and dispensed with in the shortest possible time.

PAYMENT BY RESULTS

A school administrator planning to implement an MBO program is confronted with the option of whether to link it with employee compensation. The primary reason for considering this alternative is the belief that such an arrangement will provide incentive for improved performance. This belief rests on a number of assumptions.

First, it assumes that employees operating within an MBO program need incentives beyond those integral to the program; that is, that the process of setting goals and judging performance by them (and the adjuncts of participatory goal formulation and appraisal, if these are part of the plan) are of themselves insufficient sources of motivation. This assumption requires scrutiny. Some evidence exists that target setting itself is the major influence on improved performance while subordinate participation has a positive but less potent effect.[7] Further evidence shows that criticism disrupts rather than improves subsequent performance,[8] and the danger exists that failure to receive a performance-based raise will be perceived by the employee as tantamount to a highly critical assessment of his efforts. Consequently, refining the goal setting and performance appraisal processes may be a more appropriate response to the problem of increasing motivation than a supplemental incentive system.

Second, tying performance to compensation assumes the universal attractiveness of a single kind of incentive and the efficacy of money as a motivating force. On the other hand, the ideal of providing the strongest possible incentive for *each* employee suggests an individualized approach. It is highly probable that a single kind of incentive is not the most effective for all employees, and even possible that money is a less powerful incentive than is generally supposed. The crucial question is, What kind of incentive is most effective for this particular employee? In all probability, the answer will vary among employees.

The case for a plurality of incentives can also be argued from an organizational perspective.[9] Organizations typically have available a variety of potential rewards including promotions, approval from peers and superiors, increased responsibilities, and challenging assignments. Establishing an incentive system based upon a single kind of reward has the effect of impoverishing the organization's total range of rewards, for the reward offered by the system becomes the sole indication of managerial approval.

Should the decision be made to relate MBO and compensation, a number of troublesome questions arise. Are other traditional bases of salary determination, such as experience and training and the responsibilities a position carries, to be considered in addition to performance? If so, what is the relative influence of each? Should a performance-determined raise be in addition to a guaranteed annual increase, or should raises for a position be based upon performance alone? If so, are raises awarded for hitting the target or for exceeding it, or is the raise commensurate with the degree of success? If the latter alternative is chosen, how does one deal with targets which by their nature do not permit gradation or cannot be exceeded? Is an employee penalized beyond the loss of a potential reward for falling short of his objectives? How is an employee with both individual and group goals to be rewarded? How large should a performance-based raise be to provide maximum incentive?

An adequate response to such problems requires that they be considered in terms of the impact of potential solutions upon motivation. As an example, the availability of rewards may be considered from this perspective. It is crucial to the effectiveness of an incentive system that employees feel increased effort will be rewarded. If the number which the system is able to reward is limited (that is, by factors other than performance), the character of the system parallels that of a zero-sum game.[10] This means that since the total number of rewards is fixed, if the number deserving rewards exceeds the number of rewards available, one employee is rewarded at the expense of another. This in itself has a negative impact on collegiality and morale, hence on motivation. Furthermore, under such circumstances selection among the deserving of those to be rewarded typically relies upon some form of peer comparison, such as rewarding only those who exceed their goals by a certain margin. At this point, MBO abandons its distinctive focus upon individual performance, for this means of selection entails public reckoning of the relative worth of employees, those receiving rewards having been recognized as of more value than those who do not. Finally, the zero-sum aspects of the system weaken the connection between effort and reward, for the system is incapable of expanding its capacity to reward in response to an increased number of meritorious performances. Consequently, incentive to increase effort is reduced. In contrast, maximizing the motivational power of an incentive system requires that it be possible for all members of an organization to receive rewards should they deserve them.

CONCLUSION

A major pitfall accompanying any innovation stems from taking a narrow view of the ramifications of change. Unanticipated and undesirable effects can be expected from introducing MBO into a school system. A program of this magnitude will necessarily disturb existing alignments among delicately balanced elements of the school system. For instance, one would expect the program to have decided effects upon subordinate–superordinate relationships. Such a program cannot be left to run its own course. Means are needed of assessing how well it serves its intended purposes and at what cost to other components of the school system.

REFERENCES

1. The Chicago Board of Education has implemented a management by objectives program. See *Administrative Compensation Plan,* Board of Education, City of Chicago, March 1971.

2. The discussion of student discipline from which this example is drawn is: Michael E. Manley-Casimir, "Student Discipline As Discretionary Justice," *Administrator's Notebook,* Oct. 1971.

3. This formulation of progress is borrowed from: C. West Churchman, *Challenge to Reason* (New York: McGraw-Hill Book Co., 1968), pp. 46–47.

4. Charles H. Granger, "The Hierarchy of Objectives," *Harvard Business Review,* May–June 1964, pp. 63–74.

5. *Administrative Compensation Plan,* p. 9.

6. B. Frank White and Louis B. Barnes, "Power Networks in the Appraisal Process," *Harvard Business Review,* May–June 1971, pp. 101–109.

7. Herbert H. Meyer, Emanuel Kay, and John R. P. French, Jr., "Split Roles in Performance Appraisal," *Harvard Business Review,* Jan.–Feb. 1965, p. 127.

8. Ibid., p. 126.

9. Paul H. Thompson and Gene W. Dalton, "Performance Appraisal: Managers Beware," *Harvard Business Review,* Jan.–Feb. 1970, p. 154.

10. Ibid., pp. 151–152.

MBO
in Church Organizations

Dale D. McConkey

Renewal by objectives (RBO) is a team approach designed to help us better plan, organize, and carry out His work so that we may be better stewards of our time, talent, and efforts in achieving the most desirable results for God, our church, and ourselves. As alternatives, we might also call the approach ministry by objectives or stewardship by objectives.

First, we decide what we want our church to accomplish or where we want our church to be in the future. Next, we develop an order of priorities. Which are the more important things we should do? Which should be done first? Which will result in greater benefit to the church? Then we express these priorities in the form of objectives—the results we must achieve to carry out our stewardship.

After our objectives have been established, we develop plans to achieve them. The objectives tell us *what* we want to achieve, the plans tell *how* we plan to achieve the objectives. Plans are the step-by-step explanation of the ways in which the objective will be accomplished.

Reprinted by permission of the publisher from *MBO for Non-Profit Organizations* by Dale D. McConkey, pp. 171–184. © 1975 by AMACOM, a division of American Management Associations.

Once the objectives and plans have been agreed to and we start carrying them out, we must review our progress from time to time to make sure that satisfactory progress is being made. This progress review helps us answer the questions: "Are we successfully carrying out our objectives and plans? Is it necessary to revise them?"

The value of the "team approach" lies in the proven fact that the more actively people become involved and participate in the work of the church, the more successful the church will become in carrying out its mission. The church "team" includes its pastor, its governing body, and its congregation. The congregation is especially vital to the success of RBO because, unlike the situation in many other types of organizations, the congregation is the body that must ultimately approve or pass on the totality of the results.

WHY RBO?

Most people want to see their church progress and grow. They want to do good work. They want to contribute to the church's progress in the most meaningful and rewarding manner possible.

Yet we know that some churches are more effective than others. Why? While there are probably several answers to this question, two are particularly significant to RBO.

One involves how we use our time. The other centers around how we plan and organize our efforts. Both are interrelated.

Ernest Hemingway admonished us to "never mistake motion for action." Also, we've heard people say, "He's always busy, but he never seems to get anything done." Both quotations are pertinent.

The best way to squander our precious time and effort is to become busy trying to accomplish something without first determining what it is we want to accomplish. It's rather like a postman running around trying to deliver a letter that doesn't have a name and address on the envelope.

The people in one church may stay very busy carrying out a great many activities and *hoping* that something good will happen. (This is not RBO.) The people in a second church determine what they want to happen and then align all their efforts to *make* it happen. (This is RBO.) Thus an overwhelming reason for practicing renewal by objectives is to help us accomplish the most meaningful and rewarding results for our church by first determining the most important things we want to do, by directing all the individual efforts of our team toward the things we want to accomplish, and by avoiding spending our time and energy on efforts that are not needed. Emphasis is on the results we want to achieve, not on the unorganized efforts expended.

RBO helps replace "motion sickness" with a sense of purpose and direction. Under RBO we don't get on board a ship and run around in circles hoping it will take us someplace. Instead, we first determine where we want to go and then steer a course to reach that point.

"OWNERSHIP"—THE KEY TO SUCCESS

RBO requires active involvement and participation by all members of a church. The pastor, the governing body, and the congregation—all must be actively involved and participate together to further the church's work.

Study after study has demonstrated that a person will not be really committed to helping achieve a result unless he has had a voice in determining what the result will be. Conversely, people will be more motivated to work for the success of a project if they have had a part in developing it.

Thus high commitment and high motivation usually go hand in hand with the degree to which a person believes that it is his or her project—that he or she "owns" it. "Ownership," therefore, is a big part of the foundation of successful RBO.

The late Douglas McGregor, one of the most respected behavioral scientists, emphasized the need for blending the efforts and the interest of the individual (the church member) with those of the organization (the church) when he wrote:

> Man will exercise self-direction and self-control to reach objectives to which he is committed. The most significant rewards, the satisfaction of ego and self-actualization needs, can be direct products of effort directed toward organizational objectives. The average human being learns, under proper conditions, not only to accept but to seek responsibility. The capacity to exercise a relatively high degree of imagination, ingenuity, and creativity in the solution of organizational problems is widely, not narrowly, distributed in the population. Under the conditions of modern industrial life, the intellectual potentialities of the average human being are only partially utilized.

Dr. McGregor's findings[1] highlight the value of participation to any organized group endeavor. A high degree of participation usually leads to an increased feeling of ownership. Thus all members of the church must feel they have a major voice in determining the future of their church, that they really "own" the church.

1. Douglas McGregor, *The Human Side of Enterprise* (New York: McGraw-Hill Book Co., 1960).

THE RBO SYSTEM

RBO is referred to as a system because it has several integrated components. Each must be present and must fulfill its role if the sum total is to work. The components of the RBO system are:

Establishing objectives
Developing step-by-step plans to achieve the objectives
Carrying out the plans
Reviewing progress as the plans progress
Revising objectives and plans to keep them realistic

Much like any other system, if any of these five components is missing or if it is not carrying out its proper role, the system will suffer and the desired results will not be achieved.

THE SEQUENCE IN SETTING OBJECTIVES

Figure 1 illustrates the step-by-step process for establishing objectives for a local church. Also, it indicates who in the church is primarily responsible for carrying out each of the three major phases in the sequence.

Here again, as in the section on ownership, it is emphasized that RBO will be more successful if the ideas and recommendations of the greatest possible number of people are actively sought and considered in each step of the whole process.

A high premium should be placed on getting maximum involvement by *all* members of the congregation.

Phase I   Establishing Overall Objectives

The first step in the objective-setting process is to establish overall objectives for the total church for a particular period of time. Usually these are established by a working committee comprising the pastor and the governing body. The more in tune these people are with the ideas and views of the congregation, the more successful the whole approach will usually be—especially concerning objectives that will require the later support and work by members of the congregation. This requires extensive communication and coordination with the congregation while formulating the church objectives.

Figure 1. The objective-setting process in an autonomous local church.

PHASE I

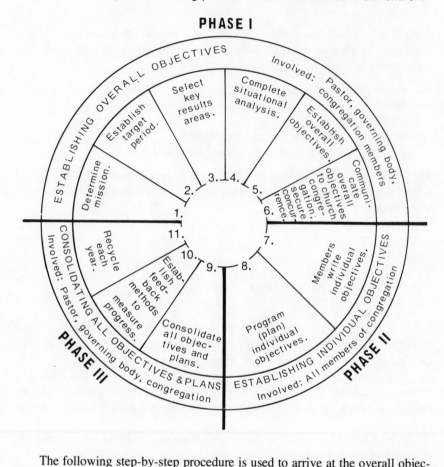

The following step-by-step procedure is used to arrive at the overall objectives of the church:

Step 1: Determine the church's mission.

Step 2: Establish the target period.

Step 3: Select the "key results areas" in which it is necessary to ultimately establish objectives for insuring the future growth and progress of the church. (These are the major "thrust" or "initiative" areas.)

Step 4: Complete a situational analysis to analyze our capability to achieve results in each of the key subject areas.

Step 5: Establish the objectives.

Step 6: Secure concurrence by the congregation of the objectives.

Once the overall objectives for the total church have been established and agreed to, they provide (1) a commitment for the total church (they state what all of the members working together must accomplish) and (2) overall guidance and direction for all members of the church as they establish their individual objectives to make the overall church objectives come true.

It is important to remember that the overall objectives for the church as a whole are not the responsibility of any one individual but, rather, the collective responsibility of all. To get action on these objectives they must be translated into individual objectives that enumerate who is responsible for what, and when. This is discussed in Step 7.

Step 1: Mission

The objective-setting process begins with the definition of the total purpose of the church. A mission statement should not be so broad that it provides little, if any, guidance, as in this example: "Our mission is to carry out God's work." This statement is so broad that it provides almost no guidance as to the areas on which the church should concentrate.

Similarly, the mission statement should not be so restrictive that it overly confines the purpose of the church. An example of an overly restrictive statement might read: "Promote a moral and spiritual atmosphere conducive to the well-being of our youth."

A balanced statement that provides a happy medium will probably include answers to these questions:

What part of God's work do we want our church to accomplish?
What is our reason for being?
What is our purpose?
What geographical area should we serve?
What people should the church serve?
What services should the church provide?

Step 2: Establish the Target Period

The target period is the length of time for which it is decided to plan and set objectives. Normally we are concerned with two target periods: long-range, which commonly means three years or more, and short-range, one year or less. Normally, long-range objectives are set first. This helps insure the growth of the church over the long pull and provides guidance as to what objectives should be set for the short range. The short-range objectives that are set within the context and guidance of the long-range objectives are the steps by which the long-range ones will be achieved; for example: A long-range objective might involve the building of a new church, which may take three years.

Annual objectives are then set to make certain the three-year objective is achieved. Examples:

First year: Secure funds and design the church.
Second year: Complete one-half of church construction.
Third year: Complete the remaining construction.

Step 3: Select Key Results Areas

These are the major areas in which the church must achieve results during the target period if it is to survive or progress, or both. They may also be referred to as the keys to success—the areas in which high performance is necessary for success. Key results areas for a typical church might include:

Level of membership
Level and sources of funds
Neighborhood acceptance
Youth participation
Membership participation
Worship facilities
Quality of leadership
Quality of services

Step 4: Complete a Situational Analysis

In this step we analyze our capability to achieve results in each of the key results areas, which we selected in Step 3. One way to do this is to take each key result area, one at a time, and discuss it in light of strengths, weaknesses, opportunities, and threats.

For example, in the first key result area (level of membership) strengths might be excellent facilities, central location, and the like. Weaknesses might be a highly mobile congregation and a high percentage of working families in the neighborhood. Two excellent opportunities could be a growing neighborhood combined with limited social and leisure-time activities outside of church. Major threats might be the possible closing of defense-related companies and a general lessening of faith and belief in religion.

A thoroughly completed situational analysis, on each of the key results areas, should provide us with excellent guidance as to what kinds of objectives we should write in Step 5. For example, the strengths and weaknesses should give us a picture of our current situation; that is, what we have to work with. They should help us answer the questions: (1) Should we have objectives that will help us capitalize on our strengths? (2) Do we need objectives to minimize our weaknesses?

The opportunities and threats are future-oriented. Questions we should ask include: (1) Should we have objectives to help us take advantage of our opportunities? (2) Do we need objectives to help us minimize the impact of the threats?

Step 5: Establishing Objectives

Having determined the major directions that we want our church to take and having arrived at a prioritized list of the key results areas in which we want to achieve better results, we are now ready to begin writing objectives. EXAMPLE: "We have determined that one of the key results areas which we want to concentrate on during 1975 is a higher degree of participation by the congregation in church activities."

The next step is to write an objective covering this key subject area.

What is an objective? For our purposes, we may define an objective as a specific statement of an end result to be achieved during a stated period of time.

An objective should always include the *what* (the end result) and the *when* (a target period or target date). EXAMPLE: "Our key result area is a higher degree of participation by the congregation in church activities."

The resulting objective might read: "By December 31, 1975, increase Sunday school attendance by a monthly average of 10 percent above the monthly average for 1974."

The date of December 31, 1975, tells by *when* the objective will be achieved. The 10 percent increase tells the *what*.

Two main categories of objectives. Although there are several different categories of objectives we might consider, the two we are interested in here we may refer to as unit objectives and individual objectives.

Unit objectives apply to the church as a whole (or to a unit of it). They are not the objectives of any one individual but are broader objectives of the organization. They set the theme and direction and provide guidance for writing individual objectives. EXAMPLE: "Increase total church membership by 100 people by July 1, 1975."

Individual objectives, as the name implies, are objectives that apply to an individual—those that he will personally carry out. EXAMPLE: "Personally secure ten new church members by July 1, 1975."

Individual objectives usually are a smaller piece of unit objectives. When the individual objectives of all members of a unit are added together, they should result in achieving the broader unit objective. EXAMPLE: "The unit objective is to secure one hundred new members; the individual objective is for ten members of the congregation to secure ten new members each."

Making objectives effective. Effective objectives should meet several criteria. They should be specific and measurable, realistic and attainable, supportive, clearly understood, have priorities assigned, and be in writing.

1. *Specific and measurable.* An objective is specific and measurable when it states exactly what is to be achieved and when progress can be gauged in the most accurate terms. EXAMPLE (poor): "Increase church membership." This is merely a statement of intent; it is not specific and measurable.

The intent could be achieved by securing only one new member or one hundred members. What do we mean? Better: "By July 1, 1975, achieve total minimum church membership of 200 (from present level of 163) and maintain at the 200 level for the remainder of 1975."

When an objective is not specific, it cannot be measured for accomplishment, we cannot formulate plans to achieve it, and we won't know what resources we will need to carry it out.

2. *Realistic and attainable*. Objectives should require us to expend more than just normal effort; they should require us to "stretch" to reach them. However, objectives should always be realistic and attainable.

The key word is "realism." Objectives that are based on hopes, desires, and wishes are seldom realistic.

3. *Supportive*. Once unit objectives have been set for the church as a whole, the objectives of all members should be established in a manner that helps carry out the church's objectives.

4. *Clearly understood*. Before starting to carry out an objective, all persons involved must clearly understand what the objective requires and what their respective roles are. Otherwise, confusion, misunderstanding, and misdirected effort will frequently result.

5. *Ranked by priority*. Like many other organizations, a church has a limit on the time and funds it can expend. Therefore, we want to make certain we are devoting our resources to the most important things and that the most important are done first. Objectives should cover these more important subjects in our work.

6. *Written form*. Objectives should always be written, to promote better understanding and to avoid confusion.

*Step 6: Enunciate and Secure Concurrence
with Overall Church Objectives*

Once the pastor and the governing body have agreed to the broad, overall objectives of the church as a whole (for a particular target period), these objectives are announced, discussed, and clarified with the congregation. The greatest possible effort should be exerted to secure overwhelming concurrence by the congregation. The success of any of these overall objectives will depend heavily upon congregational enthusiasm and support.

The objectives provide members of the congregation with the guidance they will need to write their individual objectives, which will support and help carry out the overall objectives.

Phase II   Establishing Individual Objectives

Step 7: Writing Individual Objectives

In this step, the members of the congregation write objectives for themselves, using the overall objectives written in Step 6 as guidance.

The individual objectives should support the overall objectives and should be written in the light of the criteria discussed in an earlier section, "Making Objectives Effective."

Step 8: Programming Objectives

In this phase of RBO we develop the step-by-step plans that we will follow to achieve the objectives we have written. The objective tells *what* we are going to accomplish.

Now we are concerned with the *how*—how are we going to make the objectives come true? Plans are developed in the following order:

1. *State the objective.* "Increase church membership to 200 persons by December 31, 1975."

2. *Select all practical alternatives.* There are many ways in which we might accomplish our objective. We list as many as possible of the more practical ones. They might include:

Home visits by members
Newspaper advertising
Visits by pastor
Invitations to social events
Recommendations/invitations by present members
Mailing of newsletter describing church events
Others

3. *Evaluate the alternatives.* This step consists in examining each alternative. The purpose is to boil down the list to those we want to adopt and those we want to program out. Each alternative should be examined in light of questions such as:

Is it practical—will it help us reach the objective?
What will it cost?
Have we the resources (people, time, money) to carry it out?
Is there a better alternative(s) that we might follow?
Others.

4. *Select the better alternatives.* Next, let's assume we have decided that the alternatives we will follow are home visits by members and recommendations by members. Each of these would then be programmed step by step.

5. *Program out the alternatives.* The first alternative might be programmed out as shown in Figure 2.

Phase III Consolidating All Objectives and Plans

Step 9: Consolidating Objectives and Plans

The objective-setting process began with the setting, by the governing body and the pastor, of the broad, overall objectives of the church (hopefully,

Figure 2. Plans for achieving objectives.

PERSON RESPONSIBLE: Chairman, Membership Committee

OBJECTIVE #1: Increase church membership to 200 by December 31, 1975

Major Action Steps	J	F	M	A	M	J	J	A	S	O	N	D
						January – December						
1. Visits by present members to homes of prospective members.							X					
1a. Appoint membership.	X											
1b. Determine strategy and approach.		X										
1c. Assign "quotas" to committee members.		X										
1d. Schedule the home visits.		X										
1e. Complete all home visits.			X									
1f. Committee meeting to review interim progress.					X							
1g. Hold orientation meeting at church for new prospects.						X						
1h. Induct new members.							X					
1i. Evaluate final results of membership drive.							X					

with the maximum possible recommendations and guidance from the congregation as to what these objectives should be).

Next, these broad, overall objectives were enunciated to the congregation so that its members could participate in the total RBO system.

Using these objectives as guidance, members of the congregation established their own individual objectives to support and help carry out the overall church objectives.

Step 9 involves the combining and consolidating of all individual objectives into one "package." The key question that must be answered at this stage is: Will all the individual objectives and plans add up at least to the overall objectives of the church?

Expressed differently, if all the individual objectives and plans are carried out as written, will they result in the achievement of the broad, overall objectives of the church? If the answer is "yes," our job is fairly well completed. However, if the answer is "no," we have two alternative chores to complete:

1. We must establish additional plans and objectives to make up for the void. This alternative should always be exhausted before lowering the overall church objectives.

2. We must change the broad, overall objectives of the church. Regardless of which alternative is pursued, we must conclude with objectives and plans that are *realistic* and *attainable*.

Step 10: Establishing Feedback to Measure Progress

This step is to decide when (how often) and how (with what methods) we will measure our progress as our target year begins and we start to carry out our objectives and plans.

Generally, we want to measure our progress often enough so that we will know at the earliest possible time if progress is not proceeding as planned. This permits us to take corrective action while there is still time left to take the action. If we waited until the end of the target period, there would be no time to do anything.

Therefore, interim or periodic checks during the target period are essential.

Step 11: Recycling Each Year

The last step in the process is completed each year for as long as the church is practicing renewal by objectives. We start all over with Step 1 and complete all the steps for the next target period.

Tailoring MBO to Hospitals

Herbert H. Hand
A. Thomas Hollingsworth

An increasingly difficult task faced by today's hospital administrators is the efficient utilization of employees and the retention of high performers. This article is concerned with the general problem of the administration of a hospital wage system and specifically concerned with the problems of employee productivity and turnover. Management by objectives (MBO) is suggested as a method by which administrators can best use their budgets to maximize utilization and retention of the hospital's human assets.

Hospital administrators report that hospitals have two major objectives: to provide quality patient care and to efficiently utilize financial resources. Inasmuch as salaries and wages are estimated to be 60–70 percent of the total operating costs of an average hospital, salary-wage expenditures are intimately related to the efficient utilization of financial resources. Total wage costs are, of course, a function of staff size, wage rates, employee benefits, and employee turnover. Therefore, as the effectiveness of individual employees decreases, either more staff is required (and wage costs subsequently increase) or the quality of patient care decreases and the hospital's objectives are unfulfilled.

Reprinted with permission from *Business Horizons,* February 1975.

The importance of employee turnover as a portion of total wage cost should be noted. Turnover costs contribute to both direct and indirect labor costs through inefficient job performance, improper supervision, and scheduling problems. Turnover rates for hospitals range from 36–72 percent annually.[1] Hospital administrators should be very much aware of how wages affect the vital areas of both employee productivity and employee turnover, because these areas appear to have a strong functional link to the two primary objectives of hospitals.

One could reasonably assume that hospital administrators have made a number of attempts to relate wages to productivity and turnover. However, this is not the case. The majority of hospitals base wage increases primarily on tenure. The theory underlying this practice is that productivity improvement is primarily a function of time on the job and that rewards should be given to those who remain on the staff rather than keep high producers on the job.

This practice undermines any attempt to relate wages to productivity and therefore fails to utilize the motivational potential of wages. The succeeding paragraphs will deal with the effect of pay on employee turnover and productivity. In view of the large number of variables that are thought to affect productivity and turnover, the general recommendations that follow should be tailored to specific hospitals.

PAY AND PRODUCTIVITY

Measuring Employee Output

A hospital employee's output is a difficult quantity to determine. It is often confused through the use of macro-type measures, and it is often erroneously measured by the amount of cost reduction (or addition) attained over a period of time per employee. However, before pay can be related to productivity, a viable method of measuring individual performance must be utilized.

A number of traditional measures of productivity are used in hospitals. One is patient days, the unit of measure that represents facility utilization and services rendered between the census taking time on two successive days. This measure does not take ambulatory care into consideration, so adjusted patient days (APD) are often utilized to measure the total range of services provided per day by the hospital.

Another traditional measure is the full-time equivalent employee (FTE) to patient ratio. In 1970, the national average was 292 FTEs per 100 patients. This measure allows a macrocomparison among hospitals. Unfortunately, hospitals differ to a large extent, and such comparisons are poor at best.

The preceding macro-type measures must be supplemented by more precise measures if valid indicators of both departmental and individual effort are to be realized. Since hospitals provide so many functions, there is a need for a number of measurements particularized by functional or departmental area. Such a list is shown in Figure 1.

These measures help evaluate a department's performance within the hospital, but they specify only labor input as an incremental average of total output. This may not measure an individual's effort. For instance, a single lab test may take five times as long to run as another. Therefore, weighting systems are needed. The table and corresponding weighting systems demonstrate the complexity of measuring individual performance across the numerous functional areas found in hospitals. Specific forms of performance measurement are needed if wages are to be successfully related to productivity.

Figure 1. Measures of performance in hospitals.

Department	Occasion of service
Anesthesiology	Number of patients, hours of administration and use
Basal metabolism	Number of tests
Blood bank	Number of 500-cc units prepared for transfusions
Central supply	Dollar value of processed requisitions
Delivery rooms	Number of deliveries
Dietary	Number of meals served
Electrocardiology	Number of examinations
Housekeeping	Hours of service rendered to various departments
Inhalation therapy	Number of hours that oxygen is administered
Laboratory	Number of tests
Laundry	Pounds or pieces of laundry processed
Nursing	Hours or days of service
Occupational therapy	Hours of teaching and supervision
Operation of plant	Thousands of pounds of steam produced, plus pounds of ice produced, plus kilowatt-hours of electricity produced
Operating room	Number of operations, hours of use
Pharmacy	Dollar value of prescriptions and requisitions processed
Physical therapy	Number of treatments
Postoperative or postanesthesia recovery rooms	Number of patient hours of service
Radiology/diagnostic	Number of films taken, plus number of fluoroscopic examinations
Radiology/therapeutic	Number of X-ray treatments, plus number of radium implementations, plus number of treatments by radioactive elements

SOURCE: Nicole Williams, *The Management of Hospital Employee Productivity* (Chicago: American Hospital Association, 1973).

Money as Motivator

Individual performance is thought to be a function of motivation and ability. Motivation to perform is determined by a number of variables. Specifically, how should the wage aspect of an administrator's budget affect the motivation of employees? Four conditions must be present for money to be a motivator.

First, a direct linkage must be perceived between pay and performance. Second, money must have some importance to the individual. Third, there must be a minimum of negative consequences associated with high performance. Fourth, conditions should provide intrinsic as well as extrinsic rewards.

Intrinsic rewards are those that are internal to an individual; they are provided through accomplishments. Extrinsic rewards are provided by the organization and are external to the individual (for example, a pay increase). Pay is a complex variable. Pay is important not only in absolute amount, but also in perceived equity and in the administration of the pay system. When pay is treated as a quasi-fringe benefit by management, it cannot be an effective motivator; it must be directly related to performance to be effective.

Although money is a motivational tool, there is no well-defined theory that relates money to performance in organizations. However, a number of incentive programs have attempted to relate pay to productivity.

Incentive plans, no matter how well conceived, cannot compensate for deficiencies in other variables contributing to the total output of the organization. These plans can only attempt to improve the wage–performance relationship.

For example, one study compared the incentive systems of two hospitals. The sample consisted of 146 registered nurses (73 from each institution). The extrinsic reward policies in the two hospitals were highly differentiated. In one, rewards were based on effort; in the other, they were based almost strictly on tenure. The results of the study demonstrated that the nurses' performance was significantly greater in the hospital offering rewards based on effort. The authors feel that pay was a sufficient but not necessary cause for encouraging a high degree of effort on the part of the nurses.

Another study reported an incentive plan set up in a 205-bed hospital. A cost reduction program was based solely on cost savings (not performance). The program was deemed successful, and the success seemed to be the result of two variables. First, the hospital had an efficient cost system, which reported the monthly financial status of departments.

Second, the incentives were paid within the same time period as the cost reductions. This point is important, since it attempts to link wages directly with performance.

A third study compared hospitals with and without incentive systems. The individuals in the hospital without an incentive system tended to feel that pay is a function of a number of variables *other than performance*. The workers in the hospital with an incentive system tended to feel that pay is significantly related to their performance.

PAY AND ATTRITION

Turnover is a costly problem for any organization. Hospitals are no exception. Although there is no standard measure of turnover in hospitals, estimates range from 3–6 percent per month or 36–72 percent yearly. This figure appears to be substantially higher than that for most industrial concerns.

In 1968, it was estimated that the cost of replacing a low-skilled worker in a hospital was $300 and of replacing a staff nurse or department head, $500–$1,000. These costs include separation activities, advertising, interviewing, physical examination, payroll, orientation, training, and the initial job inefficiency caused by ínexperience.[2] More recent figures are not available, but certainly costs have risen substantially.

In order to reduce turnover, the rate of turnover must be determined as well as where it is occurring in the hospital. Two methods of determining rate of turnover and whether it is localized or generalized follow:

$$\frac{\text{Total separations for the month}}{\text{Number on payroll at midmonth}} \times 100 = \text{monthly turnover rate}$$

$$\frac{\text{Number of employees continuing on payroll for full year}}{\text{Number of employees on payroll on first day of the year}} \times 100 = \text{annual stability rate}$$

These two equations have three interpretations.

Turnover localized to specific jobs and positions. This occurs when both ratios are high. A high monthly turnover rate demonstrates that there is a turnover problem. However, when this is coupled with a high stability rate, turnover for the hospital in general is not high—a few departments are causing the high turnover rate, not the hospital in general.

General turnover problem. This occurs when the monthly turnover rate is high and the annual stability rate is low. This demonstrates that turnover is high and is occurring throughout the hospital.

Acceptable turnover rate—An acceptable turnover rate can be defined by a low turnover rate and high stability rate. This demonstrates that there are no specific problems, and, in general, the stability of the hospital's work force is high.

This approach indicates to an administrator the degree of his turnover problem and tells him whether it is a general problem or one confined to specific departments or jobs. By carefully utilizing the above information, an administrator can determine the extent of the difficulty and also where his efforts should be directed.

These measures define the problem of turnover but not its causes. James March and Herbert Simon, after a review of the literature, concluded that the major determinant in the decision to leave an organization is an individual's job satisfaction. As satisfaction increases, the probability of leaving decreases. The authors also postulated a number of variables affecting job satisfaction: conformity of job to self-image, predictability of job relationships, and conformity of job and other roles.[3] Based on the preceding variables, it is theorized that when an individual is inclined to leave an organization and perceives a number of attractive or equally attractive alternatives, he is not likely to remain. This indicates the complexity of the decision to leave a particular hospital.

A number of studies in hospitals and industry have illustrated the importance of job satisfaction to turnover. A study at the Mount Sinai Hospital in New York City found four major causes of employee separations: unsatisfactory interpersonal relationships, dissatisfaction with ratings, dissatisfaction with the pay systems, and general disappointment related to expectations (actual experiences did not match hospital advertising).

A second study concluded that turnover was inversely related to job satisfaction. Two other reviews of the literature concluded that there was a consistent negative relationship between job satisfaction and turnover. However, no simple relationship was found between job satisfaction and performance. Another study, after a review of the satisfaction literature, found that there was little evidence to support any relationship between job satisfaction and productivity, but there was a relationship between job satisfaction and turnover.

The above studies exemplify the fact that the decision to leave a job, while based on job satisfaction, is a complex decision confounded by a myriad of variables. The remainder of this section will examine job satisfaction with emphasis on how it can be affected by pay and how pay can aid in reducing turnover.

Job satisfaction is a multidimensional concept. Larry L. Cummings and Donald P. Schwab, after an extensive literature search, concluded that job satisfaction is a highly variable construct and must be measured in various ways.[4] Hence, total job satisfaction is the result of a number of causal variables. Pay distribution is only one of a number of reasons for job dissatisfaction. However, it is the primary one with which we are concerned. Its contribution to total job satisfaction may vary in different situations, but pay dissatisfaction is a probable major cause for attrition and may influence turnover even when it is a relatively unimportant determinant of total satisfaction.

A number of variables are related to pay satisfaction: importance of pay, job characteristics, and perceived equity in the pay system. Two notes of caution must be mentioned. First, no well-defined relationship between satisfaction and productivity has been shown. For instance, in a classic study, David L. Cherrington, Joseph H. Reitz, and William E. Scott found that while pay did increase job satisfaction in all cases, it did not increase performance unless it was directly related to performance.[5]

Second, administrators should not rely on money to solve all their problems.

There is a tendency for hospital administrators to overemphasize the importance of economic rewards. While they rated wages as the primary determinants of employee satisfaction, employees did not. In a study of 83 nursing homes in Pennsylvania, Robert Percorchik and Borden H. Nelson found that while only 25 percent of those leaving cited pay as the cause of leaving, 40 percent of the administrators felt that pay was really the cause.[6] It might be generally concluded that all supervisors tend to overrate the importance of pay, relative to their subordinates.

These findings illustrate the complex relationship between pay and attrition. The problem for a budget director is to determine an optimum allocation of wages to minimize turnover. A variable budget approach is recommended to allow for specific differences of employees and to differentially reward superiors who are instrumental in decreasing attrition. These recommendations are covered fully in the final section regarding the implementation of an MBO program.

THE MBO PROGRAM

Management by objectives is recommended as a particularly effective method of relating salary and wages to productivity and attrition. Ideally, the program should be initiated when both the executive director and the board of directors not only establish positive support for the program, but also clearly define the overall mission of the hospital. Subsequently, the executive director should spend substantial blocks of time with the directors of the various services performed by the hospital (see Figure 2).

The purpose of these meetings is to have each director establish more specific objectives that will support the hospital missions. Upon completion of the objectives-setting task, the director meets with his or her subordinates (see Director—Division of Fiscal Services portion of Figure 1) to establish goals that are compatible with the director's objectives. This process is continued through the hospital organization until all employees have taken part in the objectives-setting process. There are a number of suggested measures of activities in hospitals, and these measures should serve as a guide whenever possible.

Figure 2. Partial organization chart showing a sample hospital.

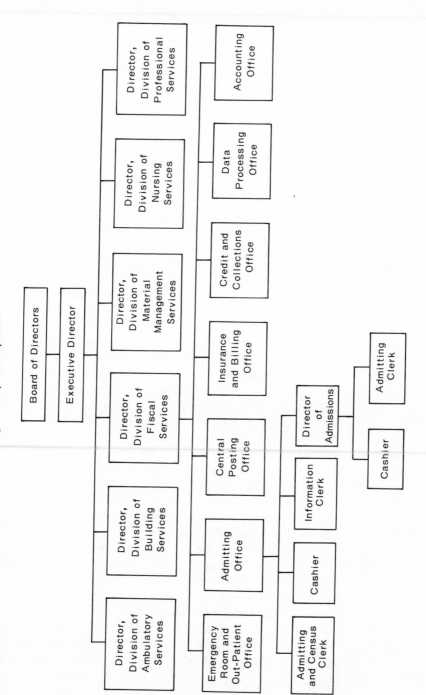

William E. Reif and Gerald Bassford indicate that the crux of MBO is setting objectives, developing action plans, conducting periodic reviews, and appraising annual performance.[7] It is incumbent upon the MBO program to take cost factors into consideration. Each supervisor should be provided financial performance records by which the performance efficiency of each individual can be ascertained. This is a very promising approach for gauging not only administrative performance in hospitals but also professional performance, such as nursing services, laboratory, EEG, EKG, inhalation therapy, pharmacy, and anesthesia.

For instance, while laundry can be measured by counting the output, a nurse's performance contains intangible items not readily measurable. An MBO program with monthly reviews is one of the best means of judging these intangible efforts. This program would require each supervisor to judge each subordinate's performance in relation to the overall objectives of the department and explicitly relate performance to objectives. Substantial evidence exists that MBO and employee compensation should be directly related.

The program recommended in Figure 3 is intended to decrease costs and improve patient care. However, quality is a major aspect of patient care and a measure of this is needed. More objective standards of quality should be utilized, such as average length of stay in terms of diagnoses, correlations between preoperative and postoperative diagnoses and between antemortem and postmortem diagnoses. Specific checklists have been established to measure various aspects of quality, such as patient welfare, patient comfort, patient charts, administering medication, and fulfilling doctors' orders.

These checklists should be established for each department so that quality does not deteriorate while attempting to cut costs. This quality feedback could originate from a number of sources, and it could be used to develop a profile of a particular department or group. For example, a number of hospitals utilize patient feedback obtained on a follow-up questionnaire after the patient has been released for approximately ten days. In order to develop a profile, a number of sources would be used, including doctors, visitors, relatives, patients, and others utilizing the department's services. These measures could aid an administrator in determining trends of performance quality.

Figure 3 shows that the establishment of an MBO program can provide a springboard to develop not only performance measures but also job satisfaction measures. Following the job satisfaction track of Figure 3 indicates how administrators may work with the job attrition problem within the context of an MBO program. In a similar manner, the reader should concurrently follow the performance measure track to compensation. It should be specifically noted that both tracks merge at the superior-subordinate conferences where *all* job satisfaction measures (including salary or wage) and performance are openly discussed and evaluated.

Figure 3. A systematic program for improving a wage administration
program.

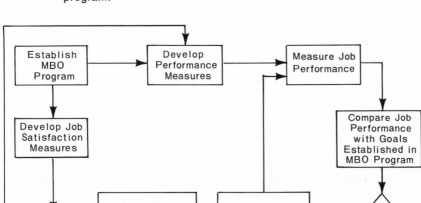

Although such a system appears to be initially simple, one should consider
that a major problem in MBO is implementation of the program. Commitment
to the precepts of management by objectives is perhaps the single most critical
factor in improving a wage administration program in hospitals.

The above program is complex. However, hospitals are complex organizations, and oversimplified measures of performance will not suffice.

The recommended MBO program considers all of the aspects commonly
associated with determining output in hospitals: individual effort, technology,
supervisory skills, raw inputs, clarity of job specifications, ability, and motiva-

tion. Any system with a high degree of validity and reliability will have to be complex and will require a great deal of sophistication on the part of all managers involved.

REFERENCES

1. Training, Research, and Special Division, *Analyzing and Reducing Turnover in Hospitals* (New York: United Hospital Fund of New York, 1969), p. 2.
2. Training, Research, and Special Division, *Analyzing and Reducing Turnover in Hospitals* (New York: United Hospital Fund of New York, 1968), p. 6.
3. James March and Herbert Simon, *Organizations* (New York: John Wiley and Sons, 1958).
4. Larry L. Cummings and Donald P. Schwab, "Theories of Performance and Satisfaction: A Review," *Industrial Relations,* Oct. 1970, pp. 408–30.
5. David L. Cherrington, Joseph H. Reitz, and William E. Scott, Jr., "Effects of Contingent and Noncontingent Reward on the Relationship Between Satisfaction and Task Performance," *Journal of Applied Psychology,* Dec. 1971, pp. 531–36.
6. Robert Percorchik and Borden H. Nelson, "Employee Turnover in Nursing Homes," *American Journal of Nursing,* Feb. 1973, pp. 289–90.
7. William E. Reif and Gerald Bassford, "What MBO Really Is," *Business Horizons,* June 1973, pp. 23–30.

A Study of
Management by Objectives
in a Professional Organization

Y. K. Shetty
Howard M. Carlisle

Introduction

During the 1960s the concept of Management by Objectives (MBO) generated widespread interest and experimentation in industrial organizations. MBO is a process whereby the members of an organization define its goals involving an identification of each subunit's and each individual's major areas of responsibility in terms of results expected. These measures are then used as guides in managing the organization and assessing the contribution of each subunit and individual. The proponents of the concept—Drucker,[1] McGregor,[2] Humble,[3] Odiorne,[4] and others—agree that a properly implemented MBO system should improve the motivation and performance of participants.

The Management by Objectives system appears to be consistent with the nature of professional organizations such as the faculties of universities. It

This study was made possible through the financial assistance from the Division of Research, Utah State University, and the College of Business Research Fund. We wish to express our thanks to our colleagues Drs. Robert Mecham and Allen Kartchner for their assistance in statistical analysis.

Reprinted with permission from *The Journal of Management Studies*, February 1975.

187

MANAGING BY OBJECTIVES

shows potential for systematic evaluation and improvement of the performance of professional employees. The research reported here was an attempt to offset the lack of empirical investigation of the applicability of such a programme within a university.

Previous Research

Although considerable literature is devoted to the general area of MBO, it includes few reports of empirical research into applications of the concept. The available research results point to four major conclusions. First, changes in attitudes, performance, communication, and interpersonal relationships appear to be positively associated with MBO. Second, certain structural and personality factors seem to influence the negative and positive aspects of the programmes. Third, problems inherent in the programme include the difficulty of linking the incentive system to the performance level, and the tendency to develop excessive formal requirements. Lastly, the completed studies noted that the administration of, or the manner in which MBO was implemented affected the perceived effectiveness of the programme.[5]

Research suggests that professionals such as engineers, researchers, and professors are more involved than nonprofessionals in their jobs and are more anxious for an opportunity to participate in making decisions relating to them.[6] Since their work is basically intellectual and creative, they perform well when considerable autonomy is coupled with a supportive environment. Their strong task-orientation also means that they want involvement, responsibility, and a high degree of self-control. They prefer not to be directed and controlled in the same way as the nonprofessional employees in the organization. MBO therefore appears to be a natural system for such employees, since it gives them an opportunity to set their own standards and evaluate their own performances.

The Present Study

In exploring the applicability of MBO to a university and to evaluating such a programme, our specific objectives were to: (1) identify the reactions of participating faculty members to the MBO programme; (2) assess the degree of variation in reactions among faculty members by professional rank, tenure status, length of service, and academic discipline; and (3) examine the influence of different implementation processes on the success of the programme.

Research Sample and Methodology

This study was conducted in a public university employing roughly 600 faculty members and having an enrollment of approximately 9,000 students. An in-depth questionnaire was administered to participating faculty members after the programme had been in progress for one academic year. The questionnaire was distributed to 236 faculty members. Of these 117 were returned and 109 had usable data.*

Findings and Analysis

The participants were asked to respond to a question that contained ten subparts. The subparts related to different criteria hypothesized to measure the success of the programme.

Programme success could have been measured through many criteria such as changes in motivation, behaviour, and performance, or as increased organizational effectiveness. The sources of data to be evaluated could include observation by others, performance records, and self-report data from the respondents. For this study, self-report data were utilized because of the nonavailability of other criteria. The answers to the ten-part question described the degree to which changes occurred as a result of the programme. The responses were scored on a five-point scale: "significant improvement," "slight improvement," "no change," "slight decrease," and "significant decrease." Table 1 presents the summary of the responses related to this question.

Faculty Reactions to the MBO Programme

The magnitude of the percentages in the No Change column suggests that the MBO programme has not caused major modifications in the areas specified. The greatest change was associated with the area of better understanding the goals and priorities of the department.

It may be that one year was not long enough to produce major changes in behaviour and actions of the participants. Nonetheless, considering the problems inherent in introducing changes of such a sensitive nature into any ongoing organization, the results were within a range that could be considered encouraging. Furthermore, the results are quite consistent with earlier studies conducted in industrial organizations.[7] The most frequently mentioned benefits in these studies were: greater awareness of organizational goals, better planning, more realistic understanding of job expectations, availability of objective performance measures, and improved communication. Results of our study indicate that objective-oriented programmes in academic environments also improve these factors.

---

* Since the programme was voluntary, less than 50 percent of the academic departments participated, involving less than half the faculty. Of the 236 faculty members participating, 117 returned the questionnaire. It is a theoretical possibility that participants with certain biases might have responded while others did not. Any such bias could not have been too strong, however, based on interviews with selected nonresponding faculty members.

Table 1. Faculty Reactions to the MBO Programme (N = *109*).

	DEGREE OF PERCEIVED CHANGE (PERCENT REPORTING)				
CRITERIA	SIGNIFICANT IMPROVEMENT	SLIGHT IMPROVEMENT	NO CHANGE	SIGNIFICANT DECREASE	SLIGHT DECREASE
Understanding of departmental goals and priorities	15.6	31.1	48.6	2.8	1.9
Help in career planning and developing professional objectives	8.5	34.9	50.9	5.7	0.0
Understanding of departmental expectations	8.6	30.5	57.1	3.8	0.0
Accuracy with which performance was measured	7.0	30.0	58.0	5.0	0.0
Performance	8.4	25.5	60.4	3.8	1.9
Support received from the department	6.7	24.0	63.5	4.8	1.0
Commitment to the university	5.6	21.5	65.4	5.6	1.9
Communication with the department head	4.9	14.6	75.6	4.9	0.0
Relationship with the department head	6.6	12.3	77.3	1.9	1.9
Relationship with the dean	5.7	12.3	69.8	4.7	7.5

Influence of Organizational Variables

The relationships between certain selected personal and organizational variables such as professional rank, tenure, length of service, and field of discipline and the perceived success of the MBO programme were examined. Toward that end, an index of "programme success" was obtained for each participant by averaging his responses on a five-point scale (from "significant improvement" with an assigned value of 5 to "significant decrease" with an assigned value of 1) for all 10 areas outlined in Table 1. Before the ten criteria were combined into an overall index of "programme success" interitem correlations were performed. Interitem correlation coefficients between criteria variables ranged from 0.37 to 0.76 with a median of 0.51. The results of the comparison of different groups—professional rank, tenure status, years of service, and the academic discipline—in one-way analysis of variance for the perceived success of the programme are presented in Table 2. Since three of the four variables examined demonstrated statistically significant differences, certain generalizations can be deduced.

Table 2. Relationship between Selected Organizational Variables and Perceived Success of the MBO Programme (N = 109).

VARIABLES	MEAN SCORES	S.D.	
Professional rank			
Professor (*N* = 24)	3.051	0.497	
Associate Professor (*N* = 29)	3.181	0.532	
Assistant Professor (*N* = 41)	3.542	0.592	*F* ratio 7.97 *
Instructor (*N* = 15)	2.864	0.386	*d/f* 3/105
Tenure			
Tenured (*N* = 62)	3.160	0.500	*F* ratio 3.07 ‡
Nontenured (*N* = 47)	3.356	0.665	*d/f* 1/107
Length of service			
1–3 (years (*N* = 32)	3.416	0.607	
4–7 years (*N* = 34)	3.335	0.537	*F* ratio 4.59 †
8 years or more (*N* = 43)	3.045	0.552	*d/f* 2/106
Academic discipline			
Business education (*N* = 5)	3.846	0.663	
Sociology (*N* = 10)	3.421	0.737	
Art, theater art, and speech (*N* = 11)	3.124	0.761	
Music (*N* = 5)	3.520	0.396	*F* ratio 1.21
English (*N* = 23)	3.183	0.566	*d/f* 8/100
Math, physics, chemistry, botany, and zoology (*N* = 18)	3.192	0.483	
Language and philosophy (*N* = 15)	3.070	0.620	
History (*N* = 10)	3.239	0.545	
Dairy and veterinary science (*N* = 12)	3.262	0.339	

* $P < 0.001$
† $P < 0.02$
‡ $P < 0.10$

Professional Rank

In the professional rank cluster, the assistant professors perceived the programme in most favourable terms. Most assistant professors are young and without tenure. Such individuals may show a more positive response to a new programme such as MBO for at least three related reasons. First, many of the assistant professors have fairly immediate professional goals and the system of MBO provides an opportunity to verbalize and communicate these goals to peers and administrators. Second, these young members are striving for organizational visibility and recognition, and the associated higher professional status and accompanying benefits. Naturally, any system that helps them to attain these will be looked upon with a favourable attitude. Third, if applying MBO is considered innovative, then it is more likely that the assistant professors, who are generally newcomers to the organization, will perceive this more positively than will the older, more established members, particularly full professors.

Instructors, compared to assistant professors, generally lack terminal degrees, and it is becoming increasingly difficult to progress in universities without such a degree. Consequently the instructors may prefer a different system of evaluation other than one emphasizing goals and concrete results. That may be why they perceive the programme negatively. Full professors, on the other hand, may be assuming that they have reached their zenith as teachers and/or researchers and little, if anything, is needed to improve their performance.

Tenure

The tenure status of the respondents is significantly related to the perceived success of the programme, with nontenured faculty exhibiting a higher level of programme success than tenured faculty. The significance of tenure to one's perception probably reflects the fact that once a faculty member acquires tenure, his resistance to controls of any type increases. Individuals with tenure and the higher academic ranks might feel that they have been adequately evaluated, and any new system of appraisal represents a threat to and a reflection on their established identity and reputation.

Length of Service

The length of service was significantly related to the criteria hypothesized as measuring the success of the programme. Faculty members with few years of service perceived the programme more positively than did those having longer service. A possible explanation is that through long-time association with the organization one favours perceiving further success as being based on strong loyalty to existing values and procedures. Also, those who are successful and satisfied with current conditions are generally inclined to maintain the status quo. Furthermore, long association with an organization can promote an identification with the past and with the existing structure that precludes a willing change to a new system. These three variables—professional rank, tenure, and length of service—are obviously related factors. Professional rank tends to be a function of length of service. In many cases tenure is similarly related. In our sample, 64 percent of the associate and full professors had tenure and 66 percent of them had four or more years of service.

Implementation Process

Many scholars [8] have noted, and other research findings also indicate, that the implementation process itself can influence the success of the programme, The most important aspects include the organization's support for developing and implementing the programme, the participant's role in the process, characteristics of the goals themselves, and the frequency of feedback to the participants. The participants in our study were asked to respond to questions relating to the implementation of the MBO programme in their departments. The questions grouped under four major areas—organizational support, participant's role, goal characteristics, and the nature of feedback. The five-point scale described the extent to which certain characteristics were found in these areas. Differences in certain characteristics of the implementation process were associated with criteria hypothesized to represent the programme success (see Table 3).

Table 3. Correlation between Certain Implementation Process Variables and Perceived Success of MBO Programme.

VARIABLES	PERCEIVED SUCCESS OF THE PROGRAMME (r)
Organizational support	
In your opinion, how much effort did your department devote to develop departmental goals and priorities?	0.257 †
How much of an interest do you think your department head has in the goal setting programme?	0.247 †
Participant's role	
How much influence did you have in setting departmental goals and priorities?	0.305 *
To what degree do you feel you had freedom to select your personal goals?	0.216 ‡
To what degree do you feel you had control over the means of reaching your goals?	0.193 §
Goal characteristics	
To what extent were you aware of the specific goals established for your department?	0.318 *
To what extent do you feel compatibility existed between departmental goals and your personal goals?	0.289 †
What in your opinion was the level of difficulty of your goals under MBO?	−0.002
To what extent do you feel you had too many goals?	0.037
To what extent were your goals sufficiently result-oriented so that anticipated behaviour was explicit and performance could be measured?	0.135
Nature of feedback	
How often were you given feedback on your progress toward goals?	0.496 *

* $P < 0.001$
† $P < 0.01$
‡ $P < 0.02$
§ $P < 0.05$

Organizational Support

The data indicate that the support given by the organization to the MBO programme, as perceived by participants, was significantly related to the programme success. The participants who felt that their departments had devoted a high degree of effort to developing goals and priorities considered the programme more beneficial than did participants who perceived otherwise $(r = 0.257, P < 0.01)$. In addition, the participants who indicated that their department head had a high degree of interest in the programme also perceived the programme in more positive terms $(r = 0.247, P < 0.01)$. These findings are consistent with the notion that an active involvement in and support by the administrators in the design and implementation of MBO can have significant impact on the success of the programme.[9]

Substantial organizational support for an MBO programme can be viewed as a prerequisite for programme success. Unless the participants believe that the MBO programme has the support of administration as demonstrated through actual effort, they will probably not take the programme seriously. Second, organizational support, in terms of effort devoted, may also influence the understanding and acceptance, as well as the commitment to, the programme. This is particularly true if the participants lack previous experience with such a programme. Under these conditions, administrators may have to devote considerable time to explaining the concept, including its objectives and procedures, and to otherwise preparing the participants.

Participant's Role

Our results support the conclusion that the degree of participant involvement in setting goals influences programme success. Participants who felt a relatively high degree of involvement in setting departmental goals and priorities also perceived that the programme yielded better results $(r = 0.305, P < 0.001)$. The participant's freedom in selecting personal goals and his control over the means to be used in reaching these goals also significantly correlated with programme success $(r = 0.216, P < 0.02, r = 0.193, P < 0.05)$. This finding is consonant with other research results and with the popular notion that participation is an important factor in the succes of MBO.[10] It contradicts, however, one of the recent findings of Carroll and Tosi,[11] who reported that the perceived amount of a participant's influence in setting goals was not related to any of the variables assumed to represent the programme success. Since their study was conducted in an industrial setting, it needs to be emphasized that the academic community in which this study took place differs in many ways from the industrial environment. In particular, values and attitudes common in the academic milieu may not prevail in industry. Research comparing industrial managers and university professors shows that strong autonomy needs and anti-authoritarian or participative bias significantly govern the attitudes and behaviour of the latter group.[12] Professionals such as university professors may therefore expect and respond to a higher degree of involvement and participation in the goal-setting process than would industrial managers.

Participation in setting departmental goals would enhance the professional's understanding of the problems and opportunities existing in the department and thereby broaden his perspective. For an individual's goals to be motivating, they must be meaningful, desirable, and meet his personal needs. Freedom in selecting personal goals and control over the means to accomplish these goals should therefore strengthen personal commitment to the programme's success.

Goal Characteristics

The characteristics that correlated with programme success were the clarity and specificity of departmental goals and priorities, the degree of perceived compatibility of departmental and personal goals, the level of difficulty of performance goals, the number of these goals, and the result and action orientation of the goals. The clarity and specificity of departmental goals positively and significantly related to the hypothesized criteria of programme success ($r = 0.318$, $P < 0.001$). This substantiates previous research which indicates that a clear statement of organizational objectives improves individual performance. The degree of congruence between departmental and personal goals, and perceived success of the programme correlated significantly ($r = 0.289$, $P < 0.01$). That is, as the level of incongruency decreases the level of perceived programme success increases significantly. This is also consistent with findings which show that when attainment of organizational objectives is a means to attainment of personal objectives the participant's motivation and satisfaction increase.[13]

The level of difficulty of performance goals was not significantly related to programme success. Likewise, no clear relationship was found between the number of performance goals, result and action orientation of performance goals, and the perceived success of the programme. A clear understanding of the departmental goals and priorities would reduce ambiguity and uncertainty relative to how individual goals fit in with organizational goals. Such understanding would also minimize role ambiguity and help the individual determine precisely what is expected of him, thus minimizing the tension and anxiety that result from uncertainty about job expectations. As personal and organization goals assume greater congruency, the attainment of organizational goals becomes the means of attaining personal goals.

Nature of Feedback

The fact most strongly correlated with MBO success is the feedback received by the participants. The frequency with which feedback is given to the participants is clearly associated with their perceived success of the programme in the expected direction ($r = 0.496$, $P < 0.001$)—the more frequent the feedback the more positive the participant's reaction. This is consistent with the findings of Carroll and Tosi,[14] Cook,[15] and Ivancevich.[16] Frequent feedback allows the participants to see how well they are progressing toward their performance goals. It also serves the purpose of systematically identifying obstacles to goal achievement and thus facilitates their removal. Further, sometimes the original goals are not realistic or sufficiently challenging, or conditions change and goals need to be adjusted. In such cases, the feedback mechanism provides opportunities for updating or adding new goals, and can thereby enhance the motivational value of the programme.

Concluding Remarks

The study shows that objective-oriented programmes such as MBO, when applied to an academic setting, increase awareness of organizational goals, improve planning, enhance understanding of job expectations, provide better data for performance appraisal, and improve performance and communication. Certain organizational variables seem to influence the perception of the participants concerning the programme success. Specifically, teachers with lower academic rank—assistant professors in particular—teachers without tenure, and those with fewer years of service consider the programme in more positive terms than do those of higher rank who are tenured and have more years of service.

Administrators must recognize the implications of these contraints when planning to implement such a programme. From an administrative point of view, decisions regarding the application of the programme cannot logically be based on an assumption of homogeneity within the group, despite the uniform nature of the work itself. Since organizational factors by their nature are not susceptible to direct change by the administrators, they must be taken into account. Furthermore, by implication, our results suggest a need to tailor each MBO programme to match the different organizational status of the participants.

The administrative processes utilized to design and implement an MBO programme, as might be expected, have a strong influence on its success. The success of an MBO programme is most strongly correlated with: the frequency of feedback, clarity and specificity of departmental goals, and the participant's influence in setting departmental goals and priorities. Our results suggest that more attention must be given to the implementation process. This is underestimated in the existing literature concerning MBO, as are other variables useful in identifying and predicting the success of the programme. Some of these variables, such as the participation in goal setting, may be comparatively more critical for professional employees in an academic environment than for industrial employees.

REFERENCES

1. Peter Drucker, *The Practice of Management* (New York: Harper & Row, 1954).
2. Douglas McGregor, "An Uneasy Look at Performance Appraisal," *Harvard Business Review,* May–June 1957, pp. 89–94.
3. John W. Humble, *Management By Objectives in Action* (London: McGraw-Hill Book Co., 1970).
4. George Odiorne, *Management By Objectives* (New York: Pitman, 1965).
5. Anthony Raia, "Goal Setting and Self-Control," *Journal of Management Studies,* Feb. 1965, pp. 34–53; —, "A Second Look at Management Goals and Controls," *California Management Review,* Summer 1966, pp. 49–58; H. H. Meyer, E. Kay, and J. R. R. French, "Split Roles in Performance Appraisal," *Harvard Business Review,* Jan.–Feb. 1965, pp. 123–129; Henry L. Tosi and Stephen J. Carroll, "Managerial Reaction to Management By Objectives," *Academy of Management Journal,* Dec. 1968, pp. 415–426; Stephen Carroll and Henry L. Tosi, "Goal Characteristics and Personality Factors in a Management by Objectives Program," *Administrative Science Quarterly,* Sept. 1970, pp. 295–305; John M. Ivancevich, James H. Donnelly, Jr., and Herbert L. Lyon, "A Study of the Impact of Management By Objectives on Perceived Need Satisfaction," *Personnel Psychology,* Summer 1970, pp. 139–151.
6. Mark Abrahamson, "The Integration of Individual Scientists," *Administrative Science Quarterly,* June 1964, pp. 208–218; Douglas T. Hall and Edward E. Lawler III, "Job Characteristics and Pressures and the Organizational Integration of Professionals," *Administrative Science Quarterly,* Sept. 1970, pp. 271–281.
7. H. H. Meyer et al., op. cit.; A. Raia, op. cit.; H. L. Tosi and S. J. Carroll, op. cit.
8. D. McGregor, op. cit.; H. H. Meyer et al., op. cit.; Ernest Miller, *Objectives and Standards of Performance in Financial Management* (New York: AMACOM, 1968).
9. John M. Ivancevich, "A Longitudinal Assessment of Management By Objectives," *Administrative Science Quarterly,* March 1972, pp. 126–138; H. L. Tosi and S. J. Carroll, op. cit.; Walter S. Wikstrom, *Management By—and With—Objectives* (New York: National Industrial Conference Board, 1968).
10. J. R. R. French, Jr., E. Kay, and H. H. Meyer, "Participation and the Appraisal System," *Human Relations,* Feb. 1966, pp. 3–19; H. H. Meyer et al., op. cit.; E. Miller, op. cit.
11. S. Carroll and H. L. Tosi, op. cit.
12. Peter P. Gil and Warren G. Bennis, "Science and Management: Two Cultures," *Journal of Applied Behavioral Sciences,* Jan.–Feb.–Mar. 1968, pp. 75–108.

13. S. B. Georgopoulas, G. M. Mahoney, and N. W. Jones, Jr., "A Path-Goal Approach to Productivity," *Journal of Applied Psychology,* Dec. 1957, pp. 345–353; V. H. Vroom, "The Effects of Attitudes on Perception of Organizational Goals," *Human Relations,* Aug. 1960, pp. 229–240; A. Zander, T. Natsoulas, and E. J. Thomas, "Personal Goals and the Group's Goals for the Member," *Human Relations,* Nov. 1960, pp. 333–344.

14. Stephen Carroll and Henry L. Tosi, "The Relation of Characteristics of the Review Process as Moderated by Personality and Situational Factors to the Success of the Management by Objectives Approach," *Proceedings of the Academy of Management,* 1970, pp. 139–143.

15. Doris M. Cook, "The Impact on Managers of Frequency of Feedback," *Academy of Management Journal,* Sept. 1968, pp. 263–277.

16. J. H. Ivancevich et al., op. cit.

The Future:
Its Challenge
and Its Promise

Dale D. McConkey

MBO is not a panacea for nonprofit organizations—or for any other organization. However, it does have much to recommend it to any organization interested in improving the effectiveness of its managers and, through their combined effectiveness, the effectiveness of the entire organization.

No attempt is made here to recommend that all nonprofit entities adopt MBO. Such a recommendation would be shortsighted indeed. It could be made only after an exhaustive analysis of the organization, its managers, their competence and motivation, and the environment in which the organization operates.

It is definitely recommended, however, that these entities give full consideration to exploring the possible benefits that MBO could bring to them. There are compelling reasons for nonprofit organizations to take a good, hard look at MBO. These reasons can be generally grouped into five broad categories:

⋄ The increasing demand for greater accountability.
⋄ The demand for a greater voice by managers.

Reprinted with permission of the publisher from *MBO for Non-Profit Organizations* by Dale D. McConkey, pp. 200–208. © 1975 by AMACOM, a division of American Management Associations.

◇ The increasing rate of change.

◇ The increasing degree of complexity.

◇ The dramatic increase in the number, size, and influence of nonprofit organizations and managers.

DEMAND FOR ACCOUNTABILITY

The demand for accountability on the part of managers has never been greater.
Both the marketplace and the owners are increasingly demanding more of business managers. Managers of churches and other religious institutions are being
required more often to justify to their congregations the effectiveness with
which stewardship is being met. Citizens, taxpayers, and organized pressure
groups are demanding that government agencies and departments achieve
meaningful, worthwhile goals. Students and parents alike are exerting comparable pressures on school managers and administrators. Volunteer groups are
being required to document the reason for their existence. Fund-raising organizations are no longer being supported blindly just because their cause is honor-
able. Social agencies in general are discovering that appreciable demands are
being made upon them for accountability. And now even the military finds itself in the position of having its objectives and performance questioned from
many quarters.

MBO can be a potent means of helping meet this increasing demand for
accountability and the challenge it poses. First, it is a means of aligning the efforts of all managers to achieve the desired ends that have been agreed upon. It
helps organizations concentrate on important matters rather than getting bogged
down in the routine, which serves only to dissipate efforts and resources and
leaves the organization subject to criticism for following wasteful practices.

Second, MBO provides the nonprofit organization with concrete means for
dramatizing the contributions it has made. It is able to point out what it intended to achieve (its objectives), and later it can demonstrate the results it actually achieved as compared against its objectives. This helps the nonprofit organization achieve one of its most crying needs—the need for credibility by its
supporters. It can also go far to at least minimizing the often unfair stereotyping
of nonprofit managers; namely, that they are inefficient, ineffective, and lacking in the competence and motivation required of their counterparts in the
private sector.

DEMAND FOR GREATER VOICE

The plight of managers—especially middle managers—has been all but overlooked in the rush to define and treat the problem at the worker level. So far,

most attention has been devoted to providing workers with more ways of gaining a greater voice in determining their futures. The same indicators used to gauge the magnitude of the problem among workers (for example, turnover, absenteeism, apathy, lack of decision-making opportunities, and a lessening opportunity to demonstrate individuality) are equally appropriate when addressing attention to managers. These indicators show that a major problem exists in the ranks of managers.

Study after study and case after case are proving that there is a potentially dangerous and costly excess of unrest and disenchantment among managers, particularly middle managers. Absenteeism, a problem traditionally associated with nonmanagement employees, is now soaring in the middle management ranks. Managerial productivity is down. One large U.S. corporation even found it necessary to conduct a special productivity improvement program for its upper-level managers. Turnover, another problem usually associated with nonmanagerial employees, is exacting a costly toll in the ranks of managers. Many are leaving business to teach, to enter public service, or to pursue other forms of endeavor where they can be their own boss or pursue their own interests.[1]

An HEW report cites additional evidence that increasing numbers of the 4.5 million middle managers in the United States are seeking a midcareer change. The report states:

> Characteristically, middle managers perceive that they lack influence on organization decision making, yet they must implement company policy—and often without sufficient authority or resources to effectively carry it out.[2]

A survey conducted recently by the Life Extension Institute in New York and quoted by Dale Tarnowieski found that "compared with 1958 figures, only one-sixth the number of middle management executives are satisfied with their jobs."[3] Tarnowieski goes on to quote from a research report prepared by the American Management Associations entitled *Manager Unions*. The report surveyed middle- and lower-level managers in more than 500 U.S. organizations. He quotes:

> If these survey results are a valid representation of what's on management's mind, there is today widespread disenchantment among American middle managers with the prevailing state of corporate affairs. This disenchantment is largely the product of the dramatic changes in life-styles throughout American society, of a painful and prolonged recession, and of increased external pressures for business and organizational reform. . . . Economic and social insecurity is at the heart of the manager's discontent, and the leaders of American business will be treading on thin ice if they ignore or deny the possibility of a revolt in the ranks of middle management.[4]

Among other findings, the same AMA report found that three out of four of the intermediate managers surveyed admitted to a substantial increase in recent years in on-the-job frustration and general discontent. Furthermore, 18 percent of the middle managers surveyed would join a manager's union today if the law or corporate climate permitted. An additional 17 percent would seriously consider union membership as a means of strengthening what they see as a fading middle management voice in corporate and organizational affairs.

A newer research report, *The Changing Success Ethic*, prepared for AMA and also quoted by Tarnowieski, adds additional dimension to the unrest among middle management. This report found that 35 percent of the more than 2,800 respondents at all managerial levels indicated that there was an occupational field other than business management in which they would rather be engaged. Among middle managers, nearly 44 percent envisaged an alternate career for themselves, and 70 percent of these managers expected to search for a way to make a career change in the near future.[5]

All these indications of managerial unrest should act as a positive incentive for companies to conduct a searching reexamination of their approaches to job enrichment. This examination should lead to answers and a positive program of action to cope with the following questions:

◇ What is the real locus of the job enrichment problem?
◇ Are job enrichment efforts being directed to this priority?
◇ How can managers be expected to enrich the jobs of their employees when they themselves often are in need of job enrichment (lack of motivation)?
◇ How can one who hasn't experienced enrichment in his own job know how to pratice it for others (lack of experience)?

Fortunately, MBO has pointed the way to several practical, effective ways for enriching the manager's job. It has within its total system the built-in vehicle and latitude for allowing the manager a major voice in determining both his day-to-day actions and his long-term future. It enables him to experience the attributes that contribute to job enrichment.

Viable objectives to be sought in managerial job enrichment should center around the following attributes to which one writer has referred as the "eight selfs." [6]

> *Self-commitment.* The manager who has a major voice in setting his own objectives will be more committed to making them become a reality.
>
> *Self-motivation.* As with self-commitment, the manager will strive harder to achieve his own goals.
>
> *Self-planning.* When a manager knows the results he must achieve, he can plan for them.
>
> *Self-supervision.* The goal-oriented manager requires less close supervision.

Self-discipline. The manager who is working with objectives and has feedback on performance tends to discipline himself.

Self-management. The manager has considerable freedom to manage his own resources to reach his objectives.

Self-development. Challenging objectives challenge the manager to more effective performance and promote his growth.

Self-reward. Meaningful rewards result from achievement and increased competency.

These, then, are the major end results that should flow from endeavors to enrich the manager's job. Working in combination and concert, they should raise the manager to the status of "entrepreneur" or "chief executive officer" of his own smaller company within the larger organization.

Probably the greatest evidence of the value of MBO as a job enricher is the vast number of top executives and middle- and lower-level managers actually working under a smoothly functioning MBO system who maintain that the most effective tool for job enrichment is management by objectives, properly practiced! MBO has built into the system the means for accomplishing all eight of these "selfs."

INCREASING RATE OF CHANGE

The continually accelerating rate of change in the world and the environment in which organizations must operate is another strong argument for a thorough study of the advisability of adopting MBO. The president of a noted school of engineering recently summarized this rate of change when he stated that everything that would be taught to the entering freshmen would be obsolete by the time they graduated. Others estimate that more change has taken place in the past ten years than took place in all the years since our country was founded.

By any measure, the rate of change has been phenomenal, and it is increasing geometrically. What was new yesterday will be old tomorrow.

Given this rate of change, no one person, or even several, can hope to successfully cope with it. What is clearly needed is the full utilization of all members of an organization—each having a segment of the entity for which he is responsible, each staying current with the changes that impact on his organization, and each constituting a change agent within his sphere of operation.

In a very real sense, MBO is a change system. It is a system designed to require the continuing review of the priorities of the organization. As these priorities change, MBO requires that objectives, plans, and budgets be changed accordingly. Thus utilizing a system that addresses itself to change, and also fully utilizing all key personnel in effecting necessary change, is an excellent means of coping with it.

INCREASING COMPLEXITY

Closely allied to the rate of change is the increasing rate of complexity involved in realizing optimum results for an organization. No long-winded treatise is necessary to convince the nonprofit manager that his is not a simple job.

The vast multiplicity of services provided by organizations such as the Department of Health, Education and Welfare is a good example. The services offered by this department—approximately $120 billion per year of them— truly range from alpha to omega, from programs designed to lower the dropout rate in schools to assistance to migratory workers and their families.

Added to this are the many interested parties who do their level best to influence the department's actions—senators, congressmen, and others with special interests. Add the lobbyists, the do-gooders, and the interests of the recipients.

Then add to these the number of persons and organizations having a part in administering the department's programs. Among these are federal agencies, state governments and agencies, and third-party reimbursement groups.

To all of this must be added the changes and increased complexity of the very services the department must deliver. Take, for example, the changing roles and methods of education, the dramatic advances in medicine, and the multiplying number of welfare programs and recipients in an era of providing some type of aid for practically everyone.

In light of all of the above, it's a small wonder that the biggest problem facing the Department of Health, Education and Welfare is the ordering of realistic priorities and the allocation of resources to them.

Once more, one of the more promising approaches to coping with this complexity is a management system that helps order priorities, and then gets all managers involved in helping cope with complexity and change. Again, no few people can hope to deal with this complexity. However, and obviously, the answer doesn't lie in merely throwing more people into the action. Only with a system like MBO can we be as sure as possible that additional numbers are needed and of the contribution they must make.

INCREASE IN NUMBERS AND SIZE

Earlier I cited the dramatic increase in the sheer weight of numbers in the nonprofit sector—increases in the numbers of managers, the increasing number of nonprofit organizations per se, the increasing proportion of the gross national product that they account for, and the increasing influence they are exerting on our daily lives. The size factor will not be further labored upon here.

It should suffice to say that these increases place an even heavier premium on following the very best and latest in management approaches. A management system such as MBO, which has been increasingly proved over a 20-year period, presents itself as a most logical candidate for consideration.

A FORK IN THE ROAD

Clearly, nonprofit organizations have come to a fork in their road. Which road they take is all-important to their future, and the choice is largely up to them.

They can adopt a "problem orientation" or an "objective orientation" in their deliberations regarding the possible adoption of MBO. The difference is illustrated by a case I recently encountered in a large municipal government organization. While the subject was different, the issue is the same.

A city manager of a large Midwest city received a proposal that would save the city several thousand dollars each year if it could be successfully implemented and administered. He called his top managers and administrators together to discuss the proposal. He soon found that his people lined up into two rather distinct groups. The essence of the thinking of the two groups was:

Group 1: Too many problems were involved in implementing the proposal. Several work procedures would have to be changed. Employees would have to be trained. The union representing the municipal employees might file grievances. Other disruptions would occur in the office. The proposal should be rejected.

Comment: This is a problem-oriented group; they first look at problems rather than at potential benefits. (Undoubtedly, they would reject any consideration of MBO out of hand.)

Group 2: The proposal seemed to have many benefits, not the least of which was the potential savings. The proposal should be investigated.

Comment: This group is objective-oriented. They first examine the issues before going to the problems. They don't let the real or imagined problems make the decision for them prematurely.

Obviously, the adoption of MBO in many nonprofit organizations won't be easy. It never is. There will be many problems that must be overcome and adaptations that must be made. But one of the primary jobs of a manager in any organization is to solve problems, not to walk away from them. The latter constitutes abdication and doesn't require very much competence, decision-making ability, or guts.

Hopefully, the vast majority of the managers of nonprofit organizations who read this book will be thoroughly receptive to:

⋄ Fully exploring the potential benefits of a well-proved management system such as MBO.
⋄ Having an objective rather than a problem orientation.
⋄ Matching MBO to the requirements and circumstances of their organizations.
⋄ Determining, realistically, what aspects of MBO can and should be adopted.
⋄ Before making the decision to implement, determining how fast and how far they want to and can go with MBO.
⋄ Recognizing that with most nonprofit organizations that are starving for better management, even a half a loaf is better than none. They won't become disgruntled if they can't realize the full benefits of MBO—benefits they might be able to realize in private sector companies.

I fervently hope that all nonprofit organizations will accept the challenge that there's always a better way of managing.

REFERENCES

1. *Dun's,* Aug. 1972.
2. *Work in America* (Washington, D.C.: Department of Health, Education and Welfare, 1972), p. 38.
3. Life Extension Institute, "Middle Managers' New Values," *Personnel,* Jan.–Feb. 1973, p. 48.
4. Dale Tarnowieski, cited in *Manager Unions* (New York: AMACOM, 1972).
5. Dale Tarnowieski, cited in *The Changing Success Ethic* (New York: AMACOM, 1973).
6. James J. Cribbin, *Effective Management Leadership* (New York: AMACOM, 1972), p. 180.

Part 4
PROJECT MANAGEMENT
AND PARTICIPATORY MANAGEMENT

Results-Oriented Management Styles

PROJECT MANAGEMENT AND PARTICIPATORY MANAGEMENT ARE APPROACHES TO the basic management process of planning, organizing, and controlling. These approaches may frequently be referred to as management styles. As is seen from the articles contained in this section, project management and participatory management can be very effectively used in nonprofit organizations.

	Government	Education	Health	Religious and Charitable	Associations and Others
Matrix Organizational Design as a Vehicle for Effective Delivery of Public Health Care and Social Services J. L. Gray			X		
Finding Answers to School Problems Gaye Vandermyn and H. Dean Smith		X			
Organizing to Overhaul a Mess Kenneth L. Harris	X				
Participatory Management: An Alternative in Human Service Delivery Systems Kenneth P. Fallon, Jr.	X		X		
Breaking the Synergism Barrier Howard L. Jones		X			

Matrix Organizational Design as a Vehicle for Effective Delivery of Public Health Care and Social Services

J. L. Gray

The use of the matrix form of organizational design has been the subject of increasing study in recent years.* Its application to business organizations is widely recognized, particularly for firms in the aerospace industry. Much of the literature has been reporting on the applicability and success of this form of organization for business firms, although perhaps its greatest fame has risen from the experiences of the United States government in the NASA organization. To date, there has been no attempt to apply this form of structure to the delivery of public health care and social services, a field that is demanding increasing attention from administrative theorists. Variations of the matrix approach have been reported on smaller scales, but it has yet to be applied as a total organizational philosophy encompassing all systems. Alternatives to the traditional bureaucratic model have been suggested (e.g., Piliavin's 1968 "entrepreneural·

* Terminology can become confusing in this relatively new area. This paper treats the terms "matrix," "project management," and "functional team" as being synonymous.

Research for this paper was supported by the Manitoba Institute of Management, Inc., and the Department of Business Administration, University of Manitoba.

Reprinted with permission from the *Management International Review*, No. 6, 1974.

model" attempts to overcome the conflicts between the professional and the demands of the bureaucratic system) but these tend to focus on the "micro" aspects of public health care and social services rather than on the total systems concept.

The purpose of this paper is to present a matrix approach to the delivery of public health care and social services. This will be accomplished by first developing the theoretical framework for the application of matrix organization to public health care institutions and, second, by presenting an example of a matrix structure that is currently being implemented in a social service organization. The major emphasis in the paper is on the development of the theoretical model; the example is presented as a descriptive case study only. The design presented in this paper has as its research base a large, government controlled public health and social service delivery system which, over the past two years, has begun to implement the matrix form of organization structure.

TYPOLOGY OF CURRENT STRUCTURES

The delivery of public health care and social services has historically been a bureaucratic activity. Rules and procedures dominated the activities of the organization and client treatment was inadequate due to the dysfunctional consequences of the bureaucratic form of organization. It is suggested here that these dysfunctional consequences have caused the emphasis in delivery systems in the past to be "symptom-oriented" rather than "client-oriented," that is, focus has been upon short-run, surface indications of organizational effectiveness (e.g., reducing the number of persons on welfare rolls) rather than upon satisfying the needs of the client. Consequently, in terms of traditional bureaucratic measures of effectiveness, the structure appears adequate; however, in terms of client need satisfactions (i.e., assisting him to better cope with his environment) the organization may be highly deficient. Client dissatisfaction therefore increases, demands are made for more participation in the decision-making process, and taxpayers decry the increasing costs of delivering public health care and social services. The end result, according to Armitage, is that:

. . . many organizations tend to adopt a "survival" type of model. This includes a primary identification with the interests of the source of finances, an avoidance of all controversy, an unwillingness to innovate or establish precedents, and an attempt to manipulate the clients so that they are contented with (adjusted to) the standard of living provided by the organization.[1]

Cause-and-effect is admittedly difficult to determine, but it is the contention of this paper that "structure" is a major source of client dissatisfaction.

The rationale for current structures lies in the basic philosophy of bureaucratic, that is, equal and consistent, treatment for all clients. Traditional hierarchical models are also noted for their efficiency in processing large numbers of clients, a factor which has been highly significant in furthering the bureaucratic system in the public health care and social service field. As the number of clients increases (due primarily to the extension of social services by governments), the need for more impersonal rules increases, there is an increased need for greater centralization of administrative systems, and decision-making becomes less discretionary.*

The bureaucratic environment, however, has changed both in terms of the bureaucrat and the client. Bureaucratic roles have become increasingly professionalized at the operative level as the professions themselves have directed efforts away from traditional custodial type functions to more preventive and diagnostic functions. These professionals are demanding more discretion in treatment methods and view the organization as a vehicle for furthering their professional attitudes and values. The potential for conflict is illustrated by this example from the social work profession as discussed by Piliavin:

> Social work has acquired many of the earmarks of a profession, including a professional association that has developed and promulgated standards, goals, and an ethical code for those providing social services. The members of this profession . . . encounter a dilemma unknown to their early predecessors: they find agency policies and practices frequently in conflict with avowed professional norms . . . Thus it appears that the unenviable fate of social workers today is that they operate within and under the control of organizations whose policies fail to maintain the values and norms of their profession.[2]

Paradoxically, then, the bureaucratic organization's orientation toward the elimination of conflict has, instead, a tendency to create it through the alienation of professional attitudes and values.

Clients, on the other hand, are collecting larger power bases and are demanding a voice in their own processing, particularly in welfare organizations. Bureaucratic structures are not oriented to mass participation in policies, nor do they provide the climate for effective change in this direction. In fact, Michel Crozier maintains that bureaucratic organizations can only change by the imposition of a solution after a major crisis, and that the accumulated pressure of the vicious circle is what finally induces the crisis.

In general, we can say that bureaucratic organization structures have the potential of generating the following types of conflict in public health care and social service organizations [3]:

---

* The term "discretion" is used here in the manner developed by Elliott Jaques in *Equitable Payment* (London: Heinemann Educational Books, Ltd., 1970).

1. Between those sections of the organization directly engaged in obtaining the organization's goals, and those which are meant to provide support systems or goal attainment (line–staff).
2. Between professional and administrative personnel over the ends–means situation (cosmopolitan–local).
3. Between the interests of the organization and the interests of the groups it is supposedly serving (helper–client).
4. Between those with power to direct the work and the rewards and sanctions given, and those affected by such decisions (manager–subordinate).

It is the author's contention that the above types of conflict are mutually reinforcing and, in total, dysfunctional to organizational effectiveness in public health and social service organizations. Suboptimization and client dissatisfaction are the primary outputs of this type of system, and it is predicted that, given a lack of satisfaction of clients' needs, intergroup conflict will increase as disagreement over goals is recognized; moreover, these conflicts are resolved either by "bargaining" or by "politics" rather than by more heuristic types of responses and this is assumed to be dysfunctional.

THE MATRIX ORGANIZATIONAL DESIGN

Shull and Judd describe the matrix in its most elementary form as a "crosshatch of structural elements, with discipline or functional units forming the vertical dimensions, and programmatic or project units providing the horizontal dimensions." [4] Or, put another way, the matrix form of organizational design is the theoretical opposite of the pure bureaucratic form, that is, the fundamental propositions underlying each are opposite. For example, the bureaucratic structure is rigid and predictable, and the matrix form is flexible and unpredictable. Bureaucracies are organized around functions and hierarchical positions, whereas matrix organizations are organized around problems (or projects) and who has the information relevant to the problem.

The underlying rationale of the matrix structure is that objectives are best met if the organization's resources can be oriented toward those objectives without regard to traditional hierarchical constraints. The organization structure is viewed as a means to an end and can be readily adapted to a changing environment. And not only is the matrix structure flexible but it is fluid as well. Since resources are organized around specific projects, the organization is in a constant state of flux as projects are completed and resources are deployed to

Figure 1. Basic diagram of the matrix organization.

Representatives of:	Project 1	Project 2	Project 3	Project n
Function 1				
Function 2				
Function 3				
Function n				
	Team 1	Team 2	Team 3	Team n

Adapted from Chris Argyris, "The Matrix Organization," *Think*, Nov.-Dec., 1967.

new or other current projects.* Diagrammatically, Figure 1 represents the basic matrix organization.

It should be mentioned that the "pure" matrix form is a theoretical extreme seldom, if ever, found in organizations. In fact, there is considerable variation within organization structures, depending upon the decision processes necessary to perform the tasks. Some decision makers have described these decision processes as being either (a) routine, (b) engineered, (c) craft, or (d) heuristic. As would be expected, decisions range on this continuum from highly prescriptive (routine) to highly discretionary (heuristic). Similarly, personnel requirements would vary from technicians (routine) to highly trained professionals (heuristic), and administrative control systems would vary depending on the orientation of the task and the personnel.[4]

Consequently, we can find in any organization a set of tasks which can operationally be differentiated from each other on the basis of decision processes. These tasks, in turn, require different administrative systems, ranging from bureaucratic to organic (matrix); it is therefore imperative that these different task units be identified and placed within that administrative system that is most appropriate.

In the final analysis, the justification for applying matrix theory to the delivery of public health care lies in the fundamentals of open systems theory. Open systems theory recognizes that all elements of an entity are interrelated; this is to say that a decision in one area has an effect on all parts of the total system in some degree. Thus, the matrix organization inherently views

* In the aerospace industry this phenomenon is illustrated by NASA's organizing around specific projects, e.g., Saturn Project, Apollo Project. As each project was completed, resources were transferred to other projects.

the organization as a system of interrelated activities, all of which have some impact on goal attainment. Moreover, the ultimate purpose of the matrix form is the assemblage of "different" resources to bear upon a common problem or objective.

It also follows from systems theory that problems have a multiplicity of sources and therefore solutions must, of necessity, be pluralistic. Yet, traditional bureaucratic models have operated essentially as closed systems and, particularly in the field of social services, have viewed "problems" as being singular in cause. Modern organization theory, however, proposes the open systems concept which provides the conceptual base for matrix organizational design and its application to the field of public health and social services.

MATRIX ORGANIZATION AND PUBLIC HEALTH CARE SYSTEMS

Consider now the relationship between the client and the organization under the traditional administrative system. The "system" processes the client as though his situation is an isolated function of a static environment. For example, if a socially disadvantaged client has no job because of lack of marketable skills (single causality), he is processed by a manpower training agency; if he has no funds to support himself, his needs are provided for by a separate agency of the organization. In short, the nature of bureaucratic institutions necessitates the treatment of the client's problems as distinct and separate entities and he would be processed accordingly.*

To illustrate what may be a more common case, consider the following hypothetical situation:

> The client is an alcoholic. He has not worked for six months and has always had difficulty in holding a steady job. His family is currently on welfare, his wife is known to be psychologically disturbed, and his three children are very slow learners in school. One of his children has been arrested as a juvenile and is currently on probation.

Under the bureaucratic system, the client would be "processed" by a total of six different social service agencies, all attempting to provide some relief for these problems. However, because of bureaucratic artificial boundaries set up according to functional areas, there may be little, if any, coordinated effort

---

* Admittedly in this case the source of the problem is being considered (assuming a closed system). Furthermore, the value of symptom relief, for example, welfare, should not be underestimated. However, the orientation of the organization should be on long-run consequences of the public health and social service systems. Bureaucratic concentration on symptom relief (a "routine" task unit activity) detracts from this long-run emphasis.

directed at his situation. Moreover, even if this case is placed in an open systems framework, system overload may prevent professional assistance, thus relegating his treatment to routinized relief from symptoms.

By referring again to Figure 1, we can now place the delivery of public health care and social service into the matrix structure. The "crosshatch" of personnel and tasks now becomes a configuration of clients (projects) and helpers (functions). By defining the client as a specific project with specific attributes, then it becomes possible to assemble the resources necessary to assist that client with his system of problems. A "team" is therefore created which is composed of professionals whose expertise is relevant to the client's need. Moreover, just as in the profit-oriented organizations where teams are disbanded as projects are completed, the social service and public health teams operate in similar fashion. If and when a client's situation has improved to the extent that professional assistance is no longer needed, the team is disbanded and the resources channeled elsewhere. If the client still is in need of processing by the organization, it will (by definition) be of a more bureaucratic nature and can be performed by technically oriented individuals.

Clearly, the matrix approach to public health care and social service delivery systems relies heavily on the professionalism of the members of the organization. The bureaucratic system, it will be remembered, is designed to eliminate conflict between functional units; the matrix organization, on the other hand, is designed to create conflict, based upon the proposition that professional conflict can be creative and productive. The lack of a formal structure, the flexibility inherent in the system, and the dependency upon expertise rather than formal administrative position in the matrix organization, all tend to inter-ject conflict into the system. The matrix organization in the public health care and social services delivery system is premised on the assumption that "professionalism" counterbalances any dysfunctional consequences that the organizational conflict may have.*

At the "macro" level of organization, matrix structure has relevancy as well, although the configuration is less predictable. The theoretical base remains the same, but the focus is upon total organizational effectiveness (i.e., delivery of health and social services within the larger environmental system) rather than the individual client. The administrative system is organized around processes of type of functions (i.e., "projects"), not according to professional functions or institutional criteria.† However, at the "macro" level there is

* While there is adequate research base to support this contention, it is necessary to point out that dysfunctional conflict may also be present in the system. For example, one might cite the traditional dominance of the physician in public health matters and the potential conflicts that may emerge as other public health occupations approach professional status. There are also other potential dysfunctional consequences of matrix organizations which are beyond the scope of this paper.

† One of these administrative systems will be the control system. At the professional level, this would be self-control, rather than a form of imposed control.[4]

greater concern with the administration of "routinized" task units; therefore, a macro structure will have more bureaucratic characteristics than will a micro structure. The theoretical foundations for the macro model can be traced back to Fisch's criticisms of the classical line-staff model in which the functional divisions are replaced by "functional teams." [5]

A SELECTED EXAMPLE

As mentioned in the beginning of this article, the research base for the theoretical model lies in an existing organization which has attempted the transition from the closed-system bureaucratic model to the open-system matrix model. Since the purpose of this section is to provide the case study as a method of illustrating the matrix model, that is, purely descriptive, the evaluation of the concept must be considered outside the scope of the present paper. Nevertheless, one can test the face validity of the model using the examples presented and the theory discussed earlier.

Figure 2 illustrates a possible macro structure that is consistent with the matrix design. Basically, the functions are organized around divisions of resources, operations, and planning. These three areas provide the framework for the administration of both professional and nonprofessional activities. Within each sub-unit it is important to note that both routine and heuristic task units will exist and will consequently require different types of administrative systems for their support.

At the micro level, Figure 3 illustrates the matrix approach to the delivery of public health care and social services that is used in conjunction with the macro system in Figure 2. It should be noted, of course, that the composition of any particular team will vary according to the objective to be attained.

SUMMARY AND CONCLUSIONS

The nature and scope of the delivery of public health care and social services has necessitated the examination of the traditional bureaucratic form of organization as a vehicle for delivering these services. One alternative is the matrix form of structure inasmuch as it allows for the discretion in the decision-making necessary for the effective employment of professionals in public health care organizations. Moreover, the matrix form recognizes that multidisciplinary forms of expertise are needed for social problems and traditional structures do not allow for the interface necessary in these situations. It is recognized, how-

Figure 2. Divisional structure of social services and public health matrix organization (macro).

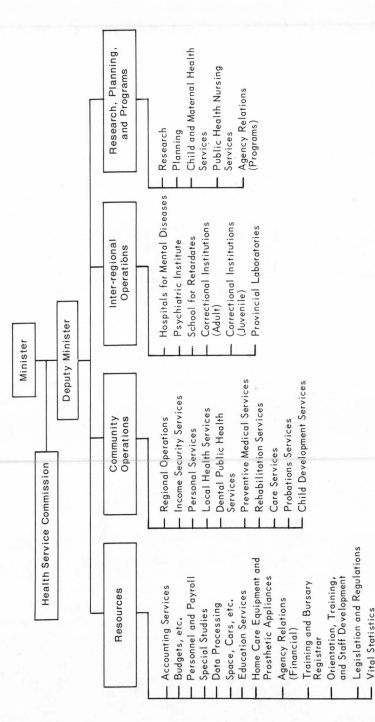

Figure 3. Social services and public health matrix organization (micro).

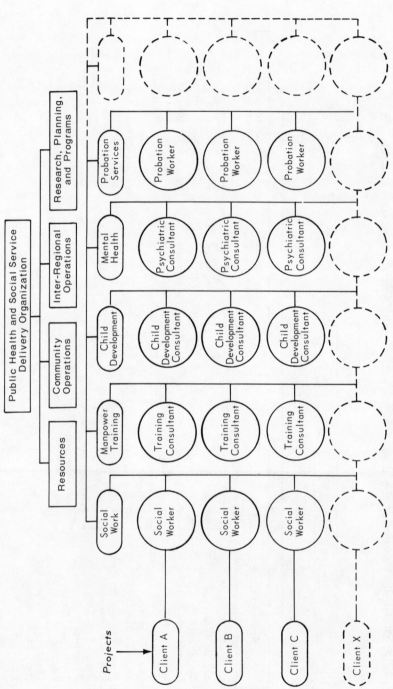

Adapted from John F. Mee, "Matrix Organization," Business Horizons, Summer 1964.

ever, that the bureaucratic model is quite relevant to routinized tasks that are present in these systems and administrative controls should be adapted accordingly.

Although an example of the matrix system applied to public health care and social service delivery systems has been supplied, it is nevertheless important to admit to Shull and Judd's comments on the matrix model that "While inductive appeal can be made to specific cases in demonstrating the matrix model, at the moment it is more conceptual and analytical than prescriptive or descriptive of organizational structure." [6] In sum, it remains to see if the theoretical bases for using the matrix model in the public health and social services field can be justified on empirical grounds. At present, it appears to be an excellent situation to test the effectiveness of the matrix model.

REFERENCES

1. W. A. J. Armitage, "A Structural View of Welfare Organizations," *The Social Worker*, July 1969, p. 172.
2. Irving Piliavin, "Restructuring the Provision of Social Services," *Social Work*, Jan. 1968, pp. 35–36.
3. Adapted from Armitage, *op. cit.*, pp. 173–174.
4. F. A. Shull and R. J. Judd, "Matrix Organizations and Control Systems," *Management International Review*, Volume 11, 1971, p. 65.
5. Gerald Fisch, "Line-Staff Is Obsolete," *Harvard Business Review*, Sept.–Oct. 1961, pp. 67–79.
6. Shull and Judd, *op. cit.*, p. 73.

Finding Answers
to School Problems

Gaye Vandermyn
H. Dean Smith

It looked like a shopping list of critical issues facing American education:

⬦ Impending financial disaster due to repeated school levy failures;
⬦ Alarming student enrollment growth rates in some areas, and
⬦ Declining enrollments in others;
⬦ Stormy relations between a school board and its superintendent;
⬦ Hostile school and community relationships;
⬦ Lack of direction in curriculum, financial, or facilities planning;
⬦ Ambitious long-range education plans gathering dust on frustrated school officials' shelves;
⬦ Teacher strikes dividing the community and school staff.

Each item on the list represented a specific problem faced by some school district in the State of Washington. As State Superintendent Frank B. Brouillet and his staff probed each problem, trying to find some effective way of dealing with it, they noticed two elements common to each situation. The first was ineffective communication between the school district (or a local school) and its

Reprinted with permission from *American Education*, June 1975.

public and thus a lack of cooperation between them. The second was ineffective communication accompanied by shaky working relationships within the district—between the school board and its superintendent, the central office and local school principals, or various other combinations.

Thus examined, each problem seemed to demand the same kind of help—a management-communications expert who was available when needed.

That conclusion really solved nothing for Dr. Brouillet, since financial reality made it impossible for either the State education department or any local school district to hire on a long-term basis the experience and expertise needed to handle effectively such complex issues. Nor was the exercise futile. It did point the way toward a cost-effective approach both flexible enough to be applied to different kinds of education problems, and structured enough to deal with "here and now" solutions. Thus, with State sponsorship and with first year Office of Education grants amounting to $140,000 under Title III and Title V of the Elementary and Secondary Education Act and in-kind contributions from the participating districts in personnel time and facilities, Project Interaction materialized.

Basically, the project has two main concerns: to provide local officials with direct consultative help on immediate problems in communication, management, and accountability; and to train local district personnel in the skills necessary for them to continue to work toward project goals or to maintain a satisfactory level of effectiveness even after the project officially ends.

Approximately half of the eighteen school districts joining the project in the first year chose to apply their efforts toward improving communications with those outside the school and toward building positive, productive relationships among community groups, parents, and the district or local school. Other districts are focusing first on internal communications, planning, and management accountability problems.

The two key management tools used in Project Interaction are Images of Potentiality (Imaging) and the Management Responsibility Guide (MRG). Imaging aids participants in expressing in concrete terms what tasks need to be done in order to attain a certain end and what priority should be given each task. The MRG process helps them work out potential role conflicts, clarify the responsibilities of each group and individual, and avoid accountability gaps.

"Because these management techniques are highly adaptable," Superintendent Brouillet says, "they help school personnel, parents, and community leaders structure workshop planning sessions. The structure process avoids dead-end disputes over who is to blame for what's wrong by focusing on what should be done to build a more effective school program and then clarifying who is responsible for accomplishing each of the tasks that must be completed to attain the desired goal."

In each participating district one school employee (usually an assistant to the superintendent, a principal, or assistant principal) is designated as the internal project coordinator. He or she is trained by six project consultants who are drawn from industry, education, State government agencies, and labor. These consultants in turn have themselves received two weeks' intensive training in project techniques, during training sessions conducted prior to the initiation of the project in September 1974, and again at midpoint of the first year's work last January. In the training, Dr. Brouillet repeatedly emphasizes the point that "the techniques used in the project are not the solution to educators' problems. They are a process, a structure, for finding the answers and making sure that effective action is taken to resolve the problems. This project shows educators a way for getting to the answers; it uncovers resources and puts the total community to work to strengthen the school program."

The twin advantages of flexibility and structure can best be illustrated by a quick look at how four of the State's school systems chose to apply Project Interaction in each of the four optional applications—or settings as they are called—that the project offers.

SETTING 1: DISTRICT EDUCATIONAL COMMUNITY

Arlington is a small, mostly rural low- and middle-income community located in northwestern Washington. Its annual special school levies based on the property tax are viewed by many of the citizens as a grossly unfair burden. Arlington Superintendent Richard L. Post agrees, but he points out, the nearly bankrupt school system simply has no other financial alternative. The levies are needed to maintain what school officials and supporters consider a woefully inadequate budget level. What's more, certain community groups continue to call for improvement in school facilities or programs, and these would have to be financed through still higher levies.

With increasing concern over narrow vote margins in passing or defeating school levy measures during the past two years, the Arlington school board turned to Project Interaction for help. The board wanted to develop better two-way communication with its patrons and more effective and positive methods for intimately involving the community in setting goals and priorities, and in implementing action plans.

Nea Toner, one of the six project consultants, and Superintendent Post, who acted as the internal coordinator, invited the community at large and particularly members of the school system to two open meetings to impress upon them that they were all in the same boat and it would be the quintessence of prudence if they were to set a common course and pull their oars in unison. More than 120 parents, businessmen, farmers, teachers, and even students showed up for the two three-hour evening work sessions.

With such encouraging community representation on scene, the techniques of Project Interaction were put to the test. In the first session, held in a local elementary school cafeteria, the group was arbitrarily divided into segments of from 10 to 15 persons each. Each segment was asked to visualize and then describe succinctly on large sheets of newsprint what it would like to see happening in their school system in a year. These ideas or "images" were then shared with the large group, after which each segment selected priorities from among the contributions of all segments and reworked the images into concrete goals. Goals were listed on the large sheets of newsprint which were posted on the walls so that the entire gathering could study them and select its priority goals from among all the candidates submitted by the several segments.

Having thus established some common goals in the first work session, participants in the second three-hour community meeting held two weeks later used a brainstorming technique in the smaller work groups to identify specific actions required to realize these goals. Using the same procedure as that used to determine its goals, the group winnowed its list of actions to the top priorities. Then each group listed positive and negative forces that would enhance or inhibit completion of the priority jobs.

One of the top goals that emerged from the labors of the group was improvement of the district's financial situation. It was the consensus that the best way of initiating action to attack this knotty problem was to assign it to a task force made up of all segments of the community and school.

The task force plunged into its job with refreshing vigor, studying the school system's money needs and its budget plans. Meeting informally each week during January with the school board and staff members, the task force carefully reviewed the school district's financial status, school officials helping in gathering and interpreting the information. The result was a community-established school-tax levy amounting to nearly twice that defeated the year before and achieved through a 65.9 percent majority vote. A building-bond issue, pushed to the top of the priority list for the 1975 ballot when the fire marshall condemned Arlington's 700-student high school as a dangerous fire hazard, collected a 57.2 percent majority vote—57 votes shy of passage. The community and school officials are confident that a second try on the issue will succeed later this year because the decisions are "owned" by the community, which now understands why it is needed.

The Arlington budget and levy study was only the first job facing the task force, however. When that work was finished, the task force fragmented itself to tackle the various jobs of developing action plans for other specific school-community goals that were established in the Project Interaction work sessions. That work includes such concerns as tax reform, construction and rehabilitation of facilities, curriculum improvement, and special program development.

The Arlington group's evaluation of Project Interaction's methods and the effectiveness of their community meetings astounded even Ms. Toner. "The critique sheets were very positive," she says. "In fact, we didn't get one negative response. Many pointed out, however, that the real test of the project's success in Arlington will be where it goes from here."

Superintendent Post is confident that the project will meet that test. He reports that an encouraging majority of participants in the original two work meetings volunteered for task force work, a sure sign that Project Interaction has not only piqued community interest in school problems but has aroused a desire on the part of many to do something about it.

SETTING 2: THE LOCAL SCHOOL COMMUNITY

Lake Washington School District, located in Kirkland, a bedroom community east of Seattle, chose the local school community setting for its first application of Project Interaction. It had a special reason for doing so.

During the two years since Kirkland Junior High was destroyed by fire, students and faculty had used borrowed facilities, sharing classroom space with other schools in the district or with schools in nearby districts. When the doors of their new building open this coming fall, Lake Washington school officials want to make sure that all members of the community share with the students and faculty the feeling of "coming home."

According to Principal Glen Carson, Project Interaction seems almost tailor-made for his own personal dream for the school. "I want to have community, staff, and students centrally involved," he explains, "not only in planning but also in carrying out the education program. It seems to me that Project Interaction is a natural. It gets the community and staff thinking in the same direction—not as foes, but as friends—on how to accomplish goals for the school."

And so last fall in Kirkland, four students, six teachers, the teacher association president, a representative from the city park department and one from the mayor's office, one school board member, and 11 parents got together for weekly two-hour Project Interaction work sessions. They began with the imaging process and worked in much the same manner as the Arlington group toward establishing priorities among their set goals and in selecting what seemed the most productive courses of action. Then Principal Carson, the designated internal coordinator, and Larry Brammar, the Project Interaction consultant, introduced the group to the language and process of the Management Responsibility Guide matrix, a management accountability tool.

A management accountability matrix lists the established goal tasks down the left-hand side of a chart. Each participant is given a specific job title which is listed across the top of the chart. In the columns under their particular titles and adjacent to a given task, participants write in their responsibility toward completing that task and how they should be involved in any decision making. This matrix is a key tool in identifying who has to do what to get the whole job done.

It is this process which Dr. Brammar credits with making Project Interaction more than just another fad that will be forgotten as soon as it is replaced by next year's fad.

"It may be that the side effects will be better than Project Interaction itself," Dr. Brammar suggests. He explains what he means by citing the experience of the Lake Washington School District: In carrying forth Project Interaction, the district recognized the need for a comprehensive five-year master plan that ties together all aspects of district operation, projects, and goals. School officials have already begun work on such a plan and propose using the Setting 3 application of Project Interaction this fall to help them complete it.

SETTING 3: BOARD/DISTRICT OFFICE INTERFACE

Faced with a hyperactive enrollment growth rate and a list of related problems that would send most school districts into shock, Evergreen School District turned to Project Interaction to knit together the threads of a necessarily ambitious and complex action plan.

Evergreen Superintendent Donald Osborne claims that the rural–suburban area just north of Vancouver is one of the fastest growing communities in the country. Current pupil enrollment is 9,000, but, predicts Superintendent Osborne, "In a decade or two we'll have 30,000 to 50,000 youngsters in our school system."

The K-12 district is located in a nonincorporated area rapidly changing from a rural to a suburban community. As a consequence there is no community identity, no support for the school base of the kind present in most established towns and cities. Furthermore there's no history to instill that solid feeling of community entity. Add to this a budget maintenance levy failure, a new superintendent, a turnover in school board members, and in the previous year a ten-day teacher strike with its lingering divisive effects on school board, administrative staff, faculty, and community, and the magnitude of the challenge facing the Evergreen school system can be readily appreciated.

The board and administration appear determined to deal with that challenge in a positive, effective manner. First, Superintendent Osborne accepted his job on a performance contract basis, one of the first superintendents in the Nation to do so. His position and salary level depend on his ability to demonstrate real progress toward clearly defined goals for education, administration, and public communication. Most of the central office administrators now have similar contracts with the school system.

According to Superintendent Osborne, results thus far have been positive. The central staff reorganized and, by applying the Management Responsibility Guide techniques, developed for each department a set of major functions that pinpoint accountability for each of the system's priority goals. This process helped establish a positive and productive working relationship within the central staff and with local school administrators.

Recognizing their own responsibility in the accountability equation, board members volunteered for training to include programs produced by the National Association of School Boards and the intensive, structured skill-building in management decision making provided by Project Interaction. Evergreen applied the project's planning, management, and communication process in two areas: management team accountability and central office and school board relationships. Getting the board involved was accomplished in the first work session by establishing the board members' own goals and action priorities. Their list included such priorities as visibly demonstrating within the community that the district successfully provides a complete education program, improving the vocational and academic balance in the curriculum offerings, and enlarging opportunities for participation of all citizens in both day and evening education programs.

The next step to be taken in the coming months in a series of board-staff work sessions will apply the management accountability matrix to the board-staff working relationship. Evergreen is making sure that each person in the system clearly understands what he or she needs to do to make the still-formidable challenge more manageable.

SETTING 4: SCHOOL/DISTRICT OFFICE INTERFACE

"It's like a map showing a road to get you from where you are to where you want to be."

That's how Clifton Johnson, Superintendent of Issaquah School District describes the Project Interaction process as applied to internal staff development needs. Once the decision to try the project was made, Issaquah school officials further decided that the most useful purpose toward which the consultant expertise and training made available through the project could be applied was a more effective working relationship between the central administration and school principals.

"You can rewrite the district's objectives and issue new operating instructions, but all that really changes are the words. What happens in the district, in the school, in the classroom doesn't change," Mr. Johnson contends. "To make changes there, where it counts, you have to involve the people who are directly responsible. They have to participate in the planning and decision making so that they understand what and why and how they fit in the overall plan."

Mr. Johnson further contends that this is exactly the need that Project Interaction answers: "It is a structure and process for efficiently and effectively involving those who are directly responsible for the education program," he says.

The first step for Issaquah placed the superintendent, his immediate staff, and their subordinates in a series of work sessions for the purpose of providing them a fresh look at roles, responsibilities, and relationships within the central office. The next step oriented local school principals to the goals and process of Project Interaction. Meeting as a group, their work paralleled the process through which the central office staff was moving. Once the central staff and the principals developed a clearer understanding and a consensus on the nature of their responsibilities and the role they play in the overall district operation, the two groups met to ponder the problem of how the two administrative levels can most effectively work together. That, too, calls for the Management Responsibility Guide process in order to reach agreement on who has what designated responsibility.

These four case histories illustrate a distinguishing feature of Project Interaction: its effectiveness in catalyzing into action the school, the district, and the community on plans that often are already on the drawing boards.

State officials readily point out other advantages:

The internal coordinators trained in the first 18 participating districts are committed to share their technical expertise in consulting services with nearby districts joining the project in the second and third years. The original project design called for adding additional districts in the second and third years.

"We don't want a short-term, one-time effort," Superintendent Brouillet emphasizes. "This progressive involvement and training of locally available consultants and school officials should help upgrade management skills on a continuing basis in districts throughout the State. This plan also enables us to share the direct benefits of the project on a cost-effective basis with as many school districts as possible."

Midyear evaluation of first-year progress indicated three problem areas: First, districts elected in many cases to apply the project to two and sometimes all four settings at once. Thus the allotted ten days for consultant's services for each of the 18 districts was often inadequate, especially in large or intermediate-sized districts. The training and assistance given the local internal coordinators in getting their projects off the ground in the local school community too often ate up most of the allotted time. That left little or none for providing the direct onsite help in developing positive and effective communication and working relationships in the additional applications.

Second, the consultants, the coordinators, and participants in the various settings have stressed the need for an application of the processes to improve communication and working relationships within the schools themselves, between principal, faculty, and students.

"We feel that eventually that's where the project will have its greatest direct impact in strengthening education in Washington State," says Superintendent Brouillet, noting that second-year plans have now been revised to include an internal school setting as a fifth option for participating school districts.

Third, internal district coordinators have requested more intensive consultant skills training for themselves and some kind of consultant pool to draw upon as needed for assistance.

By developing and putting the fifth option into operation during its second year, and by such additional improvements as the creation of a consulting team, Project Interaction might very well help the State of Washington further curtail its own shopping list of critical issues in education.

Organizing
to Overhaul a Mess

Kenneth L. Harris

The 1970s will probably present many large bureaucracies, institutions, and businesses with a painful decision: overhaul or die. As the world competitive position of the United States changes, government regulations become more stringent, and taxpayers refuse to subsidize managerial inefficiency, many organizations will require extensive surgery to survive.

Quasi-public corporations like Lockheed and Penn Central are already in jeopardy; the public is refusing to continue financing their mismanagement, low productivity, and poor service. Other highly regulated industries, notably the power utilities and airlines, will require full-scale restructuring efforts in the near future.

The pressure to overhaul has been keenest in the labor-intensive public service sector of the economy; on the federal level, the postal service is in the process of reorganizing, while on the local level, New York City has begun overhauling its "welfare" administration. In the coming years taxpayers will

Reprinted with permission. © 1975 by the Regents of the University of California. Reprinted from *California Management Review*, Volume XVII, number 3, pp. 40–49, by permission of the Regents.

demand similar measures in the area of health services and in the education system.

In 1972 the $3.2 billion, 27,000 employee, Human Resources Administration of New York City began one of the most successful and extensive overhauls to date. A unique organizational concept was developed which enabled HRA to attract over 450 management professionals and utilize them effectively during the period of reorganization. A review of the HRA overhaul experience, and the project management structure used to effect it, will provide valuable insight into the nature of overhauls in general and a potential solution to the problems of other troubled organizations in particular.

ANATOMY OF THE PROBLEM

In late 1971 New York City's welfare operation was totally out of control and heading for sure fiscal disaster. In October there were 1,255,000 individuals receiving a total of about $1.3 billion in welfare assistance and another $1.2 billion in medical assistance; six out of every seven applicants were accepted. Quality control studies revealed that one-third of all recipients were receiving the wrong amount of money and 15 percent were probably ineligible for any assistance. Approximately $150 million in taxpayer funds were being misappropriated through fraud, error, and mismanagement. Welfare rolls were climbing at the disastrous rate of 10,000 persons a month; costs were multiplying at a rate of $120 million per year.

Field operations were in a state of absolute and perpetual chaos. Welfare centers closed their doors routinely at 10:00 or 11:00 o'clock in the morning, unable to handle the crush of desperate recipients. Acts of violence against welfare workers were commonplace and police measures to protect them proved inadequate. Each of the city's forty-four welfare centers had a unique layout with a different client flow; each seemed equally senseless. Over 165,000 critical transactions were backlogged, including $27 million in cases that were supposed to have been closed. Employee productivity was below 40 percent.

The application procedures and processing system could best be described as irrational, negligent, and chaotic. A person merely had to sign his name to an application form to receive welfare, then be recertified annually by signing a statement that nothing had changed. Over $8 million a year were given to individuals who were on the rolls more than once. Another $5.5 million were lost in duplicate check frauds—when recipients cashed their checks, fraudulently claimed to have lost them, and then received replacements in addition. It took six weeks to actually "stop" a check once the decision was made to close a case.

The system inadvertently ran the world's largest heroin maintenance program for organized crime by providing $50 million in welfare funds to addicts not attending treatment programs. The system was so bad that it even allowed a dog to be accepted for Medicaid and, despite national publicity, recertified the animal six months later.

Management was virtually nonexistent. Over one-third of the employees exceeded their allotted lateness limit, at a cost of $1.3 million a year to the city. The average employee took eleven and one-half of his twelve days sick leave, with disproportionate concentrations around holidays and weekends. Absenteeism cost the city another $7.5 million per year. Although misconduct was prevalent, the agency terminated only nineteen employees for flagrant abuses.

On staff, there were no industrial engineers, less than twenty professional systems analysts, and few professional managers. In short, the system was out of control and the existing organization lacked the capability to bring it in check.

The taxpaying public witnessed the growth of the city's welfare budget from $800 million in 1965 to nearly $3 billion in 1971, and simply refused to allow the government to waste another $200 million. The taxpayers made it perfectly clear: they weren't going to accept increased personal income and property taxes or pay additional nuisance taxes to underwrite the cost of bureaucratic inefficiency and mismanagement. They demanded that the mayor "clean up" the welfare "mess."

THE DECISION TO OVERHAUL

In late 1971, faced with the appropriate political and fiscal climate and an indepth consultant's report on welfare operations, Mayor Lindsay resolved to overhaul the welfare system and bring the caseload under control. To accomplish this, the mayor brought in a new management team, authorized the expenditure of $10 million a year for professional staff and computer support, and gave the effort full political backing.

A two-year time frame was established with the goal of converting the bankrupt system known as "welfare" to something resembling a well-run, efficient, and highly-automated financial institution. To this end the following sequence of objectives was identified:

⋄ Halt the deterioration of services and arrest caseload growth.
⋄ Install a new operating system.
⋄ Establish comprehensive management control.
⋄ Computerize operations.
⋄ Secure substantial productivity gains.

To avoid fiscal disaster and maintain public confidence, the management team realized that within two years the system would have to be financially under control, with implementation of a new computer system in progress and a reduced work force. A special organization was created to design and develop the overhaul, then take over and run the operation, all within a strict time frame. Figure 1 shows the initial management organization established to develop and implement the overhaul.

Figure 1. Initial overhaul organization.

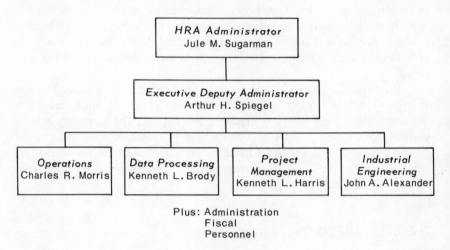

Plus: Administration
Fiscal
Personnel

Arthur H. Spiegel, a Harvard MBA who had just successfully introduced the city's rent control program, was brought in as Executive Deputy Administrator of HRA, and chief operating officer of the agency. Operation of the city's forty-four welfare centers was assigned to Charles Morris, who was given a year to learn the operation and shore up his middle management personnel. John Alexander, a former vice president of Allied Chemical, was brought in to build a staff of industrial engineers, then conduct long-term improvement and productivity studies. An assistant vice president of the American Stock Exchange, Kenneth L. Brody, was recruited to take over the data processing operation. He was given a year to clean up operations and gear up to build a new on-line computer system. Finally, a project management group was created under the direction of a consultant, Kenneth L Harris, who was given the responsibility to identify key problem areas, develop and schedule the overhaul, obtain quick tangible results, and project manage everything. This had to be done as speedily as possible.

THE PROJECT MANAGEMENT ORGANIZATION

The project management group was the pivotal unit in the overhaul strategy. It bore the major responsibility for gaining public credibility, halting the deterioration of operations, and designing the overhaul, while the other groups prepared to implement fundamental system changes. If the project management group failed to do its job the plan would never become a reality.

The application of the project management concept and techniques to an overhaul situation differs considerably from the traditional use of project management. In the aerospace or construction industries, for example, a team of highly specialized individuals from the existing organization are united to work on specific tasks according to a well-defined schedule. At the conclusion of the task or project, these individuals resume their normal assignments. In the overhaul situation, as exemplified by the HRA experience, a group of outside professionals are brought together on a temporary basis to restructure the foundering organization. The temporary project management group then becomes a permanent, integral part of the organization.

To achieve its objectives, the project management group has to go through a deliberate and unique life cycle. In the HRA overhaul, this life cycle was composed of the following three phases:

Phase I

During the first nine to twelve months, the staff, which consisted of about seventy professionals, assumed the role of an internal consultant: it analyzed problems, suggested solutions, pilot tested recommendations, and designed a comprehensive overhaul plan. In addition, the group acted as a troubleshooter.

Phase II

During the next six months the staff expanded to 200 persons, implemented the recommendations of Phase I, and installed systems in the field. In addition, certain project management individuals became line managers for the programs they had been instrumental in restructuring or developing.

Phase III

At the end of eighteen months the project management group, which by this time consisted of about 300 professionals, was dissolved and reorganized into permanent organizational functions. About a quarter of the staff was spun off as a permanent analytic unit and another third became a systems development unit. Other segments of the project management group were spun off as independent management or planning groups directly responsible to the various line operations.

ORGANIZATIONAL PROBLEMS AND STRATEGY

The manner in which a project management overhaul effort is geared up is extremely important. The following organizational problems and considerations must be analyzed and resolved in developing an initial implementation strategy for the project management effort.

♦ A critical group of qualified professionals can be amassed quickly by bringing in a consultant—but at great cost in both dollars and experience. A permanent staff, while taking longer to secure, is preferable, given the life cycle of the project management effort, since ultimately the most valuable resource the staff provides is its knowledge of the system. To achieve a successful overhaul each individual must be responsible for analyzing a particular problem, developing a workable solution, and then implementing it. Finally, the project manager must be capable of running the operation if called upon to do so.

♦ In rapidly recruiting a permanent staff, one is faced with the task of finding managers and subordinates simultaneously. Time pressures often necessitate gearing up projects with as yet unknown entities—staff members who might be classified as a "pick-up crew" as they have no previous experience in the field and lack organizational ties or loyalties. One must recognize the limitations of operating in this environment and the need to remain flexible.

♦ Detailed problems must be identified while results are being produced. Initially, only general problems may be evident to the management team, yet immediate results are demanded. The overall problems must be examined and defined in sufficient detail to permit the development of comprehensive solutions. Meanwhile, one must be prepared to "shoot from the hip" with an inexperienced staff.

♦ A strategy must be developed for implanting the new project management staff within the existing organization. The current organization must be induced to accept the new professionals either by issuing a decree or by making a mutual exchange of staff members and services. Above all, the existing staff must be prevented from interfering with the objectives of the overhaul.

♦ The success of the project management operation depends on its ability to secure "space" within the existing operation. The management group must acquire sufficient political and organizational leverage, and be able to operate without bureaucratic restraint or organizational opposition, if results are to be achieved according to plan. Therefore, the most effective means for gaining a foothold, acquiring elbow room, and establishing autonomy must be identified. This so-called "space" must be firmly established within the first ninety days of reorganization in order for subsequent actions to take place as planned.

♦ Once the project management organization is established, the initial momentum generated by the staff must be maintained so that subsequent phases of the overhaul can be completed on schedule.

The above-mentioned problems and considerations must be resolved as part of management's "gear up" strategy. Experience in the HRA overhaul revealed that the crucial factor was creating a workable environment and securing the necessary "space" to operate.

The following measures were taken by project management during the HRA overhaul to create an environment which provided enough space to produce rapid results:

Staffing Up

A decision was made to be especially critical of the initial thirty professionals hired and secure individuals who could grow with the operation, successfully pass through the project management life cycle, and operate well in an unstructured environment. Such individuals were solicited by provocative newspaper ads and a recruitment campaign at the nation's top business schools.

Because supervisory and analytic staff were hired simultaneously and both were unknown, it was essential to organize on a project basis. Figure 2 in-

Figure 2. Initial project management organization.

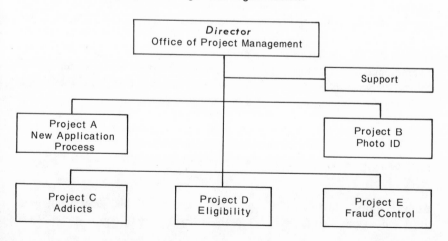

dicates the initial organization and structure. This project organization enabled us to assign clear-cut responsibility and offer individuals the "space" and autonomy they required to achieve their objectives.

Make Noise and Be Tough

A major element in the preparatory strategy was to take a strong public stance and let individuals know what was expected of them. This strategy was necessary to neutralize the opposition of the existing organization and to provide an atmosphere that would enable project management staff to operate effectively.

Go After the "Cream"

To quickly gain space, get established, and develop momentum, it was decided to begin with projects likely to have highly visible and immediate results. Therefore, three quick-results projects were implemented: a crash manual system to halt the perpetration of duplicate check frauds, a system for issuing "Photo ID" cards to recipients to discourage fraud, and a program to terminate welfare for addicts not attending treatment programs.

These projects also enabled management to identify potential leaders, and give them the opportunity to gain confidence and develop expertise before tackling the major problems ahead.

Publicize "Horror Stories"

A major element of the preparatory strategy was to structure analytic reports to read like "horror stories." Adopting that tone for the press provided the right force to bowl over the opposition and to dramatize the quick results obtained. By telling the ugly truth (for example, "We're being ripped off for $50 million per year by addicts not in treatment") and at the same time making a public commitment to solve the problem with specific steps, management left no doubt as to what its mandate was. The project managers were fully accountable to the public, should their analysis be faulty or should they fail to meet their deadlines.

THE PROJECT MANAGEMENT LIFE CYCLE

At the end of the first year, the project management staff had successfully identified and documented the system's problems, publicized "horror stories," and made appropriate recommendations. Many new systems had been implemented, special operations like "photo ID" had been completed, a comprehensive overhaul plan had been scheduled, and certain line managers had been "spun off" to run new programs.

After fourteen months, the project management staff had become a "monster" of more than 250 professionals. Fueled by some outstanding achievements, the group had attained a position of power and prominence. However, the group was threatening to sidetrack the overhaul's primary objectives—to stop the deterioration of the welfare system and to build a permanent management group within HRA, which would operate and maintain the welfare system efficiently.

The project management professionals had to relinquish their power and allow the line operations to learn and operate the new systems. The line operation had to assume its mandated responsibility and authority. This process had to take place if the overhaul was to be viable and lasting. And the project managers had to put their egos aside to allow the necessary power transfer to take place.

To precipitate this change of direction for the project management staff, the second of three reorganizations had to take place. The project management and management engineering groups were combined under a common head, several functions were added, and the stage was set for final reorganization. (Figure 3 presents this new organizational structure.)

Project management was transformed from a project organization to a functional one. Analysts from project management and engineers from industrial engineering were intermingled and assigned to new functions:

Figure 3. Phase II reorganization.

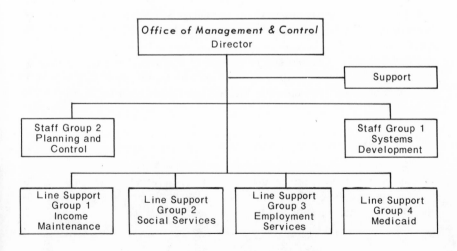

◆ A special "planning and control" group was created to program manage the different areas and to develop a permanent financial and operational analysis group. This group would monitor the system at headquarters level.

◆ A systems analysis group was formed to work on the long-term system improvements and to lay the groundwork for ultimate computerization.

◆ Finally, four special technical staff groups were created to implement and maintain the various aspects of the overhaul. Groups were established in the areas of Medicaid, income maintenance, social services, and employment planning. These four support groups were earmarked to be eventually "spun off" into the appropriate line organizations. The interim transitional grouping was known as "The Office of Management and Control."

Six months later, the final phase of reorganization took place and the four line groups were "spun off" to their respective line managers. The planning and control group became the central management group. Its function was to advise top management, establish goals and objectives for the future, and monitor the progress of all projects and programs. By this time all manual systems had been defined and either implemented or turned over to the line groups for implementation.

The only major task remaining was the computerization of the entire welfare system. The systems analysis group at this time contained a core of experienced MBAs and engineers, with a year and one-half's experience under their belts, and a firm knowledge of the new system and its operating restraints. To solidify the systems development effort, a special automation task force was mobilized by combining the systems development group in the data processing area and the systems development group of the Office of Management and Control. Figure 4 illustrates this final reorganization.

Throughout the life cycle of the overhaul, the project management/management and control staff served as a conduit, bringing highly qualified professionals into the organization, developing managers, and providing the right environment for the line operation to take control. At the end of the life cycle, the career engineers had been thoroughly assimilated into the line operation, the analysts were firmly entrenched in designing, building, and implementing the modern on-line data processing system, and the management people were finally serving in the staff positions that had been envisioned for them.

THE RESULTS

The use of a temporary project management staff to develop and implement the overhaul proved extremely successful for HRA. At the end of eighteen months, the following major results had been obtained:

Figure 4. Permanent organization.

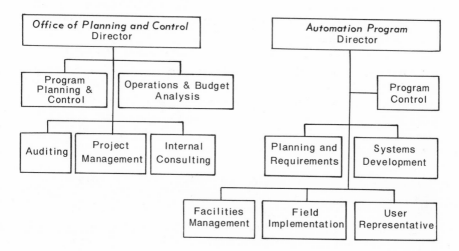

• The $5.5 million duplicate check problem was solved by referring over 1900 cases to the District Attorney for prosecution and by recouping funds from the fraudulent individuals. All recipients were summoned to a central location and given "photo ID" cards for identification and 13,000 persons were removed from the rolls in the process.

• The number of addicts on welfare was reduced from 34,000 to 15,000 by eliminating fraud, placing 90 percent in bona fide treatment programs, and developing special processing operations.

• Welfare eligibility problems and clerical errors were scrutinized and a nine-point corrective-action program prepared. This included a new application process, an annual "face-to-face" recertification, and special error control measures; rejection rates were subsequently increased from 16 percent to 41 percent in December 1972, before leveling off at 31 percent during fiscal year 1972–1973.

• Operations were analyzed and a new processing system developed; the centers were renovated and reorganized to operate in a specialized mode. Backlogs in the processing of cases were reduced from 165,000 to 50,000; employee productivity increased by 16 percent. At welfare centers, the lines of waiting clients disappeared and directors regained control of their centers. A reorganization took place which involved setting up specialized functions and replacing thirty-eight of fifty-seven line managers.

• All troublesome operations, including the Welfare Addicts Program, were put under central control. A centralized case closing system was developed, which sped up case closings from six to two weeks, thereby saving $40 million in unnecessary payments. A division of eligibility control was implemented to conduct eligibility audits and perform face-to-face recertifications. A division of location and support was established to track down missing fathers of dependent children on welfare.

♦ In the management area, administrators regained control of operations. A tough employee discipline program was implemented to enforce lateness penalties, apply absence regulations, and curtail cases of insubordination. In its first year of operation over 1,400 employees were either dismissed or fined. (Currently about 1,500 disciplinary actions are processed monthly.) A management reporting and control system monitored the operations of each welfare center and evaluated each center director on the critical operation areas under his administration.

♦ An error accountability program was instituted which measured the rate of error in each welfare center and affixed responsibility by position. A ladder of responsibility was established: from the employee to his group supervisor, then to the first-line manager, and finally to the center director. The quality of work improved and error rates declined from 35 percent to 15 percent.

♦ The world's largest municipal on-line computer system featuring on-line data, data entry, and inquiry was designed and developed. The Welfare Subsystem allows extensive transaction editing and validating to reduce error rates. The Medicaid Subsystem consists of automated eligibility determination and claims payment. The Welfare Subsystem is fully operational and the Medicaid Subsystem is partially operational, with full operation scheduled for mid-1975.

THE BOTTOM LINE

The bottom-line result of the overhaul has been a dramatic reversal in welfare expenditures. Whereas in 1971 the welfare rolls were growing at the rate of 10,000 persons a month, in 1972 this growth was arrested; the rolls remained fixed at 1,275,000 persons. In November of that year, the rolls began to decline steadily at an average rate of about 9,000 persons per month. This trend should continue through the end of 1973. The bottom line of the overall effort is a $230 million annual cost turnaround for the City of New York.

By implementing this overhaul in the brief time allotted, the City of New York was able to avert a financial and political disaster. The mayor's demand for zero caseload growth was exceeded by a large margin and the welfare rolls actually declined by 109,000 persons by the end of 1973. Since the overhaul, welfare has ceased to be a political and financial problem for the mayor and the taxpayers. Welfare mismanagement, traditionally a major campaign issue, was absent from the 1973 mayoral campaign; the candidates didn't even talk about it. In preparing its 1974 budget, the city was able to avoid further tax increases by budgeting anticipated savings in overall welfare spending.

PRESCRIPTION FOR SUCCESS

In retrospect, the most significant factor in the success of the welfare overhaul was the development of a project management staff able to adjust to each successive phase of the effort. The project management concept enabled us to quickly recruit over 400 highly trained professional managers, identify the superior ones, and achieve tangible results. A permanent management and systems staff structure was subsequently developed to ensure that the issue of welfare mismanagement does not reappear in the future.

The HRA overhaul was also successful because:

◇ There was absolute and total top management support.
◇ Adequate resources were made available as needed.
◇ Staff members brought a kind of missionary zeal to their work—a single-minded will to achieve.
◇ The new staff had no prior knowledge of welfare operations, and was therefore able to offer new and innovative solutions to old problems.
◇ Finally, the appropriate organization was created which provided the flexibility management needed to develop its strategy and implement its recommendations.

The success of the HRA effort has indicated that a top-to-bottom overhaul of a large and sprawling operation can be implemented within a short period of time; it is possible to bring in a group of professional managers without prior functional experience or vested interest and integrate them into a cohesive task force with a single-minded purpose. In fact, such a group actually serves as the best vehicle to implement an overhaul quickly.

The HRA experience has clearly demonstrated that it is important to show tangible results immediately, to concentrate on smoothing out manual operations, and to correct basic management deficiencies before installing new systems or undergoing large-scale computerization. The U.S. Postal Service commenced an overhaul concurrently with HRA, but it elected to concentrate heavily on new computer systems and cost reduction, rather than on simple systems and basic management reform. This decision has resulted in a deterioration of mail services and a further increase in costs. Now public and political confidence has been diminished and the Postal Service may have a difficult time gaining the credibility it needs to complete its programs. On the other hand, by gaining strong credibility at the outset, HRA easily obtained the funding necessary to implement its expensive and extensive data processing operation.

The project management approach is applicable to any large organization which is labor intensive and in sore need of modern technology. It is especially suitable for government bureaucracies with long-standing inertia, but it is equally suited to private industry operations where new approaches are required and immediate results demanded.

Here is a basic rule of thumb to follow in determining whether the HRA overhaul strategy and organization is applicable to your business or organization: the total staff expenditures should not exceed 5 percent of your outside potential savings and at most equal 10 percent of your best estimates. In the New York City example, a $10 million investment was made against a $200 million potential with an excellent chance of achieving $100 million in savings. In general, if an operation or organization can demonstrate that savings are potentially on the order of $50 million, then it should be able to support a 150 person/$2.5 million expenditure on a temporary overhaul staff.

WHO SHOULD BE NEXT?

The success of the HRA overhaul has indicated to the taxpayers that big government *can* do something about runaway costs without severely curtailing vital services. Government managers *can* be held accountable for their agencies and the system *can* operate with the same efficiency as analogous operations in private industry. This can be done if the taxpayers are willing to make a short-term and rather expensive investment to "clean up the mess." The New York City approach indicates that the initial investment can be recouped speedily if the overhaul is properly organized and managed.

There are other worthy candidates for overhaul in New York City. One immediately thinks of the sprawling $900 million Health and Hospitals Corporation which delivers poor quality medical services at costs 87 percent higher than the national average; or the $3 billion Board of Education, an unwieldy and uncontrolled bureaucracy. Both are ripe for an overhaul.

The transportation crisis in the eastern sector could be curtailed if the Penn Central and Metropolitan Transit Authority were subjected to a far-reaching management reform effort. Within the private sector, highly regulated industries like petroleum, utilities, and the airlines are all facing pressures analogous to those the taxpayer brings to bear on government bureaucracies.

Faced with major currency realignments, escalating labor costs, severe logistical problems, rising fuel and security costs, and strong competitive marketing forces, the nation's airlines will eventually require drastic changes in their methods of operation in order to survive. At that point, they will have to move decisively, in a manner probably foreign to career airline personnel. The HRA/project management overhaul concept is ideally suited for that situation.

Similarly, the petroleum industry is faced with a major restructuring of its business. The world's monetary and energy crises, conflicting demands of environmentalists and consumers, and the determination of Congress to eliminate the depletion allowance all portend a major organizational crisis. It is quite obvious that government regulation and consumer outcries will increase in the future. This may severely modify oil companies' business practices and alter the marketing environment in which they operate.

An extensive operations and marketing shift will most likely be required by the producers in order to maintain profits. Again, an overhaul/project management organization will probably be needed to shift gears rapidly and to provide concrete solutions. Fortunately for the oil companies, they could staff such an effort from within, since they already have the proper caliber of staff on board.

Finally, one wonders what the fate of Lockheed and Penn Central would have been had management elected to implement a far-reaching overhaul strategy using the kind of techniques HRA employed rather than continually ignoring the problem and making bankruptcy inevitable.

Whereas the fate of Lockheed and Penn Central serves as a grim warning to troubled companies and organizations, the HRA recovery offers a measure of reassurance. As New York City's welfare rolls continue to decline and its management problems are resolved, the HRA experience will continue to serve as both a suggestion and a reminder: "It *can* be done, *if* you're willing to make the investment."

Participatory Management: An Alternative in Human Service Delivery Systems

Kenneth P. Fallon, Jr.

Social service administrators have been incorporating into practice a number of methods and systems developed by business administration. These management systems have offered the agency administrator new approaches to making maximum use of scarce resources for effective service delivery.[4] Such tools as Program Evaluation Review Technique, Planning Program Budgeting System, and Management by Objectives have all had their impact on social service administration. The accountability demanded of social service management by legislators, private boards, and other consumers alike has been facilitated by these tools. Nevertheless, the greatest resource of management remains the personnel within the organization. Berliner suggested the benefits of full utilization of staff resources: "Happy is the administrator who has learned the virtues of, and techniques for, sharing of his power. Sharing of power leads to high staff morale, organizational effectiveness, and on-the-job education of a generation which inevitably must succeed him." [3]

Argyris reported in the *Journal of Business:* "Studies show that participative management tends to (1) increase the degree of 'we' feeling or cohe-

Reprinted with permission from *Child Welfare*, November 1974.

siveness that participants have with their organization; (2) provide the partici-pants with an overall organizational point of view instead of the traditional more 'now' departmental point of view; (3) decrease the amount of conflict, hostility and cutthroat competition of participants; (4) increase individuals' un-derstanding of each other, which leads to increased tolerance and patience toward others; (5) increase the individual's free expression of his personality, which results in an employee who sticks with the organization because he (i.e., his personality) needs the gratifying experiences he finds while working there; and (6) develop a 'work climate' as a result of the other tendencies, in which the subordinates find opportunity to be more creative and to come up with the ideas beneficial to the organization." [1]

Likert reported studies that indicated that "those firms or plants where System 4 (participatory management) is used show high productivity, low scrap loss, low costs, favorable attitudes, and excellent labor relations. The converse tends to be the case for companies or departments whose management system is well toward System 1 (exploitative–authoritative management)." [7]

Participatory management implies that staff will have a voice and a vote in those management decisions that affect their work. Employees who participate in this management style feel more highly motivated and tend to incorporate the organization's goals more readily than employees working in management or-ganizations that are autocratic or consultative in nature. Participatory manage-ment encourages people to stay in the organization and improve their role per-formance. [7-9]

The writer was introduced to participatory management principles at the Alaska Children's Services, a multiservice agency in Anchorage. In the sum-mer of 1972, the writer introduced participatory management to the North Idaho Child Development Center. In both agencies, the participatory manage-ment proposal was presented by the executive directors as a management alter-native, and was adopted by vote of all staff members. Both agencies were fairly new. The staff of both agreed that participatory management practices would facilitate developing programs responsive to clients' needs.

DETAILS OF PARTICIPATORY MANAGEMENT

The proposal adopted by both staffs mandated that participatory processes be applied to all major decision-making tasks, and include all elements of the staff. Democratic decision making required that decisions that affect the work of any segment of the staff be made by them. Decisions were generally to be made by voting, except in smaller staff areas, where a more liberal process (consensus) applied. The process required that, if possible, proposals to staff groups be made in writing and be available in advance to the staff.

LIMITATIONS OF THE PROCESS

Limitations of the democratic process include:

1. No segment of the staff is empowered to make any decision that affects the work of another segment. (Example: A group home staff may not make a decision affecting staff in a residential treatment center.)

2. Democratic process may not invade areas that are a matter of designated expertise of specific staff members. (Example: Speech therapists may not make decisions affecting psychometric tests used by psychologists.)

3. The competence or performance of staff is not subject to the democratic process except as applied to elected staff representatives. (Example: The professional expertise of a speech therapist must be evaluated by a speech therapist, whereas the performance of an ad hoc committee, elected by the staff to study a budget question, may be subject to democratic process.)

4. Staff may not make decisions that require expenditure of funds not under their authority. (Example: Child care workers may decide how to use recreational funds available to their particular cottage, but not how recreational funds are to be used by another cottage.)

5. Agency policy decisions are reserved for the board of directors in the case of the Alaska agency, or the administrator of the Department of Environmental and Community Services in the case of the North Idaho agency. (Example: Decisions to develop a new group home, halfway house, etc., were reserved for the board of directors of the Alaska Children's Services. Decisions regarding contracts with local school districts to develop an educational program for older retardates rested with the administrator of the Department of Environmental and Community Services in the case of the North Idaho Center.)

Basil summarized these constraints: "There is one firm rule regarding participation of subordinates in the decision-making process: that the prerequisites for participation must be ability and knowledge. Participation in decision making must be restricted to individuals with ability to comprehend what is required and the knowledge to contribute to the position." [2]

LEVELS OF DECISION MAKING

Examples of decisions to be made by each level in the agency were as follows:

1. The board of directors or the administrator: (a) agencywide policy decisions; (b) selection of a director; (c) determinations of basic program direction, with input from the community the agency serves, the board or advisory board, and the staff.

2. The administrative group (composed of designated members of each program unit, usually those with responsibility for major program supervision): (a) recommendations concerning coordination of services; (b) new service recommendations to the board of directors or the administrator; and (c) preparation of proposals to various segments of staff.

3. Ad hoc agency committees (elected by the program units to deal with specific agencywide issues): (a) all staff recommendations to the board of directors or the administrator; (b) inservice training content; (c) budget review for priorities; and (d) personnel practices such as regulations, and salary recommendations to all staff and the board of directors.

4. Program units: (a) program changes within a unit; (b) staff schedule; (c) intake into unit; (d) transfer, referral, and discharge from the service; (e) unit budget decisions; (f) changes in use of staff and of staff patterns; and (g) unit routines and rules.

5. Cross-unit staff: (a) exchange or sharing of staff for special team projects; and (b) some kinds of inservice training that may pertain to specific disciplines, programs, and so forth.

IMPLEMENTATION OF THE PROCESS

Determination of Client Need

In October 1972 the North Idaho Child Development Center held 14 meetings for professionals, consumers of service (parents and children), and interested citizens in eight communities to determine needs of children and families in those communities, and services the community felt would be responsive to those needs. At each meeting, the participants were requested to identify needs without establishing priority. Subsequently, the participants set up priorities and identified services that could be developed in response to the needs. Staff participated as resource persons but did not take part in identifying needs or service responses.

The staff reviewed the data gathered at these meetings, as well as other available data, and wrote proposals regarding program services. The proposals were summarized and sent to all participants in the community meetings. The participants were asked for their response by a community representative elected at the community meetings to represent them at a staff-community representative retreat. In November 1972 the staff proposals were considered at the three-day retreat. Programs affecting all staff were voted upon. Three new programs required funds not then available: a preschool program for handicapped children in two rural communities, a life skill acquisition program for 13- to 21-year-old retardates, and a parent training program in communication skills and infant stimulation. The community representatives set the priorities for the programs; the staff had no vote on this.

Since November 1974 all the programs have been put into operation. The first priority, the life skill acquisition program, was funded through a contract using money available through the public schools and 4-A money available to the North Idaho center. The second priority, the preschool programs for handicapped children in two rural communities, used money made available to the communities through a Title VI grant written by the Child Development Center on behalf of the school district. The third program, parent training in communication skills and infant stimulation, was developed through reallocation of existing resources within the Child Development Center and participation of AFDC recipients in infant stimulation through a special WIN program.

Full use of the participatory decision-making process allowed the North Idaho Child Development Center to develop an effective programming budget in the five-county region of North Idaho from $400,000 in fiscal 1973 to over $800,000 in fiscal 1974.

Staff Response

The initial response of staff to the participatory management practices was one of suspicion and ambivalence. As opportunities arose for the invoking of the process, staff became more committed to it. Most of those staff members who had doubts about the participatory process became committed through involvement in budget development. The give-and-take in staff's wrestling with the onerous task of developing a budget with limited funds was gratifying to both staff and management. Also, the evidence from both agencies suggests that staff are more responsible in managing their budget when they are involved in its development.

Staff are also aware that, like any other management method, democratic decision making is only as good as the administrator's intent to uphold its principles. One writer has indicated manipulatively: "An intelligent manager will, therefore, at times appoint a committee to come up with a recommendation or decision on a matter in which group deliberation is not necessary, a matter he has already decided or to which there is but one good answer. By skillful leadership or by the sheer force of facts, the group can be brought to a foregone conclusion. If the manager can avoid the appearance of 'railroading,' he is likely to obtain a stronger motivation toward acceptance in successful prosecution of a plan than if he had announced it to his subordinates without their participation." [6]

It is unlikely that staff could long be so deluded. As Basil stated: "When a manager has already made a decision, he should never ask his subordinates to participate. The subordinates will soon recognize that the executive has made the decision and is merely attempting to placate them by discussion of alternatives." [2]

A method for determining what management style is current within an organization and what the staff would desire the management style to be was made available by Likert. He devised a questionnaire on organizational performance and characteristics of different management systems.[7, 8]

This management orientation questionnaire, as modified by Comanor,[5] was administered to the staff of the North Idaho Child Development Center in June 1973. The purpose was to elicit from the staff where they thought the center was in management orientation and where the staff desired the center to be. The results of the questionnaire are shown in Figure 1.

Figure 1. Management system used and designed by North Idaho Child Development Center prior to June 1973, as seen by supervisors and nonsupervisors.

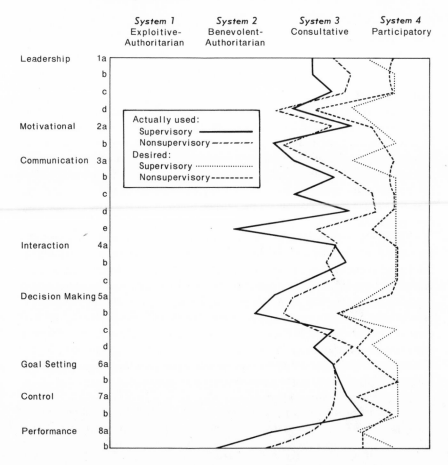

The respondents were 13 nonsupervisory staff and four supervisory staff. There are some parallels in the spikes and valleys in the figure between supervisory and nonsupervisory staff. In general, the nonsupervisory staff perceive the center's management system as more toward the participatory model than supervisory staff. Those areas where the spikes infringe in the benevolent-authoritarian area indicate problem areas to be overcome by management and staff, with management by participation as the goal.

The questionnaire was also broken down into responses by discipline and office location. This was useful in providing management with additional data in identifying specific areas where participatory management was working well and where problems existed.

The figure indicates that basically the management system at the center was consultative. It also indicates a strong desire by staff that the management be participatory.

DISCUSSION

Two months before the questionnaire was administered, the agency's former umbrella agency—the Idaho Department of Social and Rehabilitation Services—was merged by the Legislature on April 1 with the Department of Environmental Protection and Health. The new agency was named the Department of Environmental and Community Services. Its overall goal is to provide an integrated, comprehensive human service delivery system in a community-based service model. There was anxiety subsequent to the merger that the Child Development Center would lose its autonomy, and the participatory management system that had been operating in the agency might be lost to a less responsive, bureaucratic autocracy.

The staff was aware that even at best an agency that operates under the regulations of local, state, and federal government agencies has difficulty in fully implementing a participatory management system. "When the top management of an enterprise is committed to System 2 (benevolent-authoritarian) and seeks to use it throughout the company, it is extremely difficult for a manager to learn System 4 (participatory management) and to shift to it." [7] Participatory management requires a commitment in practice by management, which will also be the watchdog and guarantor of the participatory process. If that commitment is lacking or if upper management uses an authoritarian or benevolent-authoritarian management practice, middle management will have great difficulty in implementing a participatory management system in specific areas.

The staff of the Child Development Center reaffirmed commitment to the participatory management system at a staff meeting in September 1973. At a subsequent retreat (involving representatives from the Department of Environmental and Community Services in the five northern counties of Idaho), they won unanimous adoption of a participatory management proposal affecting all staff of the newly formed department. The proposal was similar to the one adopted by the Child Development Center staff the previous year.

REFERENCES

1. Chris Argyris, "Organizational Leadership and Participative Management," *Journal of Business,* Jan. 1955.
2. Douglas C. Basil, *Managerial Skills for Executive Action* (New York: American Management Association, 1970).
3. A. K. Berliner, "Some Pitfalls in Administrative Behavior," *Social Casework,* LII, 9 (1971).
4. A. W. Bradburd. "The Relationship of Systems Work to Administration," *Public Welfare,* XXV, 4 (1967).
5. Al Comanor, "Program Management Workshop," Presented at Child Welfare League of America Northwest Regional Conference, Edmonton, Alberta, 1973.
6. Harold Koontz and Cyril O'Donnell, *Principles of Management: An Analysis of Managerial Functions,* 4th ed. (New York: McGraw-Hill Book Co., 1968).
7. Rensis Likert, *The Human Organization: Its Management and Value* (New York: McGraw-Hill Book Co., 1967).
8. —, *New Patterns of Management* (New York: McGraw-Hill Book Co., 1961).
9. Joseph A. Litterer, *The Analysis of Organizations* (New York: John Wiley & Sons, 1967).

Breaking
the Synergism Barrier

Howard L. Jones

Synergism is a phenomenon that usually makes very good sense on paper. Economies are effected by doing everything in larger quantities, duplications are eliminated, and the organizations brought together bestow their best qualities on one another. Unfortunately, though, one major obstacle usually stands in the way of effective combination of organizations, departments, and groups: the attitudes of the persons affected.

Picture your first school dance when, perhaps, you were about 12 years old—with the boys standing on one side of the room and the girls on the other. Now you have a classic example of a plan for synergism that didn't gel. The problem: The two separate groups are still put off by their differences and are not yet fully aware of the benefits to be derived by their association. A veteran teacher or recreational leader knows that forcing the issue will only magnify the differences, so he is satisfied to set a climate where nature will ultimately take its course.

The above example of the difficulty of making synergism work is not at all

Reprinted by permission of the publisher from *Management Review*, July 1973, pp. 25–30. © 1973 by AMACOM, a division of American Management Associations.

distant from the story I have to tell from my own experience: the story of the merger of two prep schools—one for boys and one for girls—into a single coeducational institution with one faculty, one curriculum, and two campuses separated by the Connecticut River. Although many of the specific operating problems that we have encountered may differ from those usually experienced in the business world, the human factors involved are basically the same.

Northfield School (girls) and Mount Hermon School (boys) were both founded by Dwight L. Moody, the nineteenth century evangelist. They had been under a single board of trustees since 1912. Some coeducational classes had been in effect for ten years, and the schools had become known as the coeducational school with the five-mile hyphen many years previously.

Two Worlds

But in actuality, they were two separate and distinct schools. Each had a headmaster with a great deal of freedom in setting the course and style of his school. As headmasters, they were the top of the pyramid, with faculty and staff reporting directly to them. They lived on campus, and their homes were in a real sense the center of the adult community around them. As president, I was their reporting superior. They, as members of the board of trustees, were party to top-level policy making for the corporation.

Our decision to effect a complete merger between the two schools in late 1970 came about for two reasons. One was economic. We suffered a deficit of almost $500,000 in 1970–1971 (which was cut in half the following year and has gradually been subsiding since). The other dealt with fulfilling the objectives of education in today's environment—The needs of male and female students have become less differentiated, coeducation has become more consistent with the times, and requirements of more sophisticated curricula could be better filled with a larger aggregate student body.

When faculty, administration, and students met to discuss the future of the school, coeducation was *not* supposed to be the issue, but we found—six months before the consolidation, when these parties met in small groups to discuss it—that coeducation was the issue in the minds of most participants; it dominated the discussion in most of the groups.

The comments we heard included: "It's a more natural educational mode." "Boys—or girls—won't be such a big thing if we have daily and casual contact with them." "Who wants to go to school in a monastery—or a convent?" "Learning about people should be a prime goal of education. That doesn't mean learning only about your own sex."

Sidetracked Thinking

Fortunately these reactions, although they were not wholly pertinent, were positive ones. But more important was the fact that this was only the beginning of the kind of sidetracked thinking that would constantly crop up during the consolidation. We subsequently learned that the matters that would most stand in the way of a smooth transition would be those of a relatively minor nature. Some of the most divisive issues were:

◆ Boys had certain privileges, such as smoking for seniors with parental permission and hitchhiking, that girls did not have. How would these be reconciled?

◆ Although both schools practiced "participative democracy" for students, Mount Hermon's decision-making process was direct, while Northfield relied on committees that sought consensus. Which approach would be used in the merged school?

◆ How would students be transported between classes on the two campuses?

◆ Won't the girls want personal laundry facilities in their new dorms on the previous all-boy campus?

◆ Can the boys get their football uniforms into the lockers of the new gymnasium on the previous all-girl campus?

◆ Both campuses had programs in which students were responsible for performing various chores on campus, but the program for girls was more rigid. For example, girls were regularly assigned to cook meals under supervision, while the boys ate in a large dining hall where their function was primarily to help a commercial caterer with serving and cleanup. The internal work program for boys was more flexible, allowing time off for athletics and outside jobs. How could an equitable work program be worked out without sacrificing the values that each separate program attempted to instill in students?

Divisive Issues

In addition, we had to reconcile differences of a less minor nature. One of these was the difference in curricula between the two schools. Mount Hermon was more innovative; Northfield was more traditional. Mount Hermon was first to propose such innovations as computer math, education abroad for one term, and interdisciplinary courses. Privately, some Mount Hermon teachers felt that the Northfield teachers were behind the times, and some Northfield teachers said that those in the boys' school were wild-eyed dreamers.

Another basic problem—if it were allowed to remain one—was that the majority of Northfield teachers were women, while the majority of Mount Hermon teachers were men. This is hardly a divisive factor in most organizations today, but it was initially so in ours. Both schools had imbedded traditions and attitudes that stemmed from yesteryear's enforced differences between the sexes. Complicating this matter even further was the disparity in salaries between the schools that had developed over the years. Salaries were generally lower at Northfield, because most of the teachers were women—a practice dignified by tradition, if not just.

None of these problems—large or small, real or imagined—could be attacked effectively until the organization was knitted into a single structure. This had to start at the top, where the initial problem was redefinition of the roles of the president and the two headmasters. This problem—from the people aspect—was simplified by the facts that one headmaster was a year away from retirement and the other was offered the presidency of a midwestern school.

New Organizational Structure

In the past, my role as president was seen by students and faculty as largely an "exterior" one. Although the headmasters had been responsible to me, they had great autonomy and on-campus visibility.

We agreed finally to try out a structure that called for me, as president, to assume some of the traditional functions of the headmaster. In addition, each campus was to have a "dean of center," who would be responsible for everything on that campus except academic matters. The rationale for this was that, although we wished to retain the autonomy that fostered individuality on the two campuses, we were charged with forming one faculty and one curriculum.

For this purpose, we created the new post of dean of faculty. We already knew that a key concern of Northfield staff members was whether a fair number of women would be brought into the top level of administration, and this was our first opportunity to prove that they would. For this post, we selected an outstanding woman who was head of the science department at Northfield. Two other key positions were registrar and director of counseling. The first job went to a woman who had been administrative assistant to the headmaster; a senior master was selected to supervise counseling activities on both campuses. He has since been appointed associate headmaster at another school and succeeded by a woman.

Our next step was to appoint a chairman to bring each department together. It was important that each department's chairman be acceptable to its members, so the opinion of every teacher in every department was solicited. Once the chairman was appointed, discussion of the course content and methods was much easier. Although there were still differences of opinion, the split was no longer along school lines but genuinely on differences in professional approach, which could be discussed with less emotion. New alliances were forged, which cut across the potential gaps of age, sex, and former school, allowing substantive and manageable discussions on the direction each department would take.

Participative Management

Even with the school's administration and faculty consolidated, there were many problems that remained to be solved. More than once, we encountered the question, "Why doesn't the administration make all the decisions based on the knowledge and experience that it is supposed to have?" We could have done just that. It would have been easier for us. But we realized that our teachers, as dedicated professionals, had to be consulted on most matters. We deliberately attract some teachers with unorthodox ideas about teaching methods and course content; any management structure that does not encourage original thought from such persons is self-defeating. Also, our product—the student—has a mind of its own.

So we decided to go the participative-management route, which had the secondary effect of bringing together the separate groups of administrative personnel, faculty, and students. A "Committee on the One School" was created, consisting of teachers, students, and administrative staff. Spinning out from this committee were task forces assigned to study various aspects of the school and recommend plans. These task forces covered such areas as curriculum; international involvement; the arts; rules, ethics, and customs; and governance.

The task force on governance, for example, settled on a senate with a complicated but equitable election process. Every class, every dorm, and every shade of opinion of faculty and staff are represented. I must say that this participatory democracy is a bit more than I like to bear at times, and sometimes I can even doubt Benjamin Franklin's assertion that democracy—bad as it is—is better than all the other possibilities. However, the senate has functioned as the main legislative body of the school, and there's hope that it will develop into an effective forum and source of ideas for future planning. Also we considered participatory involvement a necessary part of the educational process.

Presently, with about 150 boys residing on the former all-girl campus of more than 500 students and 150 girls on the former all-boy campus containing roughly the same number of total students, the two campuses are subdivided into clusters, where the single-sex dorms are each part of a coeducational cluster of dorms. Each cluster is responsible for making its own rules, within limits set by the senate, to which they send elected representatives.

Analyzing the Results

Through this total approach to participative management, many of the minor problems have been solved. Many have not; for example, we will always have the considerable expense of transporting students between classes on the two campuses daily. Even so, such problems are now of less concern to the parties involved, because they have participated in reaching decisions through the most painless approach possible.

The salary discrepancy between male and female teachers has not disappeared entirely. While the Northfield teachers have been classified into the salary ranges that had been used for Mount Hermon teachers, they tend to be below the midpoint of the range, while the Mount Hermon teachers tend to be above it. In many cases, this is justified by the men having additional duties as coaches. In any case, the framework is set for the discrepancy to disappear gradually.

And some of the petty problems have benefited from benign neglect. The girls have their washing machines; the boys don't. Neither group seems concerned about this inequity any more.

Part 5

MANAGING . . .

...The Art Museum

...The Generosity Business

...The Presidency

...The Naval Shore Establishment

...The Professor

...The Judicial System

THIS SECTION IS ORGANIZED DIFFERENTLY THAN THE PRECEDING SECTIONS. Parts 2, 3, and 4 discuss techniques and styles of management as they are being applied in a mix of organizations. The articles in this section focus on special nonprofit organizations not heavily covered in earlier sections. These special kinds of organizations appear to be unique because of special characteristics associated with them. Articles on these organizations have been highlighted and singled out because of their emphasis on particular problems of managing in that sector or organization.

	Government	Education	Health	Religious and Charitable	Associations and Others
Management Problems Enter the Picture at Art Museums Walter McQuade					X
Determining Results in the Generosity Business Robert J. Dubin				X	
How to Make the Presidency Manageable Peter F. Drucker	X				
The Naval Shore Establishment and Parkinson's Laws Donald A. Morton	X				
The Administration of Professors as Decision-Makers Martha A. Brown		X			
At Last—Innovation in the Federal Judicial System Warren E. Burger	X				

Management Problems Enter the Picture at Art Museums

Walter McQuade *

Managers may find the present time exciting, challenging, or otherwise rewarding—but certainly not serene. Inflation, various kinds of militancy, and pressures to show "social responsibility" have introduced a degree of turbulence
into the task of managing almost any kind of organization. The turbulence extends even to what might be thought to be just about the most sheltered of all
managerial posts, the job of running an art museum.

Not so long ago most art museums were primarily elegant tombs of culture
past. The men who ran them, the museum directors, lived lives of gloved serenity. In the summer they traveled through Europe in search of acquisitions. In
winter they did some discreet social arbitrating among members of the upper
crust, from whom they drew their boards of trustees. It was all very genteel.
Things had been like that for a long time. The Metropolitan Museum of Art
was organized in New York in 1870 by a committee whose avowed purpose
was to afford "to our whole people free and ample means for innocent and

* Research associates: Varian Knisely and Jane Mull.

Reprinted with permission from *Fortune,* July 1974.

refined enjoyment," but it was not until twenty-one years later that the Met bothered to stay open on Sundays, the only day most working people had off at that time. There were no evening hours at the Met until 1968.

Today the pace of life for museum directors is geared high. Most of them must deal with a range of problems, including severe financial troubles and labor unrest, that would be familiar to any corporate executive. The cost pressures are so great that many museums are now being forced to shorten their hours again and curtail elaborate exhibitions. The directors even face a cultural equivalent of the consumer movement, with the public demanding greater probity in the ways museums buy and sell that noble commodity, art. And just as corporate chief executives must sometimes reexamine the purposes of the organizations they head, museum directors are having to ask themselves what their institutions ought to be.

These issues have combined to create a great deal of day-to-day tension between the thousand or so directors of art museums in the United States and the small army of trustees who try to guide the directors. This tension is bringing changes in the requirements for the post of museum director. No longer are trustees satisfied with a charming, articulate scholar and connoisseur of art; now they are demanding, in addition, high competence and experience in a wide range of managerial arts.

Museum directors today are expected to be masters of personnel management, superb public-relations men, and competent merchants (most sizable museums operate their own shops for art-related goods). They must be skilled bargainers with art dealers, effective lobbyists for government support, and deft politicians able to deal with bumptious neighborhood or ethnic groups demanding special consideration. And if their museums are to increase their stocks of art, as most of them are eager to do, the directors must be agile at a very old game. They have to be what John Walker, a former director of Washington's National Gallery of Art, refers to as "collectors of collectors," in order to inveigle private owners into donating their Rembrandts and Picassos.

Rolling Out the Upper Crust

To some extent, the directors' growing difficulties derive from the fact that art museums have in recent years become increasingly popular with adult Americans. (Schoolchildren, of course, have always been herded through in droves.) The increased attendance is partly a result of some basic changes—many art museums no longer display only paintings and sculpture, but put on highly sophisticated exhibitions offering many other kinds of visual experiences. Museums exhibit posters, printed fabrics, industrial designs, photographs, architecture, furniture, and even movies.

The Associated Councils of the Arts, a nonprofit organization formed in 1965 to provide guidance for state and community councils, commissioned a poll last year to measure the upsurge of interest in art. A cross section of the American public was asked what they did with their leisure. It turned out that more of them went to art museums than to sports events. The upper crust, it seems, has been rolled both thick and wide.

Popularity, however, is not bringing prosperity. Museum directors are hard-pressed to keep up with rising costs of operation, and must constantly seek added revenue. Whereas prices of paintings and sculpture have gone to the sky, the institutions that own them get no financial relief from the appreciation of their stored assets. In fact, the rise in prices penalizes the museums by making it more expensive for them to add to their collections. In the past ten years the value of the collection at Manhattan's Museum of Modern Art has probably doubled. But William S. Paley of CBS, who is the museum's chairman, says that "deficits are eating us up." The museum's endowment now comes to about $16 million; in the past three years, operating losses have reduced it by $3 million.

Even the admission charges imposed by many museums have not stemmed the flow of red ink. Most museum directors argue that only ever increasing governmental subsidies, for both public and private institutions, can help them satisfy the appetite for art. Legislators at all levels of government seem to be responding with money. Last year the National Endowment for the Arts sponsored a survey of American museums, including those devoted to history and science. The survey determined that no less than 37 percent of the museums' income came from cities, counties, states, or the federal government. That represented more money than came from any other source. The average museum got 29 percent of its income from operating revenues, including admission charges, 13 percent from endowment income and other nonoperating revenues, and 21 percent from contributions by private citizens, foundations, and corporations.

Although both directors and trustees seem to regard government support as necessary and inevitable, many of them don't really like it. For one thing, they cannot count on having the money when they need it. In times of pinch, art may seem highly dispensable from a political viewpoint. Museum officials worry that with support will come control, and they understandably dislike the possibility of government interference in their selection and presentation of art. They are aware that few politicians fully share their tastes (a contempt for nonrepresentational painting was one thing that Harry Truman and Dwight Eisenhower had in common), and some of them are not reassured by the knowledge that art has remained unstifled by the past support of museums by governments in the United States and Europe.

One veteran trustee on the West Coast says the more remote the governmental source, the less dangerous: "At the county level, I'm scared. On the state level, I'm less scared. At the federal level, I'm not scared." Others take a less sanguine view of federal support. Says the director of a midwestern museum: "By the year 2000, the federal government will give more funds and have more control. I for one am glad that I'll be dead. I would hate to have to explain a piece of art to a Congressman."

A Loss of Esteem

That, no doubt, would be about as difficult as explaining to today's museum employees that they should be content to work at low salaries because their surroundings on the job are so rich. One reason art museums find their budgets strained is that pay scales have been rising inexorably in response to increased demands by their professional staffs. Salaries remain meager, however. At the Museum of Modern Art a college graduate with a general knowledge of twentieth century art, a reading knowledge of French, and some skill at typing starts at $6,500 a year. Guards start at $6,317.

Museum directors themselves work for salaries that are low by corporate standards. Last year a survey by the American Association of Museums disclosed that the median pay for directors of art museums was just $17,500 a year. Only 25 percent earned more than $24,000, and the highest salary reported was $49,500. Few directors have much job security; contracts are a rarity. And directors no longer enjoy a full measure of the old-time recompense of assured public esteem.

There has been much criticism recently of the methods some museum directors have used in stocking their museums. Even the Metropolitan, the country's greatest single art treasury, and its mesmeric director, Thomas P. F. Hoving, have been battered by the New York *Times* for the way Hoving "deaccessioned" some painting two years ago. (He traded them to an art dealer in return for other art objects that the *Times* and its sources regarded as being less valuable.)

The aplomb of many acquisitive museum directors has been badly upset by public reaction to disclosures that their collecting apparently encourages the looting of ancient art and artifacts all over the world. The controversy has engaged the critical attention of the television networks, usually reliable allies of the museums in their effort to disseminate culture. An ABC documentary special in May showed Hoving fending off sharp questions about a $1.1-million collection of old Lydian silver and gold pieces that the Met had bought. Hoving did not say where the museum obtained the collection, but Turkey's deputy director of antiquities, Burhan Tezcan, declared that the Met's acquisition is a national treasure which belongs in his country. On the same program, Richard

F. Brown, director of the Kimbell Art Museum in Fort Worth, was asked to name the seller from whom he had purchased two classic Mayan carvings displayed in his galleries. Brown stonily refused.

Cries for a new morality in collecting have grown so insistent that Congress is now considering legislation to drastically restrict importation of archaelogical art. Museum directors say that if the bill passes, they will be virtually unable to expand their collections of antiquities.

The directors are vulnerable to bad publicity because, among other things, it stirs up their bosses, the trustees. At many museums, trustees and directors live in a state of increasing mutual unease. During board meetings, trustees frequently stare in puzzlement at the director, wondering why so many problems are lofted to them from the operating level. The director may smile back politely, but his mind is likely to be filled with wonder at the innocence of trustees who cling, as some do, to a belief that the museum world is much the same as it was when their governesses walked them through the marble corridors fifty years ago.

No Place for Artists

Often there are so many trustees on a board that arriving at clear decisions is difficult. As large a corporation as Xerox finds it can function with thirteen board members, but many art museums have thirty-five trustees, or more. This means that the crucial decisions must be hammered out by a small executive committee, then sold to the rest of the board. Museum trustees traditionally have been successful businessmen, prominent professionals in medicine, law, or the church, and people who are plumaged in inherited money and dwell in the upper branches of old family trees. Just as hospital boards generally have few physicians as members, museums have few art scholars and almost no artists on their boards.

Museum boards are usually self-appointing, thus self-perpetuating, and are often weighted with members much older than the usual art-museum audience. At the Metropolitan, for example, it was only last year that the trustees revised their bylaws concerning age, and then only to state that people more than seventy-two years old are not eligible for nomination to be new trustees.

Important as the trustees are to art museums, they are sometimes selected in a casual manner, with little regard to the overall composition of the board or the institution's needs. Ralph F. Colin, a Manhattan lawyer who is also a noted art collector and an experienced trustee, has developed a prescription for balanced boards and has urged it on various museums. "First," says Colin, "you need about one-third composed of the very rich, to pay the bills and make up deficits. It would be lovely if you could get along without them, but you can't.

Another third should be distinguished people who lend luster to the museum and are an effective means to tap outside sources. The final third should be people who know something about art, and are willing to contribute time, enthusiasm, and work." So far Colin has found no museum interested in adopting his formula.

Colin believes that museum trustees, as a group, are neither better nor worse than members of the corporate boards he has served on. "They mean to be constructive, but they can also be arbitrary on occasion, gutless, or just plain apathetic—going through the motions."

Passions often run high on institutional boards. After fifteen years on the Museum of Modern Art's forty-member board, Colin so strongly disapproved when Paley fired the museum director in 1969 without calling a meeting of the trustees that he resigned from the museum's board. As a result of the disagreement, Colin lost Paley as a private law client, lost the corporate account of CBS, which his firm had represented for forty-two years, and had to relinquish his seat on the CBS board.

A Nuance of Control

No such brouhaha among the trustees has ever disturbed the serenity of the grand neoclassic building that houses the National Gallery of Art. The director, J. Carter Brown, thirty-nine, has only nine trustees to answer to. They include Paul Mellon, who is also president of the gallery, and John Hay Whitney, the vice president. Both men are knowledgeable collectors of art as well as generous philanthropists.

Like a number of other art museums, the National is an odd combination of public ownership and private control. The site, between the Washington Mall and Pennsylvania Avenue, is government-owned, and so is the building itself. But when Brown, a brilliant art scholar and capable administrator, is asked whether the National is a public or private institution, he replies, "There is a nuance here."

The National Gallery was established in 1937 by Andrew Mellon, who had served as Secretary of the Treasury in the Harding, Coolidge, and Hoover administrations. Mellon shaped the National's charter, paid for its building, and primed its galleries with masterpieces. The maintenance of the building, most salaries, and the costs of some exhibitions are paid for by congressional appropriation. The money to pay the five top members of the executive staff comes from a private endowment, established by the Mellons and others; the size of that endowment is kept secret.

No taxpayer's money has ever been spent on purchasing art. After Mellon started the collections with his contributions, other wealthy Americans gave generously—among them Samuel H. Kress, of dime-store fame; Joseph Widener, whose money came from streetcars; Chester Dale, an investment banker; Lessing J. Rosenwald of the family that controlled Sears, Roebuck; and Averell Harriman. Paul Mellon is now adding a building, at a cost to him of about $70 million, to the institution founded by his father.

One of the ways in which Carter Brown is more fortunate than most museum directors arises from the relative clarity of the National Gallery's reason for being. It is an acknowledged national treasure, a repository for great art, where individuals can contemplate the best of the past. Other museum directors in the United States are being forced to redefine the proper function of their institutions, and there is considerable disagreement among them as to what that proper function is. Some believe the art museum to be basically an educational instrument to be used in socially aggressive ways. They see their job as being one of energetically promoting cultural wares. Others, more traditionally inclined, believe that active promotion of art compromises its contemplative value.

The leader of the latter school of thought is Sherman E. Lee, director of the Cleveland Museum of Art. Lee is a tall man of fifty-six, of distinguished appearance and tailoring, unbending in manner. He insists that the true purpose of the museum is to provide the setting for the confrontation between one work of art and one person. He paraphrases a Latin paradox: "Never is he more active than when he does nothing, never is he less alone than when he is by himself."

Lee argues that the art museum "is not fundamentally concerned with therapy, history, social action, entertainment, or scientific research. The museum is comparable to a permanent storage battery. It is a primary source of wonder and delight for mind and heart." He puts on an extensive educational program for slum schools, but his is essentially an upper-middle-class operation. Lee says people should learn about art by reading about it before they visit a museum to see it, and he deplores Acoustiguides, the small amplifiers of recorded lectures that some museums provide for visitors to plug into their ears.

"Disgusting" is Lee's word for the recorded lectures. The experience, he says, is "like listening to a Beethoven quartet with pictures thrown on the wall. It is simply another activity—something happening. If museums follow this route, they may destroy themselves." Lee thinks an art museum should be like a woodland preserve, free of distractions: "A wilderness area, the highest and purest realm of nature. It cannot become a Disneyland."

A Means of Communicating Values

The director of the Los Angeles County Museum of Art, Kenneth Donahue, takes an approach that is quite different from Lee's. An informal, friendly person and an excellent art scholar, Donahue believes in actively promoting community interest in his museum's many outstanding paintings and sculptures. "The Los Angeles Museum is a ten-ring circus, but a very serious one," Donahue says. "All Los Angeles is a kind of circus."

He thinks of a work of art as a "means of communicating values, as helping toward an understanding of history, of man himself. I am as concerned with ideas as I am with the work of art as an object." Donahue makes sure that his art museum gets frequent exposure on morning television shows. He recently staged an exhibition of Chicano art that was attended by 70,000 people, most of whom, he said, had never before passed through the doors. He is now planning a historical show of black artists. "What does this accomplish? One, it brings more black people into the museum. Two, it lets these people know that their tradition is important."

Donahue measures a museum's success by its attendance figures, and most other museum directors would agree with him. Tom Hoving called last fall's show of tapestries at the Met—a lecture by Hoving on the tapestries was available on Acoustiguides—the most successful in the history of the museum because it set a new attendance mark. More than 375,000 people visited the show in ten weeks.

Richard Brown of Fort Worth's Kimbell was Donahue's predecessor as director of the Los Angeles County Museum, and like him wants to attract the broadest possible audience. "The next real job of the museum is not to get the educated, leisured person who can and does come, but to go out into the countryside to minority groups, and bring these people in. You can't expect them to take in new forms without any background. We should get little kids in, and by momentum, all the people who might never think of coming into a museum."

What Does the "Best Possible" Mean?

With the museum world so divided as to purpose, it may seem surprising that there is considerable agreement among today's museum directors and their trustees as to how tomorrow's managers should be trained. They all, of course, see as paramount the need for advanced training in the fine arts, but many grant the need for something more. When Hoving interviews applicants for jobs at the Met, he says, he looks for people who have degrees in both fine arts and business administration, and perhaps law as well. When Ken Donahue was asked how he would educate a son who wanted eventually to run an art museum, he replied, "Doctorate in the history of art, then a master's in public administration."

But Cleveland's Sherman Lee thinks too much emphasis is being put on business management these days. "A museum shouldn't be run inefficiently," he says, "but you must realize there is hardly any decision that is not—once, twice, or three times removed—an aesthetic decision. For example, the choice of using high-gloss polish versus wax is not just a fiscal choice. Regardless of the price of either, there are totally different shines and effects. This is a hard thing to get across to a business manager. The museum is not in business to be efficient. It is in business to be the best possible art museum it can be.''

But what it means to be the "best possible" museum remains to be defined by the directors, their trustees, and their restive publics. The answer is not to be found on the Acoustiguide.

Determining Results in the Generosity Business

Robert J. Dubin .

Nonprofit organizations that are devoted to the betterment of mankind through projects in education, culture, health, and other vital social areas seldom see themselves as businesses. Considering the selfless nature of their work, this attitude is perhaps understandable; but because of it, countless public and private institutions spend or administer billions of dollars in projects whose goals are loosely defined at best and whose end results are some intangible betterment of the individuals who participate in them.

The foundations, corporations, government agencies, and individuals who allocate an annual wealth of funds for nonprofit purposes are involved in what could realistically be termed the "generosity business." Research techniques by which profit-making businesses measure the marketability of their products are equally applicable in the generosity sector.

No funding source, not even the U.S. government or the Ford Foundation, can fulfill anywhere near the number of requests for grants that it receives. And when money is given, the donor needs to find out if it is helping to accomplish

Reprinted by permission of the publisher from *Management Review*, January 1973, pp. 17–26. © 1973 by AMACOM, a division of American Management Associations.

the noble objectives that the receiver of the grant so eloquently stated in its application. Funding organizations and the groups that are the recipients of public and private largesse must face the thorny issue of finding some yardstick by which to measure the results of the programs with which they are concerned.

MEASURING THE INTANGIBLE

Developing such a yardstick has posed few problems where the results or "product" of a program are tangible. In a capital-funding project, for example, sufficient money either is raised or it isn't; the building gets built or it doesn't. Similarly, a public campaign to raise money to eradicate widespread disease lends itself to relatively simple measurement: Money is or is not raised to conduct research; the research produces a cure or fails, or is deemed significant enough to merit continued support.

The problems of measuring results—and thus of sound financial management—are much more difficult for organizations involved in programs that have less tangible "products." Few, if any, of the organizations that back these programs have developed a credible method of determining which are worthy of support and how well those that are funded achieve their goals.

Compounding this problem is the attitude, long prevalent among so many institutions devoted to "good works," that somehow funding for such programs is above the mundane considerations of cost controls and effectiveness. Most organizations in this segment of the nonprofit community view money spent for art or other cultural enrichment as money spent for its own sake and behave as if distribution of these funds is excepted from established management practices by virtue of the programs' lofty goals.

Competition seems a harsh word applied in the context of nonprofit funding. However, proliferation and even duplication of programs in many areas has created increasingly heated competition for the attention and dollars of funding institutions. Donors and recipient organizations now find themselves in a desperate search for information that will help them in making decisions about which programs to continue and which to abandon. No organization in the generosity business can afford to feel secure in the confidence that somehow the worthiness of its cause will attract the unfailing benevolence of those who have money to give.

The first reaction from some of the "do-gooders" to the idea of marketing research is skepticism and possibly even hostility.

Could, in fact, the same concepts of marketing research that go into the development of a better deodorant soap be adapted to the development of better

"cultural enrichment"? Could the audience for "human betterment" be as effectively measured for acceptance of the "product" and changes in "buying"
patterns (behavior modification) as the audience for cake mixes?

The National Endowment for the Arts, a government agency, and the
Sears-Roebuck Foundation, one of the country's largest and most innovative
foundations, were willing to fund an experiment to test this concept. These two
funding sources sought a means of evaluating two programs they supported in
the past and which were due for a major decision on continuation of that support. Young Audiences, Inc. and Affiliate Artists Inc., the funded organizations, are similar in program and goals. Both seek to aid performing artists in
their artistic growth and employment opportunities, and both seek to introduce
the performing arts to new audiences.

In each case, emphasis is placed on musicians and their music. Young Audiences, however, directs its program to children in the public schools, while
Affiliate Artists seeks to introduce professional but relatively unknown young
performers to college and adult audiences. Young Audiences involves several
hundred performers in dozens of cities across the country. Affiliate Artists supports a single performer in a given community for a period of weeks under the
sponsorship of a local organization.

When J. R. Taft Corporation was called in to conduct a study of these programs, the information we sought about each was basically the same: Are the
programs successful? Are they accomplishing their objectives? Do they deserve
continued support, or should support be abandoned, redirected, or expanded?
What are the weaknesses and strengths of each program? How might they be
improved?

TESTING GROUND

These programs afforded an excellent opportunity for us to test our theory of
market research in the nonprofit community. The audiences for their "products" are sufficiently diverse (school-age children, college students, and adults
in several major "markets") and their goals (enriching lives through involvement in listening to and performing music) sufficiently intangible to present a
fair statement of the kind of problem most frequently encountered in the decision-making process by nonprofit organizations.

The first task was to develop the parameters of the research design, difficult though it is, when dealing with human endeavor, to determine the quantitative differences between success and something less. There is no one individual or group of individuals whose perceptions of a project and its results
provide a whole answer to the question, "Did we succeed?" Just as in the

marketplace, research must reflect the attitudes and perceptions of a wide range of individuals from the manufacturer of a product to its consumer, to people who have never used the product or one like it, so too, our research had to reflect responses of all of the "publics" touched by the program.

The obvious "public" for the Young Audiences program is school children in grades one through six. Their response is tempered, however, by the attitudes of other equally significant participants in the program. We determined that to develop a total picture of the program's effectiveness with some accuracy, it also would be necessary to elicit the attitudes and response of the sponsoring organization itself, the artists who perform in the program, the officials who decide when and to what extent their school systems will participate, and teachers in the classrooms who play an important role both before and after the experience of a musical performance.

Continuing the evolutionary process of defining our "publics," we also discovered that each of the program's audiences was composed of identifiable segments, or "subpublics." Clearly, children in grades one through three who might be experiencing the Young Audiences program for the first time would respond differently from children in grades four through six who had seen the programs in the past. Distinctions were determined to exist among children for whom attendance was compulsory and those attending voluntarily, among inner-city children and urban middle-class children, among groups of children from urban families and those from suburban middle-class families, and among children with access to a wide selection of cultural experiences and those with limited cultural opportunities.

Similarly, there were distinctions in attitudes and perceptions among national headquarters personnel and local chapter volunteers, artists participating in the programs, school officials and teachers.

VARIED RESPONSES

Another factor affecting the shape and scope of the research was the diversity of programs conducted by Young Audiences. The organization for many years has enabled public school children to experience live performances of "serious" music and to interact with both the music and the performers. In its "standard" program, musical groups perform one to three concerts per school year, each unrelated to the other. In its "depth" program, musicians perform five or six closely integrated concerts, each building upon the musical experience of the one before it. Obviously, there would be significant differences in the response of children exposed to the two programs and in those expected from children who either had or had not experienced any kind of program at all. We determined the "audience" in fact was made up of five distinct "publics":

The Children: school children in grades one through six exposed to the programs; and school children in the same grades, of similar socioeconomic backgrounds, who had not been exposed.

The Performers: artists in the "standard" program and artists in the "depth" program.

Young Audiences, Inc.: members of the board of directors, local chapter leaders, and national staff members.

The Funding Organizations: the National Endowment for the Arts, Sears-Roebuck Foundation, and other donors.

Peripheral Publics: music teachers, classroom teachers, principals, and superintendents from participating schools; music teachers, classroom teachers, principals, and superintendents from schools not participating, and musicians' union members directly involved in the Young Audiences program.

Two important questions were raised by the nature of the publics to be studied and the program itself. First, what was the best method for eliciting information, and would the techniques that worked for one sub-public work for another? Second, since frequency of exposure to the program was an obvious parameter of the survey, what should the research strategy be: longitudinal or cross-sectional?

Taking these questions in reverse order, we determined that a cross-sectional survey was the best way to proceed. To be valid, a longitudinal study must follow specific individuals through a number of concert seasons and record responses both before and after different exposures to the program. It was neither desirable nor practical to stretch out the study over a period of years. Moreover, because of the nature of the Young Audiences program itself, it was possible to study communities where the program was just being introduced and at the same time investigate school systems where the program had been in operation for some years.

Thus, a cross-sectional survey was an opportunity to talk concurrently with a number of publics representing different stages of exposure and different backgrounds. This approach provided all the advantages of a longitudinal survey while eliminating some of its potential drawbacks. Data could be collected over a relatively short period of time and thus avoid the problems of sample attrition. We also were able to avoid the effect on audience response of the interview itself as a factor in heightening awareness or altering attitudes toward the program. The cross-sectional survey enabled us to avoid conditioning the respondents to our areas of interest and permitted greater flexibility in measuring changes in behavior at each level of exposure to the program.

Our strategy determined, we turned to the question of how to get the information we sought. It was clear that a method that might be successful with the musicians involved in the program might prove less successful in surveying the children exposed to their performances. We adopted two methods of collecting data: a self-administered questionnaire, supplemented by a limited number of depth interviews for the children, and depth personal interviews alone for the adults involved in all levels of the program. Because of the ages of the children, we relied heavily upon nonverbal measures. The self-administered questionnaires were designed with a combination of "smiling face" rating scales and structured questions to which children could respond by circling pictures, thus minimizing reliance on reading and writing skills.

The technique of depth interviews was used with musicians in each of the Young Audiences programs and with the organization's personnel in its national headquarters and local chapters. Different questionnaires were developed for use with local members and national personnel to measure variances in perceptions of goals, personal reactions, and organizational structure. Other questionnaires were developed for the peripheral publics, including school personnel and musicians' union officials. All interviewing was done in five chapters—Boston, Kansas City, New York City, Portland, and Arizona State—which were selected on the basis of geographic location, type of program(s) offered, maturity of the chapter, and its size. About 1,000 people were interviewed.

As is often done in market research, we constructed cells of analytical size for each of the populations from whom we sought information. We then developed a series of "précis" tables that enabled us to bring into sharp focus the kinds of information we needed and permitted measurement of a range of factors at the same time.

While we measured children's perception of the "entertainment" and "educational" values of the concert programs, we also made a comparative analysis of reactions to the standard and depth of the concerts and the distinctions in response that existed among children from various social and economic backgrounds. We constructed précis tables for such relatively simple comparisons as attitudes toward listening to music and favorite type of music, as well as more complex questions such as "entertainment" and "educational" values over three years of exposure, both for the total population and for ethnic subpopulations. The orientation simply was to adapt commercial marketing research techniques to a nonprofit program by generating as much valid, relevant data as possible to permit managers of the program to make a rational decision about its funding.

Local chapter officials were given the responsibility of selecting "equivalent" nonparticipating schools to serve as a control group in the study. Children not exposed to either the "standard" or "depth" program but who had usually attended other kinds of musical concerts were matched on the basis of sex and ethnic and socioeconomic background with those who had been exposed.

PROBLEMS IN CONTROL

A number of unanticipated factors complicated the effort to establish a control group in the strictest scientific sense of the term. For example, the schools steadfastly refused to disclose specific socioeconomic data on individual children. Furthermore, the program tends to have greater impact on children who have few cultural opportunities, and this is particularly true of the "depth" program, which focuses on black, inner-city children in New York and Boston. Thus, there were substantial problems in gathering strictly comparable data on "exposed" and "not exposed" groups.

To ensure that the conclusions from comparing the groups were statistically valid, we sought the aid of an independent statistical analyst. His report indicated that we were, in fact, measuring "real" differences among the subpopulations of children, while restating our own perceptions about the scientific shortcoming of our "control" group. In effect, the control group was really more a model against which to measure the perceptions of our survey population.

What, then, did all this preparation and theorizing finally tell us? Out of the mass of data collected there emerged a comprehensive picture of the organization and its strengths and weaknesses; a broad understanding of how the program is perceived, not only by its "users" (the children), but also by the musicians, organization officials, and educators who are involved in determining its success or failure; and a sharply focused measure of the program's effectiveness in terms of modified behavior by the individuals whom it is intended to benefit.

For the purpose of this analysis, it will be sufficient to concentrate mainly on the reactions and behavior changes of the children who participated in the study.

For example, we found that children exposed to either Young Audiences program, "standard" or "depth," rated their experience at a significantly higher positive level than the children in the model/control group rated their outside musical experience. The data demonstrated the superiority of the programs in providing both "entertainment" and "educational" value. But they also indicated that the "depth" program has been even more successful than the "standard" program in achieving these results, a fact of some importance to a fund manager who must determine where and how to spend the money entrusted to him.

We also discovered, with little surprise, that black children favored "soul" music, while white children expressed greater appreciation for "pop rock," with some predisposition toward "serious" or "classical" music. It was interesting to note then that black children derived less "entertainment" value from the programs, which were classical, than did white children. It was even more interesting, however, to discover that black children perceived that the programs had substantial "educational" value.

When the programs were examined in terms of the "value" they have for children exposed to them, we discovered that the program as a whole was perceived more positively by middle-class children who were likely to have some experience with "serious" music. Neither upper-class nor lower-class children attribute any greater value to the programs than did their counterparts in the model/control group who had experienced classical concerts outside of school.

In contrast, we found that a specific program, the "depth" series, did have "entertainment" and "educational" value for both upper- and lower-class children. We hypothesized that upper-class children derived value from the "depth" program because they came to it with a degree of sophistication that enhanced their appreciation, while lower-class children found the "depth" program stimulating because, for them, it represented a new experience.

A key question the survey sought to answer was whether the programs have had an effect on behavior. Specifically, did exposure to the Young Audiences program upgrade a child's attitude toward serious music? The statistical evaluation supported the conclusion that the programs produced measurable enrichment of their audiences. Perhaps more important in terms of our goal of providing management information, we found that the "depth" program is more culturally enriching than the "standard" program.

RESULTS OUT OF SCHOOL

We established one tangible criterion of cultural enrichment that represented a measure of a specific goal of the program. That criterion was the effect of the program on children's interest in, and actual attendance at, concerts outside the school setting. The findings indicate more children exposed to the Young Audiences concert series attend outside concerts than do children who have not been exposed. These findings do not purport to show that these children attend more concerts of "serious" music. In fact, given their predisposition toward soul and pop rock, that hypothesis would border on the absurd. Nevertheless, the findings do indicate that Young Audiences is achieving its goal of orienting children toward live musical performances.

Further the "depth" program was shown to have considerably greater effect on this question than did the "standard" series. Almost twice as many children from the "depth" program than from the "standard" attended three or more concerts in a year.

Further analysis of concert-attendance responses verified the findings in other areas of the evaluation: The Young Audiences program is more effective in influencing the habits of black children than of white in attending concerts outside the school. While there is no measurable difference between white children exposed to the Young Audiences program and whites not exposed, there is significant difference among blacks.

More than half the blacks exposed to the Young Audiences program attended outside concerts this year in contrast to less than a fourth of the blacks not in the program. Further, there was shown a significant difference in the number of Young Audiences blacks who have attended three or more concerts (30 percent as opposed to 7 percent in the "control" group).

The same positive effect from the Young Audiences program is seen among children identified as from the lower class. Twenty-five percent of the lower-class children in the Young Audiences program attended three or more concerts, as opposed to only 7 percent of those not exposed. Finally, giving strong support to the superiority of the "depth" program in influencing behavior is the impressive 43 percent of the lower-class children who attended three or more concerts in contrast to only 18 percent of those not exposed.

The study yielded a substantial number of data, scientifically collected through techniques adapted from the commercial marketplace, that enabled the administrators of the funding institutions to make a rational decision about the program's effectiveness and worthiness for continued support. We clearly demonstrated that the "depth" series motivated changes in behavior patterns that were more closely attuned to the program's goals than did the "standard" series. Thus, the basic theory, put into practice, resulted in a tangible measurement of less-than-tangible program goals. (A similar research project was conducted to examine the program of Affiliate Artists, and it achieved similar results.)

The findings, including those pertaining to the structure and mechanisms of the funded organization itself, resulted in the National Endowment for the Arts and the Sears-Roebuck Foundation renewing their financial support. They did so, however, on the basis of the recommendations, arising from the research, that their support take the form of grants for specific projects rather than unrestricted funds. Furthermore, Young Audiences, Inc. itself adopted several of the recommendations for changes in structure and approach.

We believe we successfully demonstrated that commercial marketing-research methods can be adapted to nonprofit programs whose results heretofore have defied quantitative measurement. Moreover, these methods result in "hard" data on the effectiveness of such programs and enable donor and recipient institutions to make more precise decisions about what programs to fund and how to spend that money once it is given.

We also believe that this study indicates that commercial marketing strategies can be applied to programs at the proposal stage, before funds have been granted. Nonprofit money managers can determine in advance which programs are worthy of funding and which will result in the greatest benefit to the individuals, many of them desperately in need, to whom they are directed.

We view this research as a pragmatic review of organizational effectiveness and program success, rather than as an academic exercise in human behavioral response. The research design focused on those aspects of each program that are most important, in terms of the program's aims, and was tailored to develop reliable, scientifically valid data in sufficient depth and detail to aid decision makers in their choices.

The basic point of view of the researcher has substantial effect on the results of his research. We were not seeking to determine success in terms of the degree of acceptance of the program, or, in other words, whether more individuals liked it than did not. Rather, the research goal was addressed to a specific management problem: Is the funding agency spending its money wisely?

How to Make the Presidency Manageable

Peter F. Drucker

A great deal of the advice so generously offered to President Ford these days seems to imply that a charm school would be a good place to prepare for being President of the United States. There is a lot of talk about the President's "style." He is told to be open, informal, and accessible. He is told not to be arrogant, but humble. Above all, he is told to be a man of candor—not to be secretive.

Insofar as this advice means that the President is so highly visible, and under such close observation, that he had better not start telling lies, it is sound advice indeed. But most of the advice does not jibe with American experience or with the facts of American politics during the last forty years or so. A President's style is much less important than most of the advice assumes it to be; and, to the extent that style does matter, the advice is mainly wrong.

The President, it seems almost to be forgotten, is first of all a manager. And if President Ford is ultimately to be effective, he might be thinking hard about some management lessons that can be learned from the record of recent

Reprinted with permission of the author and publisher from *Fortune*, November 1974.

presidencies. It seems to me that the record suggests six basic rules for the chief executive's job.

1. There Should Be No Central Operating Staff in the President's Office

Such a staff always looks good on paper, but it cannot work in practice. The practical difficulty is rooted in the fact that the President is concerned with many different activities, from farm-subsidy payments to military organization, and from international monetary policy to desegregation of a local school district. No central staff can serve the President in all these areas. If the staff had experts in every major area, it would have to be even larger than the one President Nixon built. The staff would then be totally unmanageable, taking up more and more of the President's time and yet keeping him essentially uninformed (which clearly happened at times during the Nixon Administration). Or, if the staff is small, it becomes essentially a group of amateurs and busybodies who can easily be manipulated by the knowledgeable people in the various departments and agencies.

More important than the futility of any such central operating staff is the damage it can do. The staff people inevitably become courtiers, putting loyalty to the chief above the content of the job. They adopt the courtier's rule: "Don't ever tell the boss anything he doesn't want to hear." Their own places in the pecking order of the court become their greatest preoccupation, and this leads them to insulate the chief executive. Anyone whose position and power are not dependent on the favor of the chief executive, or on his place at the chief executive's court, is viewed by the staff people as a threat and becomes, in effect, an "enemy."

The staff people have no job and every job. They have the fullness of their chief's power, yet are not accountable. They are totally insecure, having no grounds of support except the boss's favor. And so, in the end, they always act irresponsibly, immorally, and with at least a touch of paranoia. For their basic position is irresponsible and in the last analysis immoral—as power without responsibility always becomes.

There is nothing new in what I am saying. I have only paraphrased the arguments that led the U.S. and British armies to reject the philosophy of the German General Staff system when they reorganized their own staff systems around the turn of the century.

Nor is there anything very new in two rules for organizing his office that any chief executive, in business or government, must observe if he wants to be an effective manager.

Never let the central staff get between the chief executive and the key men in his administration who are responsible for managing major activities.

Limit staff operations to activities that are the direct personal chores of the chief executive himself, i.e., as opposed to activities that he is supposed to guide, control, and supervise. Keep the number of staff people to the absolute minimum and always make sure that they have clearly defined responsibilities. As recently as 1939, Franklin D. Roosevelt got by with eight staff people: the budget director, the head of the National Resources Planning Board, a press secretary, an appointments secretary, a congressional liaison officer, a personnel director, and two general assistants. That number still seems about right (although the particular responsibilities would be different today).

They Used to Last Longer . . .

The fact seems almost incredible nowadays, but some members of Franklin D. Roosevelt's original Cabinet still had their jobs when F.D.R. died in his fourth term. And except for Secretary of the Treasury William Woodin and Secretary of War George Dern, both of whom died during the first term, every member of the original Cabinet served at least five years. (Woodin was succeeded by his deputy, Henry Morgenthau Jr., who then served out the rest of the Roosevelt Administrations.) This remarkable "job security" for Cabinet members had one large advantage: the officials heading major government departments were around long enough to learn how their bureaucracies worked.

In later years, there was far more concern about making the bureaucracies responsive but far less of the required continuity in direction from the top. By October 1973, not one of Richard M. Nixon's original Cabinet appointees was still in his job.

---

2. The President Must Work Hard to Get Fresh Thinking

Not all our successful Presidents have organized their efforts the same way, but all of them have clearly recognized the *need for a steady supply of ideas.* Without some such supply, they become the *prisoners* of White House *routine and ritual.* Until World War II, Franklin D. Roosevelt's "thinking input" came primarily from a few individuals: Eleanor Roosevelt, Bernard Baruch, Felix Frankfurter, and Adolf Berle were among the most important. As occasion demanded, Roosevelt called in other people for advice on particular problems—Anna Rosenberg, for instance, on labor matters. At that, F.D.R. was only following the example of his distant cousin Theodore who, as President, had turned for ideas to such independent outsiders as William Allen

White, the unconventional editor of the Emporia *Gazette;* Columbia University President Nicholas Murray Butler (then still highly unconventional); and the British diplomat, Cecil Spring-Rice.

Franklin D. Roosevelt, like Teddy Roosevelt before him, was criticized for the haphazardness of the methods he used in his search for ideas. Providing ideas for the President, it was argued, is much too important a task to be left to the accidents of personal acquaintanceship with outsiders—the function ought to be organized. Some such argument played a role in the formation of the Council of Economic Advisers, for example, and the Office of Science and Technology.

It is not entirely clear that these more formal arrangements work better. At least, some of the recent Presidents seem to have had doubts. J.F.K. supplemented the formal arrangements by bringing his own counselors in major areas into the White House—for example, McGeorge Bundy as Special Assistant for national security affairs. Nixon had several such counselors, including Arthur Burns for economics, Henry Kissinger for foreign affairs, and Daniel Patrick Moynihan for issues affecting welfare and the poor.

But this approach has some disadvantages too. It rests on a false analogy between the counselors and staff executives in business and the armed forces. These executives, who oversee such operations as personnel in corporations and logistics in the military, often have substantial responsibilities. But they are not responsible for the basic operation of the enterprise: personnel is not a "business" and logistics is not a military operation. The handling of foreign affairs, the economy, and social welfare *are* basic operations of government. Thus the President's counselors have jobs that parallel operating functions and, inevitably, they compete with and tend to undermine these functions.

But no matter how he organizes his effort to get ideas, the chief executive will fail if he has a central operating staff. Anyone providing fresh ideas is, almost by definition, critical of the accepted wisdom and will therefore seem obviously disloyal. A central operating staff will always resent and fight him.

3. The President Needs Strength and Ambition in His Key Executives

It is the first managerial task of any executive in any organization to use the strengths of the people working for him. To be afraid of strength in subordinates, and to discourage it, is to weaken the chief executive himself.

The Nixon Administration was curiously ambivalent on this account. On one hand, it cultivated "superstars"—Henry Kissinger and George Shultz—which is not necessarily the most effective way to use strong executives. And except for the superstars, the Nixon Administration seemed to prefer mediocrity to strength.

A President needs strong subordinates because he must rely on them to keep him "educated" about their operations. The chief executive must demand of key subordinates that they think about and then convey to him whatever he needs to know and understand. He must demand that they protect him against "surprises," that they tell him well ahead of time of new problems, opportunities, and changes that are looming on the horizon. A weak subordinate cannot be counted on to perform this educational role adequately; he will be too inclined to fear that bad news, or reports of new problems in his area, will displease the President.

Strength in executives is not an unmixed blessing. Strong executives can be proud and may tend to feud. Harold Ickes, as Roosevelt's Secretary of the Interior, or Henry Wallace as his Secretary of Agriculture, must have been sore trials for their boss. But they performed.

The President needs strong subordinates for another reason: only the strong are apt to dissent from existing policy. The President needs dissent within the administration, and all effective Presidents have recognized the need. The chief executive who insists on "consensus" deprives himself of understanding. He becomes a poll taker and conciliator rather than a decision maker. In effect, he abdicates.

F.D.R. generated dissent by putting his key executives into competition with one another—a practice that actually dates back to George Washington. A chief executive can use two or three key men separately: Truman discussed major issues separately with Dean Acheson and George Marshall, apparently without letting one know what the other had proposed. President Eisenhower insisted on "completed staff work" on the part of one man, and work was not considered completed unless it included a recommendation. But once Ike had a recommendation from one executive, he submitted it for comment, criticism, and, above all, for dissent to other members of his executive team.

4. There Has to Be a Lot of Continuity in Key Positions

Nixon and his staff complained bitterly about the unresponsiveness of the federal civil service and its tendency to go its own way rather than carry out the President's policies. Unresponsiveness to broad policy direction is indeed a problem of any large, diversified organization. The individual units can easily become "bureaucracies"—that is, ends in themselves and laws unto themselves. And there is no doubt that Nixon had a special problem. The upper levels of the civil service were—and are—heavily staffed with people who were not sympathetic to his announced policies and who had, in all likelihood, voted for his opponent in 1968.

Yet Nixon primarily has himself to blame for the fact that during his Administration the civil service remained largely unmanageable and resistant to policy direction from the top. With few exceptions, his appointees, the Cabinet and sub-Cabinet officers, did not stay in any one job along enough to learn it, to understand it, and to get control of it. During his Administration, the median length of service in Cabinet jobs dropped to around 18 months (versus a median of forty months for Cabinet officials during 1933–1965).

The federal government depends for its managerial control and direction on "political appointees," that is, on outsiders who, as a rule, have only the scantiest experience in organizations as big and complex as the ones they now head. The political appointee in policymaking positions is an American invention—and one of the better ones. The appointee serves to inoculate the bureaucracy against its deadliest disease, the smug arrogance of a closed elite. He provides for new thinking, different approaches, and different points of view. He keeps the civil service in contact with the "real world," indeed, reminds the civil servant that the "outside" *is* the real world.

But the political appointee can work effectively only if he has enough time to learn the job, to find out what it is all about. He also needs an expectation of a reasonable tenure in order to have a chance of being taken seriously by the civil servants. Without that expectation, they will decide to outwait him and proceed to outwit him. What is the point, after all, of patiently educating a newcomer if he will only be replaced by another, equally green and equally ignorant, long before he has learned the ropes himself?

The President under whom political appointees had the longest tenure was Franklin D. Roosevelt. One of the ten Cabinet members he appointed when he took office, Secretary of the Treasury William Woodin, died within the first year; Secretary of War George Dern died after three years. Everyone else served at least five years. Ickes and Labor Secretary Frances Perkins still held their original posts when F.D.R. died. Henry Morgenthau Jr., who had been Woodin's Under Secretary and succeeded him, was still running the Treasury when F.D.R. died. Henry Wallace, first at Agriculture, then as Vice President, then at Commerce, also held office during virutally the entire Roosevelt era.

Among sub-Cabinet officers, the continuity was greater still. In fact, F.D.R. probably did not have enough turnover; toward the end, his Administration was badly in need of new people, new faces, and new ideas. But the continuity provided by Roosevelt's political appointees accounted in great measure for the control his Administration had over an explosively growing civil service.

Within the Nixon Administration, there was really only one example of the benefits of continuity. And the example was provided by the department that probably resisted the Nixon approach most and that was least enchanted by Nixon's announced policies—the Department of Defense. Melvin Laird as the new Secretary of Defense and his Deputy, David Packard, had to slash manpower, reform procurement practices, and liquidate the war the military had lost in Vietnam—hardly a program to make them popular in the Pentagon.

But Laird and Packard did not have the problem of an ''unresponsive'' or ''unmanageable'' bureaucracy. One reason was that they kept a large number of seasoned sub-Cabinet people from the previous Administration, including John S. Foster Jr. as Director of Defense Research and Engineering and Barry Shillito, who became Assistant Secretary for Installations and Logistics.

5. The Chief Executive Must Protect the Confidentiality of the Advice He Gets

An effective chief executive should not let ''experts'' make decisions for him, as John Kennedy learned to his sorrow at the Bay of Pigs. The responsibility for the decision is his, and he cannot abdicate it. But he has to depend on experts for information and advice. He must be able to trust in their good faith, in their willingness to give him the best advice they can think of, and in their readiness to take an unpopular stand.

Which means, in turn, that the advisers must have confidence in the integrity of the man they advise. They must know that he will not throw them to the wolves to save his own skin. They must be able to count on their advice remaining confidential. If an adviser wonders whether he will find himself lambasted in a Washington column, vilified in Congress, or otherwise made into a political football, he will trim—he will write his memos so that they will look good to Jack Anderson. Above all, he will eschew anything controversial and play it safe. He will not only lose his usefulness, he will become a menace to the President.

One violation of the principle that confidentiality should be protected occurred during the Eisenhower years. In order to appease the McCarthyites in Congress, John Foster Dulles let them have confidential reports and recommendations of American diplomats. This did not buy off McCarthy—paying blackmail never does. But it severely damaged the morale and effectiveness of the Foreign Service. Overnight, every Foreign Service officer learned the lesson: don't tell the truth; tell them what they want to hear; above all, don't be controversial.

The Nixon Administration seems never to have understood the principle involved in confidentiality. The central principle is the reciprocity of obligations. The giver of advice owes good faith and candor to his client, the recipient of advice. But the recipient owes the protection of confidentiality to the adviser. To install hidden tape recorders without the knowledge of the people the President called in for advice was a breach of privacy; but even more, it was a gross breach of the principle of confidentality without which advice cannot be rendered.

One major piece of damage done to the presidency by Watergate was the discrediting of the doctrine of executive privilege. As we now know, Richard Nixon invoked the doctrine to cover up some indefensible actions of his own. And because the doctrine was improperly applied, it is now generally discredited. But if the presidency is to be made manageable again, "executive privilege" must be reestablished. Advice rendered to the chief executive, or to any of his key advisers or Cabinet members, must not be made public except with the consent of the adviser.

6. The President Should Forget About "Style" and Just Be Himself

One of the myths of modern American politics is that we now elect Presidents because of their style, or because they have charisma, rather than because of their ideas. In fact, and with the single exception of John F. Kennedy, who won in 1960 by the thinnest of whiskers, those with style have been losers rather than winners. If style were decisive, Dewey would have beaten Truman hands down, and Adlai Stevenson would have given Eisenhower at least a good run for the money.

Furthermore, most of the specific advice about style now being offered President Ford is highly dubious. No chief executive can really be "accessible" or "informal." He has much too big a job for that. Every one of our Presidents since Franklin D. Roosevelt has been a highly secretive man. He either confided in no one (like Roosevelt himself, Eisenhower, and Lyndon Johnson) or in no more than one or two people (e.g., Truman in Dean Acheson and George Marshall, Kennedy in his brother Robert). In fact, the last President who was really a man of candor, who was truly informal and easily accessible, was Herbert Hoover—very likely the best of the lot as a human being, but still hardly the model for a new President.

To be sure, a President should not be arrogant. But it is probably even worse for him to be humble. For a President, like any other chief executive, has to be self-confident. He had better be convinced that the country needs him; he had better be convinced that he is more often right than wrong. Indeed, he requires self-confidence to a degree that in anybody else would properly be called "arrogance."

In any case, a man who is not naturally humble can hardly act the role for four years. A chief executive is respected only when he is himself and acts like himself. For an executive to pretend to be somebody else, to play-act, not only cheapens him; it weakens him. Once he himself knows that he is a phony, it can only be a question of time before everybody else discovers it too.

It is not the President's job to be soothing, or agreeable, or even inspiring—although all these qualities are surely desirable. His *job* is to be a manager. He must run the largest and most complex organization in the world. The job is tough enough without play-acting.

The Naval Shore Establishment and Parkinson's Laws

Donald A. Morton

In 1957, Cyril Northcote Parkinson—Englishman, scholar, author, humorist, and civil servant—developed explanations for bureaucratic growth tendencies. While studying the British Admiralty, Professor Parkinson found that the Admiralty staff (dockyard workers, clerks, and officials) had grown 5.75 percent annually, irrespective of the size of the British Fleet or the number of officers and men in the Royal Navy. Subsequent studies of other British agencies confirmed his findings and led to the conclusion that in any organization the number of subordinates multiplies at a predetermined annual rate, regardless of the amount of work the staff does, even when the final output decreases. From these observations, he derived several principles which have come to be known as Parkinson's Laws.[1]

One must quote these laws with tongue planted firmly in cheek, for they were written in that manner. But their deeper message is not amusing, not when it describes so well what has happened in our own Navy. Here are Parkinson's Laws:

First Law: Work expands so as to fill the time available for its completion.

Second Law: Expenditure rises to meet income.

Third Law: Expansion means complexity and complexity, decay—The more complex, the sooner dead.

Reprinted from *Proceedings* by permission; copyright © 1975 U.S. Naval Institute.

Growth Principle: In any public organization growth will average 5.75 percent per year, regardless of the amount of work to be done.

The mission of the U.S. Navy is to control the seas. A truism perhaps, but it has been overlooked lately. The welter of Navy tasks and programs often obscures the reason for its existence. Many navymen ashore, burdened with minutiae while pursuing their narrow specialties, often regard fleet problems as an unwelcome intrusion into their routine. Unfortunately, however, wars are not won by sheer force of correspondence. The fundamental Navy unit of measure is, as it always has been, the ship, and sea power is still a function of the size of the fleet.

The shore establishment comprises land, facilities, and employees—both military and civilian. Because land and facilities were acquired over many years at different costs, are maintained at different standards, and are operated at different efficiencies, plant value was not selected as the unit of measure of the size of the shore establishment.

The number of officers and men ashore is likewise not a valid indicator of shore establishment size. The percentage of navymen ashore is nearly constant with respect to total shore establishment manning. Also, the number of officers and men in the Navy is highly sensitive to the size of the fleet.

Navy civilian employees are another matter. It is fundamentally they who operate and maintain the shore establishment. Navy policy requires it. And, although sailors are ashore, there are virtually no civilians at sea. That's why, for the purposes of our analysis, the permanent, full-time civilian work force has been chosen as the basic shore establishment size indicator.

What has happened to the fleet—the consumer of the shore establishment product—over the last 30 years? While there was an increase of 860 percent in the number of ships during World War II, and an 85 percent increase during the Korean War, there was only a 6.4 percent increase during the Vietnam War. As one might expect, there has been a close correlation between the number of ships and the number of officers and men.

Now let us examine civilian employment. Post-World War II demobilization caused a fast 35 percent cut in the number of civilians, understandably much less than the 82 percent fleet reduction. The Korean War caused increases of 65 percent in civilians and 85 percent in ships. After Korea, both ships and civilians declined uniformly at about the same rate and remained closely correlated until 1960. Both increased again during the Cuban Missile Crisis, and at roughly the same rate.

Between 1964 and 1968, the fleet grew slowly and regularly, by 6.4 percent. During the same period, however, civilian employment grew 30 percent. This odd phenomenon is partly explained by the 1966 establishment of the Office of Civilian Manpower Management (OCMM) and the initiation in 1967 of the Civilian Substitution Program. Establishment of OCMM enhanced the prestige and influence of Navy civil servants. It provided centralized civilian personnel policies and procedures and increased the civilian voice in top Navy management.

The purpose of civilian substitution was to convert as many military billets as possible to civilian positions so that more military men could be sent to combat areas. In 1967, 1968, and 1973—the three years during which the program was implemented—36,125 civilian positions were substituted for 41,000 military billets.

The ascendancy of federal government unions has increased the power of Navy civilian employees. Membership in Navy unions increased from 33,955 in 1962 to 179,505 in December 1973, a 423 percent increase. With their paid staffs in Washington and increased bargaining leverage in the field, the unions effectively resist reductions in force.

Two other disturbing phenomena which indicate lack of control of civilian personnel have been grade escalation or "grade creep" and the increased percentage of graded (white collar) workers. The average grade of Navy white collar employees in 1960 was 7.26. In 1973, it was 7.88, an 8.5 percent increase. This grade increase alone cost the Navy approximately $112 million over the period, or about $8.6 million per year. Although some increase may have been warranted—as professional, technical, and administrative requirements increased—much of it was caused by management's lack of awareness of, or lack of will to resist, grade increase pressures. The price paid is unacceptable.

In 1969, 39 percent of the Navy civilian work force were graded. In 1975, 52 percent are graded. This trend means that the number of managers, administrators, clerks, secretaries, and other overhead personnel increased in relation to the number of welders, painters, equipment operators, electricians, warehousemen, and other "wrench-pullers."

In the aggregate, these examples strongly indicate that Navy management has tended to pay its civilian employees more than necessary to obtain and hold their services, causing an increase in payroll costs that is not the result of inflation, local wage surveys, collective bargaining, or threat of personnel loss to the private sector. Since 1969, federal salaries have, on the average, been higher than those of comparable positions in business and industry. For example, since 1964, when rough comparability existed, average federal civilian pay has increased 99 percent while private industry pay has gone up only 74 percent.

There was another interesting, related condition occurring at the same time. From 1954 to 1972, the number of admirals increased 13 percent, while the number of ships declined 41 percent. No judgment is made here about the need for this many admirals. However, it is noteworthy that, since 1954, when there was one admiral for each 3.96 ships in the fleet, there will, in 1976, be one admiral for every 1.76 ships. This should give us serious pause. But two points about this situation are relevant. First, it may be an indicator of the Navy's lack of personnel management discipline, an example which carries over into the shore establishment, and second, its impact upon the size of the shore establishment. The growth in the number of admirals has led to creation of a bureaucracy to serve them. Thus, we find ourselves at the first of Parkinson's Laws, ''Work expands so as to fill the time available for its completion.'' The law has two axioms:

Officials strive to multiply subordinates.

Officials make work for each other.[2]

No doubt these have been major factors in the large size of the shore establishment.

From the 1968 Vietnam peak to the present, the fleet has dropped 49 percent. But from the 1969 civilian peak to the present, civilian employment has dropped only 26 percent. Again, odd. Whereas the fleet has declined 45 percent from its pre-Vietnam size, the shore establishment has been reduced less than 4 percent. Very odd indeed.

Figure 1 is a comparison of ships in commission and Navy civilian em-

Figure 1. Shore establishment civilians per ship supported.

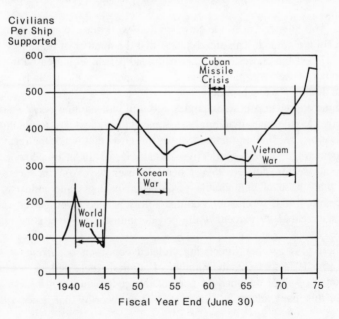

ployees (the shore establishment) by fiscal year, beginning in 1938. This relationship is the essence of this analysis—the number of shore establishment civilians per ship. World War II was an aberration. Its magnitude, nature, and full national mobilization imposed unusual constraints. It also allowed huge economies of scale. Central allocation of scarce manpower among the military services and defense industries limited the size of the shore establishment. But World War II data are useful nonetheless. As a revealing indicator of what was achieved, the average number of Navy civilian employees-per-ship supported was 130.

Note the similarity for World War II, the Korean War, and the Cuban Missile Crisis. The number of civilians-per-ship declined during each conflict. There are a number of ready explanations:

◇ Rapid fleet buildup
◇ Deferral of maintenance
◇ Economies of scale caused by application of unused plant capacity, and increase in labor (variable) as a percentage of overhead (fixed) production costs
◇ Increased efficiency resulting from wartime motivation (patriotism, overtime pay, etc.)

The increase in number of civilians-per-ship after each crisis is understandable: ship scrapping/mothballing, need to restore readiness after degradation caused by wartime operating tempo, drop in variable workload resulting in high overhead and excess yard capacity. The graph was at least rational until 1965.

During the Vietnam War—unlike World War II, the Korean War, and the Cuban Missile Crisis—the number of civilians in the shore establishment per-ship increased sharply, consistently, and nearly uniformly. The increase from 356 to 614 civilians-per-ship between 1965 and 1975 suggests a serious imbalance, a discontinuity, and a loss of control. It cries out for explanation, particularly since the fiscal year 1976 budget indicates there will be as many as 635 per ship.

A continually increasing civilians-per-ship ratio might be expected. Ships are becoming more complex. We now have nuclear power plants, missiles, computerized weapons systems, and more "black boxes" in general. But if the fleet is now a more capital intensive operation, is not the shore establishment also? Obviously not. And there does not appear to have been a productivity increase, which would tend to lower the civilians-per-ship ratio. Apologists might well say that the mix of ship types has changed and, with it, the fundamental character of the fleet. Not so, as Table 1 indicates.

Table 1 lists the number of ships by type and percentages at five-year intervals from 1945 to 1975. Since 1950, the percentages have been remarkably

Table 1. *Fleet Mix, by Fiscal Year.*

SHIP TYPES	1945	%	1950	%	1955	%	1960	%	1965	%	1970	%	1975	%
Carriers	138	2.5	15	2.4	24	2.4	23	2.9	25	2.7	19	2.5	15	3.0
Battleships	23	0.4	1	—	3	—	0	—	0	—	0	—	0	—
Cruisers	72	1.3	13	2	17	1.7	13	1.6	14	1.4	10	1.3	27	5.4
Frigates	0	—	0	—	5	—	7	0.8	27	2.8	25	3.2	64	12.8
Destroyers, Destroyer escorts	365	6.7	147	2.4	308	30	260	32	246	27	198	26	73	14.5
Amphibious ships	1,256	23	91	15	175	17	113	14	135	14	97	12	64	12.8
Minesweepers	611	11.2	56	9	112	11	81	10	85	9	64	8.3	3	0.6
Submarines	237	4.4	72	11	109	10	113	14	134	14	146	19	116	23
Auxiliaries	1,256	23	190	31	262	26	197	24	262	28	194	26	126	25
Patrol ships	1,469	27	33	5.3	15	1.5	4	—	6	0.6	16	2.1	14	2.8
Totals	5,427		618		1,030		811		934		769		502	

constant. Notable exceptions are the elimination of battleships, introduction of frigates, and the increase in the number of submarines. Nor has the average manning of ships changed much; the correlation between Navy ships and men is close.

What, then, was different about the Vietnam War? Many things, but it was not really that different from World War II and Korea. There was shore bombardment. There were carrier air strikes, tactical air support, and coastal patrolling. Riverine warfare and the "brown-water Navy" seem to be the only significant Navy variations. The fact that the North Vietnamese had almost no Navy, and no Air Force operating at sea or over South Vietnam, vastly simplified our fleet air, surface, and antisubmarine defense effort.

Still, as Figure 1 shows, the number of civilians-per-ship increased 44 percent, and this cannot be justified by the peculiarities of the Vietnam War.

This developing condition was known to top Defense Department and Navy decision-makers. In 1973, Admiral Elmo R. Zumwalt, Jr., Chief of Naval Operations, testified:

> . . . I began to report to my superior, the Secretary of the Navy (1) that we were headed for serious reductions in ships and aircraft, and (2) that we had for nearly a decade not taken any reduction in shore establishments, and (3) that the shore establishment was so large in comparison to the dwindling Navy that I felt it was immoral not to make some dramatic reductions in the shore establishment." [3]

Secretary of the Navy John W. Warner addressed the problem in a 22 June 1973 statement:

> . . . When Secretary [John] Chafee and I joined the Department of the Navy, February 1969, we had not been there more than a few weeks until Admiral Moorer, the then Chief of Naval Operations, impressed upon us the imbalance between the shore establishment and the operating fleets. . . . When I took over as Secretary in May of 1972 I was determined to move forward with this [naval shore establishment] realinement. I could clearly see the waste of dollars and I would not be a party to the continuation of this waste." [4]

It appears then that the problem has been apparent for years. Why was action to restore the balance not taken sooner? The following explanation was given by Secretary of Defense Melvin R. Laird on 6 December 1972:

> . . . it is not the military that is fighting for the particular base structure or the particular support facilities that are associated in our defense budget. There are others in governments and in our Congress that really felt a halt had to be called to these massive reductions affecting so many people." [5]

This justification is unsatisfactory. There are many actions which can be taken over time by wise management to reduce the size of the shore establishment, actions which are well below the threshold of congressional concern and which do not have a harmful local community impact. Vast changes can be wrought by good management, through careful planning, patience, and attrition. The latter averages about 10 percent a year in the Navy civil service.

The Navy shore establishment realignments announced by Secretary of Defense Elliot Richardson in April 1973 have done little to reduce the size of the shore establishment. The reductions have, over a two-year period, reduced civilian employment by 14,552, about 4.5 percent. At the same time, the shore establishment realignment has eliminated 1,228 officer and 5,969 enlisted billets, which total almost half as many military men as civilians being cut. Hence, it was an overall Navy cut, not just a shore establishment reduction. The liquidation of these facilities has reduced the shore plant about 5 percent. The maintenance backlog has also declined by only 5 percent ($21 million). These reductions do little to solve the basic problem.

Why did the shore establishment get so out of hand? Those best able to answer are the commanding officers who are the direct employers and managers of the vast majority of civilian employees and, therefore, have the greatest influence on the shore establishment. The reasons, not in any particular order of significance, include political pressure, super-loyalty to command, appropriated fund philanthrophy, *status quo* management, institutional disincentives, liberal funding, preoccupation with public affairs, the over-readiness syndrome, abdication of decisions to the civilian hierarchy, investment fixation, over-concern with morale, mesmerization by management systems, and poor management itself. These command management frailties are not the author's creations. He has repeatedly seen archetype practitioners of each throughout his career.

Political opposition is assumed to exist to all reduction in the civilian work force, regardless of size. This is a major deterrent to reduction by commanding officers. In fact, however, small reductions seldom attract political attention, and, when they do, good reasons are often acceptable. Congressmen have to respond to constituent complaints. But congressional inquiries are pressure only if commanding officers choose to consider them so.

The federal government buys votes by distributing employment. And the Navy is part of the federal government—a fact of life. But the Navy must still recommend closures when it believes they are necessary. To keep naval installations open purely for political reasons, or to maintain inflated payrolls, robs the Navy of funds needed to keep in fighting trim, encourages bad management, and in general creates—well, what we have today.

The growth and success of the Soviet Navy in the last decade have been fantastic. The Russian method of achieving this ought to tell us something. The

Soviets build their defense installations and manage them in order to achieve their objectives in the most efficient manner. It is doubtful that they operate their naval shore establishment for social benefit, to create jobs, or to spread the ruble evenly around the U.S.S.R. Our naval planning system places us at a serious disadvantage with respect to the Soviets.

A second serious commanding officer fault is placing the welfare of the command ahead of the Navy's interests. Its principal result is maintenance of the payroll at almost any cost, fighting every change that could diminish the budget, prestige, or influence of the command. The costly corollary to super-loyalty is that philanthropy and humanitarianism with tax dollars costs the Navy dearly. Many commanding officers fear hurting their employees. The old "of course everyone knows Joe is incompetent, but he can retire in only eight more years so let's keep him until then" trick has no place in a good manager's bag. Still it is a commonplace in the Civil Service.

Another problem is the conventional officer wisdom which holds that one cannot fire a civilian. Civilian personnel managers perpetuate this myth. In fact, it can be done—by properly documented unsatisfactory performance, by patience, and by determination. The Navy discharges officers and enlisted men for unsatisfactory performance, but of late we have not shown equal determination to do it to our civil servants. The humanitarian commanding officer must be made to realize that Civil Service regulations provide each employee with ample protective rights, but absolute security is not one of them. A good CO must call them as he sees them—then let the system take over.

Status quo management is the norm in the shore establishment. The whole Navy system encourages and contributes to it. Our incremental budgeting system requires justification primarily for changes from the previous budget. Savings resulting from command innovation may result in embarrassment to headquarters by reducing obligation rates. They often result in lowering future budget bases. Personnel cuts taken unilaterally by an aggressive commanding officer may be followed by across-the-board cuts dictated by Washington. If there is no fat left, flesh or bone must go. The fat command next door can take the cuts easily.

The economy-minded commanding officer attracts headquarters attention to himself—often unfavorably. He may be viewed as "negative" or a troublemaker. The most career-enhancing style is that of growth management. The most successful commanding officers are usually those who create new programs and manage to have their budgets increased. Expansionary management is laudatory, whether or not mission requires it. Hence the prudent CO avoids reductions. He keeps a low profile and doesn't rock the boat.

The local Civil Service hierarchy exerts great pressure on the commanding officer to constantly increase, or at least to maintain, the payroll. Recommendations to reduce the force rarely reach the commanding officer through the civilian chain. Reductions not only eliminate jobs, they result in (or should result in, although it does not often happen) reduced grade levels for many who remain on the payroll. So when personnel reductions are mentioned, the protective civilian screen goes up. Few commanding officers have a good enough military staff and management information system to find out where cuts are possible. Fewer yet are tough-minded enough to start reduction actions when the need becomes clear.

Many commanding officers have had little experience working with Navy civilian personnel. They do not know civilian personnel regulations and procedures and thus feel inadequate in this area of their responsibility. They therefore tend to accept too readily recommendations of their civilian advisors. They do not question civilian solutions to problems in the same way they do those presented by their military staffs. Commanding officers should recognize the strong vested interest of their civilian managers and their tendency to solve most problems by simply "putting more men on the job," with all the benefits, such as promotion, which flow to the civilian hierarchy by doing so. This tendency does not necessarily imply evil motives to our civilian administrators. It is as natural as ambition. But commanding officers must recognize it and make allowances for it.

Civilian positions which become vacant should never be filled routinely, as is commonly done. Each should be regarded as a new position being filled for the first time. Questions should be asked: Is the work done by this position necessary? What other position can do it? What will happen if the position is not filled? The one fundamental criterion should be the contribution the position makes to the command mission. If the relationship is too indirect or obscure, the position should not be filled. With sufficient time, commands can be reduced and reorganized in this manner.

There are a number of administrative barriers to cuts. Whereas increases require only money and civilian ceiling points (neither of which were problems during the war in Vietnam), cuts of magnitude (over 50 positions or 10 per cent) require headquarters approval and congressional notification. Reductions cause inefficiency and turmoil. For each employee terminated, an average of four employees is affected. Civil Service "bumping" often knocks the best people out of positions. Poorly qualified employees fill positions for which they have low aptitude or require long training. This causes production slowdown and general low morale. These are powerful disincentives, to be sure.

The availability of funds is unfortunately the basic reduction consideration. If the budget supports the payroll, the payroll won't change. If the budget won't support it, the commanding officer has a ready excuse. He can tell his employees that he couldn't help it. They should blame headquarters. He is making cuts only because Washington made him do it. His command loyalty survives, but at the expense of his management competence.

Among those things most galling to a manager ought to be being told by headquarters to do something which he knows he should have done on his own initiative. But, alas, as long as the budget supports the organization in most naval shore installations, the organization remains unchanged. Note conformance with Parkinson's Second Law: "Expenditure rises to meet income."

"Over-readiness" is the cause of much waste. The country cannot afford in times of relative peace to maintain in the shore establishment in large quantity all the skills and capabilities required during war. Idle production capacity and a civilian work force stand by or work at half speed. Many skills in the civilian economy can be quickly mobilized. And contracts can be awarded quickly for the manufacture of war material.

The maintenance of a huge shore establishment fits neither of the extreme war scenarios. In the event of a fast nuclear exchange, with the decisive action completed in a few hours or days, a large shore establishment counts for nothing. In the more likely event of a protracted Vietnam-like limited war, there is ample time to recruit, train, and produce.

Fleet Admiral Ernest J. King, CNO during World War II, attributed much of the Navy's success in that war to the fact that his wartime organization had to be recruited from scratch. In his autobiography he said: "There were no civilian employees with fixed habits to consider. 'Empire builders' were conspicuous by their absence." [6] Our naval and national leadership might be well advised to reflect on this lesson. If we have to build up rapidly for mobilization, we will have a younger civilian force able and willing to learn and not encumbered by traditional methods. There is a point at which experience becomes a liability.

Parkinson's First Law comes into full play under these readiness overmanning conditions: "Work expands so as to fill the time available for its completion."

The naval shore establishment should not be considered a simple means of distributing the federal largesse equitably among congressional districts. The price in waste and inefficiency is too great. Many commanding officers cannot reconcile the two conflicting objectives of managing effectively and maintaining the payroll.

There is also a morale problem caused by keeping a large, underemployed work force. Make-work jobs are created. Employees find nonproductive ways to use their time. At many overstaffed commands, civilian employees simply hide—with the knowledge and tacit approval of top management. Also, management goes to great pains to continually justify its inflated work force, overstating its needs or fabricating new ones. But here is the real danger: After years of sloppy management and inefficient work methods, it may not be possible for an organization to suddenly become alert and efficient when an emergency occurs. Good management ability atrophies when not used regularly.

With a shore establishment whose current value is $40 billion, there is an understandable reluctance to retire any of this plant. But this attitude reveals an inability to recognize that these costs are "sunk" and cannot be recovered. What are important are maintenance and operations costs—future, controllable costs—which compete dollar for dollar with other needs. The backlog of real property maintenance was estimated at $398 million in June 1973 and it is increasing at the rate of $50 million per year. An acceptable backlog is $35 million. Hence, the annual backlog increase is greater than what the total backlog should be. And the Navy is worsening the situation by adding new construction at several times the rate at which facilities are disposed of. For example, in fiscal year 1974, only $33 million (5.4 percent) of the $609 million Military Construction Program was for replacement of facilities. This increased to 26 percent in fiscal year 1975, but it is still much too low. The cost of plant maintenance and operation alone should be a great motivator for the Navy to reduce the size of the shore establishment. Our choice is to continue to operate a large, inefficient, materially degraded plant or a smaller, efficient, well-maintained one.

Commanding officers can be overconcerned with morale. It leads many of them to bad decisions, or worse, the avoidance of decisions. Morale is mercurial—and highly perishable. Several major (and costly) decisions favorable to employees can result in a happy, motivated work force. Then a single incident can cause morale to plummet. Optimism beats strong in the human breast. Low morale tends to rise. But sustained high morale is unachievable, and attempts to achieve it can be unacceptably costly.

A few commanding officers have a fundamental inability to regard appropriated funds as money. They think of command as something entrusted to them as a reward for long and faithful service, rather than as a great responsibility, a charge to manage (and conserve) public resources. Our tendency to manage everything as a system has resulted, in many cases, in organizational constipation: inability either to digest or eliminate the mass of data produced. This tendency accounts in large measure for the increase in graded employees at the expense of ungraded workers. Unfortunately, many of the systems have never proven themselves to save money or improve effectiveness. What they have done is become institutionalized and develop a clientele.

The most serious fault of all is simply poor management. Management is the ability to equate work and resources, of which the most expensive resource is manpower. When work changes, so must the work force. As we have shown, the work (the fleet) has diminished dramatically with very little change in the work force (shore establishment). By definition, this is poor management. To be sure, every command does not have ideal, well-defined work units, measures of effectiveness criteria, and a management information system to reveal quickly variances from its plan, whether caused by workload or work force. A product may be intangible. Only our industrial (productive) commands have good, quantifiable standards. But if a commanding officer doesn't at least have some seat-of-the-pants techniques to tip him off, he is not a manager and should be kept at sea, where his resources (ship and crew) are fixed, and his product (training) places elastic demands upon time.

Perhaps the Navy has lost sight of its fundamental objectives. It has created so many programs of secondary and indirect relation to its mission that is has diluted its efforts and squandered its energies and resources. It has become bogged down in trivia. It has become too complicated. It has in many cases made the decision to spend money for a vast officialdom and huge bureaucracy, instead of for weapons and fighting effectiveness.

Recall Parkinson's Third Law. It may be the most revealing, alarming, and damaging of all: "Expansion means complexity and complexity, decay— The more complex, the sooner dead." Put another way, if youth is character- ized by vigor and imagination and maturity by inertia, rigidity, and stagnation, the naval shore establishment must surely have reached senility. A static orga- nization is indeed a dying organization.

Let us again examine Figure 1 to remind ourselves how fast the ratio of civilians to ships has grown over the years. In the 35 years between 1940 and 1975, the ratio has grown from 199 to 620, a 210 percent increase, or 6.0 per- cent a year, remarkably close to, but surpassing, the 5.75 percent estimated for the Royal Navy by Professor Parkinson.

When he became Chief of Naval Operations, Admiral Zumwalt said that it might be necessary to give the Soviet Union naval superiority for five to ten years while the U.S. Fleet is modernized. He paid for this modernization mostly by reducing the size of the fleet. Would it not have been wiser to reduce the size of the shore establishment—at least an amount corresponding to the present smaller fleet size? A 16 percent cut in the shore establishment, 50,000 civilian employees, would reduce the support ratio to 530 civilians per ship, still much higher than the 450 average for the last 25 years. It would allow for a sizeable increase due to ship complexity, increased administrative require- ments, and civilianization, and would release about $1.5 billion a year for new ship construction and modernization. It might also create a like number of jobs elsewhere, perhaps in a different region or sector of the economy, but where they could be of better use to the Navy, not in the bloated shore establish- ment.

Our Navy is now second best. If we are content with that we need not worry. But if we want to meet the Soviet maritime challenge, ever larger ap- propriations are not the only solution. There is another way. We can awaken, stir ourselves, and shake free from the bureaucratic impediments, complacency, and excesses we have acquired in 30 years of being first. We must renounce our business-as-usual shore establishment nonmanagement. We must return to our founding principles and regain our former clear eye and steady hand. We must firmly engage ourselves in the cause, for to achieve greatly, one must feel strongly and strive mightily.

The place to start is the shore establishment, and the time to begin is long past.

REFERENCES

1. C. N. Parkinson, *Parkinson's Law and Other Studies in Administration* (Boston: Houghton Mifflin Co., 1957), pp. 2, 12; *The Law and the Profits* (Boston: Houghton Mifflin Co., 1960), p. 4; *In-Laws and Outlaws* (Boston: Houghton Mifflin Co., 1962), p. 233.
2. C. N. Parkinson, *Parkinson's Law,* p. 4.
3. E. R. Zumwalt, "Hearings Before the Subcommittee on Military Construction of the Committee on Armed Services, United States Senate," 93rd Congress, 1st Session, Part 3, 28 June 1973, p. 136.
4. J. W. Warner, "Hearings Before the Subcommittee on Military Construction of the Committee on Armed Services, United States Senate," 93rd Congress, 1st Session, Part 2, 22 June 1973, pp. 239–240.
5. M. R. Laird, news conference during meeting with NATO Defense Ministers, Brussels, Belgium, 6 December 1972.
6. E. J. King and Walter Muir Whitehill, *Fleet Admiral King: A Naval Record* (New York: W. W. Norton and Co., 1952), p. 359.

The Administration of Professors as Decision Makers

Martha A. Brown

The constant and overarching goal in the administration of professors in public colleges and universities is to align the objectives of the institution (organization) with the needs and aims of the individual professor. This general goal has received considerable attention and study from a number of investigators in administrative and management writing (Maslow, 1943; Ansbacher (on Adler), 1956; Schacter, 1959; White, 1959; Herzberg, 1959; McClelland, 1961; McGregor, 1967). Three studies conducted in the university setting among professors seem to support the more general investigations. Hill and French (1967) tell us department chairmen are relatively powerless. Etzioni (1965) suggests that instrumental leaders should be subordinated to expressive leaders in socializing institutions. Patterson (1966) adds that only one-fourth of the professors she queried felt decisions should be made by deans or chairmen or both. Both groups of researchers apparently found that the gentler the leading the more satisfaction for the followers (particularly where those followers are

Reprinted from *Public Personnel Management,* September/October 1973 by permission of the International Personnel Management Association, 1313 East 60th Street, Chicago, Illinois 60637.

highly educated and more motivated by self-actualization), and therefore the more opportunity for accomplishing both sets of goals.

Another general area of research pertinent to this question is the study of role. More particularly, a relationship can be established between studies or ideas covered in role literature and the accompanying data resulting from questioning professors about their roles as decision-makers in their department or division. This line of questioning follows naturally from research by Morse and Reimer (1965) conducted in an industrial setting to test hypotheses concerning the relationship between the means by which organizational decisions are made and the individual's satisfaction and productivity. These two researchers found that satisfaction and productivity increased when autonomous rather than hierarchically-controlled methods were used. Scott (1966) delved into role conflict associated with the difference between bureaucratic and professional models of organization. Assuming these differences place the location of decision-making functions in different persons, the accompanying data also speak to Scott's work. On the other hand, Kornhauser (1966) makes the point that professional persons' needs must adapt to institutional forms in our advanced technological society. Still another view held by Clark (1966) in this area of decision-making is that the major form of organization and authority found in the faculties of American colleges and universities is now neither predominantly collegial nor bureaucratic. All of these studies deal to some extent with the amount of influence various levels of the hierarchy in different organizational forms have in decision-making. The accompanying material deals directly with this subject by asking the professor-respondent to define his self-perceived role by recording how often he feels he influenced decisions that came up in his department.

A general summary of writings in the area of the role of the professor lead to an inescapable conclusion. The total role of the professor is composed of three subroles: the institutional role, the research and consulting role, and the teaching role. These three subroles come from an organization of the role literature on the following bases. The institutional subrole of the professor grows from the multitudinous writings concerning roles in organizations generally. The research and consulting subrole is fed by studies in the professionalization and socialization of the role. A picture of the teaching role stems primarily from investigations into the public school teacher role and directly into the college professor role. Notice that Table 1 in the results following divides the decisions about which the professor was queried into those associated with the teaching role and those more directly related to the institutional role. Decisions related to the research and consulting role are largely individual and thus relatively unrelated to decision-making in the department of a university or college.

METHODOLOGY AND PROCEDURE

Since the population to be studied is regarded as highly literate and accustomed to filling in forms, a questionnaire was devised to query the three upper ranks of professors (professors, associate professors, and assistant professors) in twenty-eight public colleges and universities in the states of Arkansas, Louisiana, Oklahoma, and Texas. The sample selected included institutions controlled for region and size of teaching staff.

The questions upon which the accompanying data are based simply asked the professor how often (quite often, fairly often, seldom, or never) his department chairman, division chairman, or department head talked with him about ten different decisions. Then he was asked how often he thought his superior *should* have talked with him. Each response was given a numerical weight (e.g., +2, +1, 0, −1, −2), so that numerical differences could be calculated for the discrepancy between actual and ideal influence, as represented by the two questions outlined above. Thus, the term "discrepancy" as used in the following analysis simply refers to the numerical difference between the way the professor actually sees his influence and the way he would like to see it for each of the ten decisions.

For each decision the contingency coefficient (C) and its maximum value were calculated to give a measure of the *extent* of association or relationship between the two variables in addition to the typical chi-square association test. (See Table 2, as this applies, of course, only where the two variables, influence on decisions and satisfaction of professors, are considered.)

RESULTS

All of the professors were asked to indicate the exent to which they actually influence certain decisions as opposed to the amount of influence they would like to have on the same group of decisions. Note that Table 1 naturally divides into two of the three subroles of the professor. Most research-oriented decisions are made by the individual professor, so this table does not cover that subrole. But the first five decisions listed fit into the general teaching subrole, and the last five cluster around the institutional role of the professor. Thus, the decisions with which the respondents indicate most satisfaction are all in the teaching category, while those with which they express relative dissatisfaction are all generally institution-related.

Table 1. The Professors' Satisfaction with Their Influence on Decisions.

DECISION	DISSATISFIED WITH INFLUENCE * (%)	SATISFIED WITH INFLUENCE † (%)
Teaching Role		
Selecting a textbook for a multiple-section course offering.	20	80
Supervising procedures within the classroom.	21	79
Recommending titles in subject field for library acquisition.	22	78
Initiating changes in curriculum by addition, deletion, or revision of courses.	30	70
Determining prerequisites for courses to be offered.	32	68
Institutional Role		
Selecting graduate assistants or lecturers for the department.	34	66
Determining recipients of financial aid for student scholarships.	41	59
Evaluating qualifications of applicants and deciding to issue an invitation to join the faculty of the department.	43	57
Seeking applications for prospective faculty members.	44	56
Determining long-term department policy.	48	52

* While "dissatisfied" includes both those who want more influence and those who want less, the number of professors who want less influence on decisions was so small that the figures were not useful alone. Thus, the great majority of the professors represented in this column want more influence.

† When asked the amount of influence they actually have and the amount they would like to have, the professors represented in this column recorded the same rating, while those in the other column noted a different rating.

With three decisions—selecting a textbook for a multiple-section course, supervising procedures within the classroom, and recommending titles in their subject field for library acquisition—approximately eight out of ten professors were most satisfied. Only about two in ten were dissatisfied with their influence on these three decisions.

About two out of three respondents were content with their influence on initiating changes in curriculum, determining prerequisites for courses, and selecting graduate assistants or lecturers for the department. Thus, about one-third of the professors were dissatisfied with their influence on these decisions. The great majority of these wanted more influence.

Less satisfaction was felt when considering three other decisions—determining recipients of financial aid for students, evaluating qualifications of applicants for the faculty, and seeking applications from prospective faculty members. Almost six in ten of the respondents expressed satisfaction with their influence on these decisions, leaving four in ten who were dissatisfied.

A few more than half of the professors were satisfied with their influence on the final decision—determining long-term department policy. It is significant, however, that for decisions about which they were asked, at least half (and as high as 80 per cent) of the professors were satisfied with their influence on those decisions.

INFLUENCE IN DEPARTMENT DECISIONS

In addition to the frequency distributions regarding satisfaction with decision-making influence (Table 1), some information was gathered relating the professor's influence on department decisions and his satisfaction with the leadership style of his superior (in Table 2). Chi-square and the accompanying contingency coefficient tests were applied to distributions for each of the ten decisions. In Table 2 the resulting probabilities and contingency coefficients indicate the degree of relationship between the professor's satisfaction with his influence on decisions and his satisfaction with the leadership style of his superior.

Using a probability of .05 for acceptance, only two decisions, the ones concerning textbook selection and classroom supervision, were tentatively accepted as independent of the professors' interaction with their chairman. Thus, the first eight decisions listed in Table 2 are associated with the professor's interaction with his superior and the last two decisions listed there are not so associated.

Note that the two decisions for which the two variables are independent (selecting textbooks and supervising classroom procedures) are both related to the teaching role (see column on the right in Table 2). Also three of the first four (seeking and inviting men to join the faculty and determining department policy) are institution-related rather than associated with teaching. On very scant evidence then we may see a bit more association between his satisfaction with influence on decisions and his satisfaction with the leadership style of his chairman when the decision is related to the institutional role.

For only five of these ten decisions (determining long-term department policies, recommending titles in subject field for library acquisition, determining prerequisites for courses to be offered, seeking applications from prospective faculty members, and evaluating qualifications of applicants and deciding to issue an invitation to join the faculty of the department) this study profiles the more professionally satisfied professor as generally older, tenured, and higher ranked.

Table 2. Relationship between Influence on Decisions and Satisfaction of Professors.

	PROBABILITY	CONTINGENCY COEFFICIENT (MAXIMUM $c = .707$)	DEGREES OF FREEDOM	SUB-ROLE †
Decisions Associated with the Professor's Interaction with His Superior				
Seeking applications from prospective faculty members	.0000	.417	3	R
Determining long-term department policies.	.0000	.386	3	R
Determining prerequisites for courses to be offered.	.0001	.340	3	T
Evaluating qualifications of applicants and deciding to issue an invitation to join the faculty of the department.	.0001	.331	3	R
Initiating changes in curriculum by addition, deletion, or revision of courses.	.0039	.260	3	T
Determining recipients of financial aid for student scholarships.	.0040	.260	3	R
Recommending titles in subject field for library acquisition.	.0204	.223	3	T
Selecting graduate assistants or lecturers for the department.	.0401	.205	3	R
Decisions Independent of the Professor's Interaction with His Superior				
Selecting a textbook for a multiple-section course offering.	.1474	.166*	3	T
Supervising procedures within the classroom	.1520	.165*	3	T

* In the case of these two decisions only, because the hypothesis of Independence has been tentatively accepted, these values of C have not been shown to be significant. They have little meaning in the analysis.

† Indicates the institutional subrole: R is the research and consulting subrole and T is the teaching subrole.

DISCUSSION AND IMPLICATIONS

The department chairman can be reassured that at least 50 percent (and up to 80 percent) of his faculty is satisfied with the amount of influence they have on these ten decisions. Caution should be exercised, however, in generalizing this result to *all* possible decisions. These ten were selected because they appeared to be more individually-oriented to the professor. Replication studies considering other decisions are strongly advised.

The professor's satisfaction with the leadership style of his superior is related to his satisfaction with the amount of influence he has on the following decisions: seeking applications from prospective faculty members, determining long-term department policies, determining prerequisites for courses to be offered, evaluating qualifications of applicants and deciding to issue an invitation to join the faculty of the department, initiating changes in curriculum by addition, deletion, or revision of courses, determining recipients of financial aid for student scholarships, selecting graduate assistants or lecturers for the department, and recommending titles in subject field for library acquisition. Whether it is much or little, the professor is satisfied with the influence he has on these decisions. Note that the first seven of these decisions are clearly department-oriented.

Satisfaction with his influence in selecting a textbook for a multiple-section course offering and with supervising procedures within the classroom is not related to his satisfaction with his superior. Note that these two decisions share a student-teacher-classroom association that is very little influenced by the department head, i.e., these kinds of decisions are simply not in the domain of professor-superior relationship. Of the eight decisions on which his influence was adequate, only one—recommending titles in subject field for library acquisition—may be considered in this area. But recommending titles is usually approved by the department chairman; thus, the professor-superior relationship is part of the transaction. In Table 1 it is clear these three decisions, which did not seem to be in the domain of the professor-superior relationship, garnered the highest satisfaction rating, eight in ten professors.

INDIVIDUAL NEEDS AND ORGANIZATION OBJECTIVES

In the administrative literature the contention is held that the administrator contributes to the motivation of his followers by understanding their needs, and clearsightedly aligning those needs with the objectives of the organization. In this study admittedly the *only* considerations are the needs of the individual—the self-perceived picture the professor has of his role and the way in which he fulfills that role. This study assumes professors have a profound influence on their superiors. One social scientist has suggested:

> There is some justification for regarding the follower as the most crucial factor in any leadership event and for arguing that research directed at the follower will

eventually yield a handsome payoff. Not only is it the follower who *perceives* both the leader and the situation and who reacts in terms of what he perceives. And what he perceives may be, to an important degree, a function of his own motivations, frames of reference, and "readiness" (Sanford, 1950, p. 4).

A perusal of the data from this study by the administrator would acquaint him with the need of the professor for more influence in some decision areas: determining long-term department policy, seeking, evaluating, and issuing invitations to prospective faculty members, and determining recipients of financial aid for student scholarships. Thus this study delineates particular needs of the college professor, compared with employees in other organizational settings, i.e., now the college and/or university administrator has some decision needs of the professor with which he may begin to work in the direction of aligning them with the needs of the organization.

Among the studies reviewed in the area of administration of colleges and universities two seem to have some relevance to the present study. Hill and French (1967) found that professors imputed a generally low power position to the average department chairman. In this study the need for more influence among professors shows some support for the Hill and French position. If professors want more influence in departmental decisions, they also appear to want less influence (power) vested in the position of department chairman.

IDEAL DECISION UNITS

Patterson (1966) asked professors to indicate the ideal decision units for a number of decisions. A large number think the professor acting alone is the ideal decision unit for supervising classroom procedures and choosing equipment and textbooks. These two decision areas are the ones with which the professors queried in this study were most satisfied. In the Patterson study most professors want the department faculty as a whole to participate in long range planning, currculum improvement, setting course prerequisites, encouraging competent students to pursue advanced study, and choosing their future colleagues. With these very decisions professors in the present study are more dissatisfied. Thus there is some support in this study for the Patterson findings, although in this study satisfaction with decisions was measured, while in the Patterson research the ideal decision unit was selected.

The material profiling the more professionally satisfied professor as generally older, tenured, and higher ranked (based on only five decisions) may suggest two feasible avenues of action on the part of administrators. They can alter ranking and tenure policy to include in the higher ranks and the tenured group younger professors that they feel are able to make judgments in these decision areas. Or at the very least they can talk with younger professors about their feelings in this area. If the younger professors feel administrators do discriminate against them according to age, rank, and tenure, they can attempt to at least communicate this to administrators. The question here is, of course, have the results indicated by this study been communicated to department chairmen, for example, or is this latent, unexpressed dissatisfaction? If communication is unproductive, then the younger professors always have the alternative of looking for an environment that will better satisfy them.

Thus this study adds the dimension of professors in public universities and colleges to the already existent administrative literature. It largely supports the general position of the writings. More precisely, it finds a majority of professors (from 52 to 80 percent, depending on the particlar decision) satisfied with the influence they have on selected decisions; additionally, for eight of ten decisions considered there is an association between the professor's satisfaction with that decisioc influence and his satisfaction with the administrative style of his superior.

The acute need is for additional studies in this general area of college and university department faculty management to guide the administrator through the maze of ingrained tradition and rigid and often inaccurate perceptions of the view the professor has of his role.

REFERENCES

H. L. Ansbacher and R. R. Ansbacher eds., *The Individual Psychology of Alfred Adler* (New York: Basic Books, Inc., 1956).
Burton R. Clark, "Faculty Organization and Authority," *Professionalization,* edited by Vollmer and Mills (Englewood Cliffs, New Jersey: Prentice-Hall, Inc., 1966), pp. 283–291.
Amitai Etzioni, "Dual Leadership in Complex Organizations," *American Sociological Review,* Oct. 1965, pp. 688–698.
Frederick Herzberg, Bernard Mausner, and B. Snyderman, *The Motivation to Work* (New York: John Wiley & Sons, Inc., 1959).
Winston W. Hill and Wendell L. French, "Perceptions of Power of Department Chairmen by Professors," *Administrative Science Quarterly,* March 1967, pp. 548–574.
William Kornhauser, "Scientists in Industry: Conflict and Accommodation," *Professionalization,* edited by Vollmer and Mills (Englewood Cliffs, New Jersey: Prentice-Hall, Inc., 1966), pp. 292–303.
A. H. Maslow, "A Theory of Human Motivation," *Psychological Review,* Vol. 50 (1943), pp. 370–396.

David D. McClelland, *The Achieving Society* (Princeton, New Jersey: D. Van Nostrand Co., 1961).

Douglas McGregor, *The Professional Manager* (New York: McGraw-Hill Book Company, 1967).

Nancy C. Morse and Everett Reimer, "The Experimental Change of a Major Organizational Variable," *Journal of Abnormal and Social Psychology,* Jan. 1965, pp. 121–122.

Laura Marguerite Patterson, "Preferences in Administrative Styles Based on an Inquiry into Perceptions of the Ideal Structure of the University Department and the Ideal Role of the Department Chairman," Unpublished Ph.D. dissertation, College of Business Administration, The University of Texas at Austin.

F. H. Sanford, *Authoritarianism and Leadership* (Philadelphia: Institute for Research in Human Relations, 1950).

Staley Schachter, *The Psychology of Affiliation* (Stanford, California: Stanford University Press, 1959).

Richard W. Scott, "Professionals in Bureaucracies—Areas of Conflict," *Professionalization,* edited by Vollmer and Mills. (Englewood Cliffs, New Jersey: Prentice-Hall, Inc., 1966), pp. 265–275.

Robert W. White, "Motivation Reconsidered: The Concept of Competence," *Psychological Review,* Vol. 66, No. 5 (1959).

At Last— Innovation in the Federal Judicial System

Warren E. Burger

I have always been puzzled that a nation so willing to adopt and adapt and innovate, so committed to better mousetraps, up-to-date business machines, the latest in medical equipment, and the spending of billions on space exploration, nevertheless tolerates judicial procedures and methods that many people considered too cumbersome even 100 years ago. If John Marshall, Thomas Jefferson, Alexander Hamilton, or John Adams—all very good lawyers—came back today, they would require only a small amount of briefing on procedure to go into court and try cases. (I limit this assessment to the *courtroom* because it is in procedure and method that the law has experienced the least change. Corporate law, tax law, administrative law, and regulatory law constitute a totally new world, of course.)

What has kept the judicial system so resistant to innovation in terms of administration or "management" is, I think, a widespread refusal to realize that in some very basic ways the judicial system resembles a business system, a

Reprinted by permission of the publisher from *Management Review*, June 1974, pp. 14–19. © 1974 by AMACOM, a division of American Management Associations. This article is adapted from an address presented by Chief Justice Burger to the Economic Club of New York.

health care system, or any other human institution. Complex human institutions can either adapt to new needs and changing conditions or falter and fall in a world of flux and transition. They need constant analysis and a willingness to adapt and change. With courts, as with any other complex social, commercial, or governmental organization, a little tinkering here and there and urging everyone to work harder will help, but it is no substitute for hard thinking, serious administrative analysis, and willingness to cast off old habits of thought and patterns of work.

Thirteen years on the United States Court of Appeals in Washington, D.C., persuaded me that our system of justice was overdue for changes, some substantive, but for the most part in the areas of method, procedure, and attitude.

When I assumed my present post in 1969, I made a series of suggestions and proposals, all directed toward having the judiciary face up to three great needs: the need for continuing research and analysis of our methods, the need for development of new methods, and the need for forums to exchange and implement new ideas. Some of these proposals are already beginning to make a difference in the way the federal court system is operating.

STRUCTURE AND FUNCTION

As a first step, I suggested to the American Bar Association that Congress create a commission to examine immediately the structure and organization of the 11 federal circuits and also to study the internal functioning of the federal judicial system and coordinate with the Congress on legislative matters affecting the courts. Congress responded by creating a commission designated one-fourth by the President, one-fourth by each house of Congress, and one-fourth by the Chief Justice.

Senator Roman Hruska of Nebraska is chairman and Judge J. Edward Lumbard, former Chief Judge of the United States Court of Appeals of the Second Circuit, headquartered in New York, is vice-chairman of that commission. It has filed its first report, in which it recommends a partial restructuring of the system, dividing the country into 13 in place of 11 circuits. The commission also is now conducting hearings on the entire process of appeals in the federal courts; the hearings include consideration of a new court to relieve the Courts of Appeals and the Supreme Court.

Another step was the creation of a National Center for State Courts so that the state court judges would have a national facility to operate a clearinghouse for research and development on their problems and for education of their new judges and court personnel. Fortunately, we had a pattern to serve as a guide:

the Federal Judicial Center that was established in 1968 to serve as the R&D and educational facility for federal courts. This center was an innovation that created no little skepticism among established federal judges, but they were won over by the prestige and zealous leadership of retired Justice Tom Clark and his successor, Judge Alfred P. Murrah. With this experience to guide us, we helped the state judges—who had had no advocate or common forum—to organize a comparable center to serve the state and local courts. The State Center, now three years old, has grown to the point where it has a staff of 73 and regional offices in five states. A national headquarters for the Center is soon to be established on the campus of William and Mary College in Williamsburg, Va., where its initial organizing committee first met.

Why were we concerned with state courts when we were focusing on the federal judicial system? The reason is simple and not entirely altruistic: Long delays in the overcrowded state courts were contributing to a trend by litigants to use the federal courts. In 1969, a study by the American Law Institute concluded that we needed to reexamine the allocation of the workload between federal and state courts and to restore the federal courts to their traditional role as courts of special and limited jurisdiction.

Another important long-range proposal we have made to Congress is to remove from federal courts those cases in which the reason for federal jurisdiction rests on the fact that the two litigants are citizens of different states. The tendency to try such cases in federal courts is a carryover from the 1787 view that a citizen from New Hampshire or Massachusetts could not get a fair trial in the state courts of Virginia or Georgia. We have outgrown most of that parochialism, but the doctrine still clings to us long after the reason for letting it govern federal jurisdiction has altered. These diversity-of-citizenship cases are largely claims for personal and property injury, and they have little more place in a federal court than an overtime parking ticket case.

Since a large-scale reexamination of federal jurisdiction must come, and changes must be made, it will be necessary for the state courts to assume a greater proportion of the total judicial burden. The National Center for State Courts will now be available to help upgrade and modernize the state courts and make them ready for new tasks.

COOPERATION ON COMMON PROBLEMS

Beginning in 1969, we urged the chief justices of the 50 states to join in creating state-federal judicial councils consisting of the chief judges of the federal and state courts in each state. More than 40 states have done this, and these councils have been of incalculable benefit in reducing the friction and hostility that had grown up between the two systems, and in producing long-overdue co-operation.

Another step was to create the Conference of Metropolitan Chief Judges from the 22 largest federal courts—who have common problems and handle 60 percent of all the federal cases. The purpose—and happily the result—was to have these very experienced judges pool their total experience and develop a more or less common attack on their problems. These 22 judges meet twice each year and maintain continuing communication with each other. Their efforts have already helped save several millions of dollars and have substantially improved productivity.

The role of a judge today is far more complex at every level than it was 30 or 40 years ago; the average workload is probably about double, and many of the cases bring up totally new problems on which there is little guidance from precedent. With this in mind, we now bring all newly appointed federal judges to the Federal Judicial Center in Washington (mentioned earlier) for an intensive two-week indoctrination with experienced judges as their mentors. After three or four years we bring them back again for a week. Apart from giving the new judges information on the mechanics of their new craft, this procedure results in having improved techniques developed by a judge in New Orleans or Texas, for example, transplanted to New York or Boston, and vice versa. The value of this cross-fertilization is enormous.

Finally, we have been seeking ways to develop management-trained specialists to help ease the courts' administrative burdens. Corporations long ago abandoned the fiction that any "bright young man" can master all the complexities of a sprawling, multifaceted business establishment. The days are also past when a chief judge, with help from a secretary and the clerk of the court, could manage the amazingly complex and varied tasks required to keep courts functioning effectively.

In 1969, we asked the American Bar Association to help persuade Congress to create a new office: that of court executive or court administrator to act as a managerial officer for each circuit and for each of the larger trial courts (26 positions in all). The flaw in this proposal was the fact that there were no trained court administrators available except in a few states; we needed to create an institution to train such specialists.

By the fall of 1969 we had the Institute for Court Management in operation. Organizing the institute was done with the help of Roger Blough, a lawyer who had been president of the U.S. Steel Corporation; James Webb, former director of the Budget and of NASA; Dr. George Graham, executive director of the National Academy of Public Administration; and Herbert Brownell, former U.S. Attorney General. In each year since 1969, the institute has trained about 75 court administrators in an intensive six-month course, and virtually all of these graduates have been absorbed into the state and federal judicial systems.

Of course, not all of them are in the precise court executive positions we had envisioned; Congress created only 11 circuit executive positions rather than the 26 we had asked for. Congress also, however, in 1971 established the post of administrative assistant to the Chief Justice of the United States. (Does it surprise you that there was no such position until then?) The total cost of the circuit executives for each of the 11 circuits and the administrative assistant to the Chief Justice is less than $500,000 annually.

CHANGE AND PRODUCTIVITY

To measure the value of any or all of these steps in terms of numbers of cases and judges is difficult. To put the situation in terms that have been found useful in business, however, the average productivity per judge improved 30 percent from 1968 to 1973. Our studies show that this improvement can be attributed to many changes besides those I have mentioned, including better calendar methods that center responsibility for each case in one judge, consolidation of all pretrial motions into a single hearing, better utilization of jurors, and the use of six-member juries.

Regarding the last two factors, one well-informed person has estimated that up to 20 percent, or $100 million, of the total costs of jurors for our federal, state, and local courts can be saved by better management. Here is an area where the newly created National Center for State Courts and the Federal Judicial Center can work together.

Meanwhile, two study groups sponsored by the Judicial Center have surveyed the processes of reviewing cases. One study examined state and federal court appeals and the other concentrated on the Supreme Court; both focused on the solutions as well as the problems. Although there is virtually universal acceptance of the diagnosis of our ailments, lawyers and judges being what they are, we do not yet have unanimity on the cures—which should not surprise anyone.

We have, then, a great deal of ferment and some accomplishments and changes in the federal court system.

Just as a poorly run hospital is a danger to the community and to its patients, a poorly run judicial system will in time undermine public confidence in the entire system of government. Our judicial systems—state and federal—have been teetering on the brink of that stage for 10 to 20 years. I confess I have little patience with those who are fearful that modern methods and improved efficiency will undermine justice—that somehow an *efficient* court system will be mechanistic, heartless, and insensitive to human needs. We cannot "deliver" justice without efficient means any more than we can deliver medical care or satisfy other essential human needs without methods and means that work. It is not necessary to use obsolete, inefficient nineteenth century methods in the courts in order to be "humanistic."

So we are moving toward efficiency and we are innovating in many ways. This forward movement is slow at times, but it is there, and our hard-working federal judges are giving it their full support.

Biographical Notes

WILLIAM G. AKULA is Acting Chairman of the Department of Management and Industrial Relations at the University of Bridgeport, Bridgeport, Connecticut. He holds a Ph.D. in Management from New York University.

ROBERT N. ANTHONY, Ross Graham Walker Professor of Management Control at Harvard University, is the author of many articles and books, and the coauthor of *Management Control in Nonprofit Organizations* (1975).

RICHARD BOLLING, of the U.S. House of Representatives, is the author of *House Out of Order* (1965) and *Power in the House* (1968), rev. ed. (1974). He resides in Kansas City, Missouri.

MARTHA A. BROWN is an Associate Professor at Stephen F. Austin State University. She received her Ph.D. from the University of Texas. In addition to her academic life, Dr. Brown has had experience in advertising and broadcasting. She has published articles in various professional journals.

WARREN E. BURGER is Chief Justice of the United States. He is also (by law) chairman of the Federal Judicial Center—the research and development arm of the judicial system—and chairman of the Judicial Conference of the United States, which operates as the judicial system's "board of directors." He studied law at St. Paul College of Law. After private practice, he was appointed Assistant Attorney General of the United

States for a time and then became judge of the U.S. Court of Appeals for the District of Columbia Circuit.

HOWARD M. CARLISLE is head of the Department of Business Administration at Utah State University. He began his business career in 1953 with the U.S. Atomic Energy Commission where he served as budget analyst with the San Francisco office. In 1958 he joined the Wasatch Division of Thiokol Chemical Corporation to head its budgets and business planning department. Mr. Carlisle's articles have appeared in many management periodicals. In 1962 he won an Author Award for "How Budgets Control MINUTEMAN Procurement" in *Aero-Space Management*.

PETER F. DRUCKER is a noted writer, consultant, and educator. He is Clarke Professor of Social Science at the Claremont Graduate School in California. Among his many books are *The Practice of Management* (1954), *Managing for Results* (1962), *The Effective Executive* (1967), and *Management: Tasks, Practices, Responsibility* (1974).

ROBERT J. DUBIN is executive vice president of J. R. Taft Corporation. He had been president of Comlab, Inc., a market research subsidiary of Columbia Pictures; vice president and director of research services for Post-Keyes-Gardner, a Chicago-based advertising firm; and a senior vice president of Schwerin Research Corporation. In the nonbusiness world, Mr. Dubin was a research associate at the Yale Center for Alcohol Studies. In his present capacity at the Taft Corporation, he is responsible for developing marketing strategy for many clients and also conducts program evaluation studies for foundations, federal agencies, and nonprofit groups.

ROBERT ELKIN is principal in the Washington, D.C. office of Peat, Marwick, Mitchell & Co. and coordinator of the firm's consulting practice in the social services field. Dr. Elkin holds degrees from American University.

KENNETH P. FALLON, JR. was director of the North Idaho Child Development Center, Department of Environmental and Community Services, Coeur d'Alene. He is currently executive director of the Panhandle Child Development Association in Coeur d'Alene.

JERRY L. GRAY is Associate Professor and Acting Head of the Department of Business Administration, The Faculty of Administrative Studies, at the University of Manitoba, Winnipeg, Canada.

THORNE HACKER is staff associate at the Midwest Center of the University of Chicago, Chicago, Illinois.

HERBERT H. HAND is a faculty member in management at the University of South Carolina, Columbia.

OWEN B. HARDY is currently president of Medicus Planning, Inc. in Bethesda, Maryland. He was formerly vice president of Gordon A. Friesen International, Inc., Washington, D.C. Mr. Hardy received an M.B.A. degree from George Washington University in 1964, where he was elected chairman of the student governing board of the Programs in Hospital Administration. He served as administrator of Mitchell County Hospital, Camilla, Georgia, from 1950 to 1954 and occupied the same position at

Phoebe Purney Memorial Hospital in Albany, Georgia, from 1954 to 1964. A past president of the Georgia Hospital Association, he has received several noteworthy honors and awards. He is a Fellow of the American College of Hospital Administrators, holds associate membership in the American Association of Hospital Consultants, and is the author of many articles published in professional journals.

KENNETH L. HARRIS is director of Project Interaction, Bellevue, Washington 98004.

A. THOMAS HOLLINGSWORTH is a faculty member in management at the University of South Carolina, Columbia.

MICHAEL J. HOWLETT is former Secretary of State of Illinois, the only Democrat in Illinois history elected to four consecutive terms of statewide office. He was previously auditor of public accounts in which capacity he served for 12 years, after which he held the position of regional director of the Office of Price Stabilization. From 1952 until 1960 he was vice president of the Sun Steel Company.

HOWARD L. JONES became president of Northfield–Mount Hermon School in 1961. He won his doctorate in education from Syracuse University. He was a member of the Colgate University faculty, where he became vice president in 1958. Dr. Jones also taught and coached at the East Hampton and Waverly (New York) high schools. During World War II he served with the Army Air Force and spent three years as a pilot in the Air Transport Command in Europe.

L. KEITH LARIMORE is chairman of the Division of Business Administration at Missouri Southern State College, Joplin, Missouri, and president of Professional Management Services, Inc. He holds a B.S.B.A. from Kansas State College, an M.B.A. from the University of Oklahoma, and a Ph.D. from the University of Arkansas. Dr. Larimore was awarded a Certificate of Merit for the article that appears in this volume.

FREDERIC V. MALEK, former director for the Office of Management and Budget, Washington, D.C., is currently senior vice president of the Marriott Corporation, Washington, D.C.

DALE D. McCONKEY is Associate Professor of Management at the University of Wisconsin in addition to heading his own international management consulting organization. He is recognized generally as one of the pioneers in the development of Management by Objectives and has been one of its most active practitioners, having helped install the system in many organizations in the United States, Europe, and Japan. Previously, he had served as group vice president with the United Fruit Company, and as vice president of Beech-Nut Life Savers, Inc. The author of several books and many articles on corporate management, he is director of two corporations.

WALTER McQUADE is an editor residing in Port Washington, New York. He is on the Board of Editors of *Fortune*. He is the author of *Schoolhouse* (1958) and *Cities Fit to Live In* (1971).

DONALD A. MORTON is Commander of the Civil Engineer Corps, U.S. Navy. A Naval Academy (Class of 1954) and Naval War College graduate, he served on destroyers before transferring to the Civil Engineer Corps. In the latter he has had staff, planning, engineering, construction, public works, and Seabee duty. His most recent assignments have been as executive officer of Navy Mobile Construction Battalion Five, Management Course Director and Development Programs Officer at the Naval War College, and executive officer of the Construction Battalion Center at Davisville, Rhode Island. He is now in Washington on the staff of the Navy Comptroller.

EDMUND D. PELLEGRINO, M.D., formerly Vice President for Health Affairs and Chancellor of the Center for the Health Sciences, The University of Tennessee, Memphis, Tennessee, is currently Chairman of the Board of Yale–New Haven Medical Center, Inc., and Professor of Medicine at the Center.

DANIEL H. PERLMAN is Dean of Administrative Services, Roosevelt University, Chicago, Illinois. During 1972–1973 he was Fellow of the Academic Administration Internship Program of the American Council on Education.

HOWARD L. SAMPSON is the director for the Division of Administrative Services at the Madison, Wisconsin Public Schools. His responsibilities include the departments of Systems Services, Computer Services, Office of the Registrar, Printing Services, and Instructional Support Services. Dr. Sampson earned his Ph.D. from the University of Wisconsin–Madison. He is a professional member of ASM, past president of the Madison chapter of ASM, and a recipient of the ASM Merit Award. In addition, he is president of the Madison Association of School Administrators and a member of AEDS, WAEDS, and ARMA, respectively. Dr. Sampson has work experience in government and industry and has major interests in the fields of systems management and organization planning and development. He serves as a management consultant to the Wisconsin Interscholastic Athletic Association.

ROBERT M. SCHAFFNER is a government official assigned to the Food and Drug Administration, Washington, D.C. He received his Ph.D. from the University of Pittsburgh.

Y. KRISHNA SHETTY is Associate Professor of Management at the College of Business Administration, Utah State University. He received a Ford Foundation fellowship in 1966, and his Ph.D. in Business Administration in 1967. Currently, he holds positions with the U.S. Forest Service and the Oregon State System of Higher Education.

H. DEAN SMITH is director of Project Interaction, Bellevue, Washington 98004.

GAYE VANDERMYN is a writer in Seattle, Washington.

JAY A. VORA is Assistant Professor, Department of Management and Industrial Relations, University of Bridgeport, Bridgeport, Connecticut.

Index